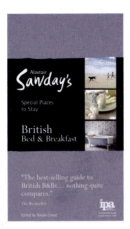

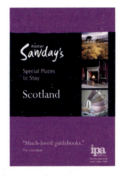

Seventh edition
Copyright © 2009 Alastair Sawday
Publishing Co. Ltd
Published in 2009
ISBN-13: 978-1-906136-08-6

Alastair Sawday Publishing Co. Ltd,
The Old Farmyard, Yanley Lane,
Long Ashton, Bristol BS41 9LR, UK
Tel: +44 (0)1275 395430
Email: info@sawdays.co.uk
Web: www.sawdays.co.uk

The Globe Pequot Press,
P. O. Box 480, Guilford,
Connecticut 06437, USA
Tel: +1 203 458 4500
Email: info@globepequot.com
Web: www.globepequot.com

All rights reserved. No part of this publication may be used other than for the purpose for which it is intended nor may any part be reproduced, or transmitted, in any form or by any means, electronically or mechanically, including photocopying, recording or any information storage and retrieval system, without prior written permission from the publisher. Requests for permission should be addressed to: Alastair Sawday Publishing in the UK; or The Globe Pequot Press in North America.

A catalogue record for this book is available from the British Library. This publication is not included under licences issued by the Copyright Agency. No part of this publication may be used in any form of advertising, sales promotion or publicity.

Alastair Sawday has asserted his right to be identified as the author of this work.

Series Editor Alastair Sawday
Editor Nicola Crosse
Assistants to Editor Tara Roney-Dougal, Rebecca Thomas
Editorial Director Annie Shillito
Writing Jo Boissevain, Nicola Crosse, Alastair Sawday
Inspections Neil Brown, Sinéad Connelly, Nicola Crosse, Catherine Hogan, Aideen Reid, Angie & Kenneth Reid, Alastair Sawday
Accounts Bridget Bishop, Amy Lancaster
Editorial Sue Bourner, Jo Boissevain, Wendy Ogden, Claire Wilson
Production Julia Richardson, Rachel Coe, Tom Germain, Anny Mortada
Sales & Marketing & PR Rob Richardson, Sarah Bolton, Bethan Riach
Web & IT Joe Green, Chris Banks, Phil Clarke, Mike Peake, Russell Wilkinson

We have made every effort to ensure the accuracy of the information in this book at the time of going to press. However, we cannot accept any responsibility for any loss, injury or inconvenience resulting from the use of information contained therein.

Maps: Maidenhead Cartographic Services
Printing: Butler, Tanner & Dennis, Frome
UK distribution: Penguin UK, London

Alastair Sawday's

Special Places to Stay

Ireland

Contents

Front	Page
Our office & culture	6
ASP – a green company	8
A word from Alastair Sawday	9
Introduction	10
How we choose our Special Places	13
Inspections	13
Feedback	13
Subscriptions	14
Disclaimer	14
Using this book	16
Finding the right place for you	16
Maps	16
Ethical Collection	16
Sawday's Travel Club	16
Symbols	17
Quick reference indices	17
Practical matters	18
Types of places	18
Rooms	18
Meals	18
Prices and minimum stays	20
Telephoning	20
Booking and cancellation	21
Payment	21
Tipping	21
Arrivals and departures	21
Closed	21
Maps	22-31

Guide entries	Entry	Map
Ulster		
Co. Antrim	1-6	2, 5
Co. Armagh	7	2, 5
Co. Donegal	8-17	1, 2
Co. Down	18-27	2, 5
Co. Fermanagh	28	1, 4
Co. Londonderry	29-31	1, 2
Co. Monaghan	32-33	1, 2, 4, 5
Co. Tyrone	34	2, 5
Connacht		
Co. Galway	35-52	3
Co. Leitrim	53-54	1, 4
Co. Mayo	55-61	3
Co. Roscommon	62-63	4
Co. Sligo	64-69	1, 4

Guide entries

	Entry	Map
Munster		
Co. Clare	70-79	3
Co. Cork	81-109	6, 7
Co. Kerry	110-135	6
Co. Limerick	136-141	6, 7
Co. Tipperary	142-151	4, 7, 8
Co. Waterford	152-166	7, 8
Leinster		
Co. Carlow	167-168	8
Co. Dublin	169-175	5
Co. Kildare	176-178	4, 5
Co. Kilkenny	179-185	8
Co. Laois	186-187	4
Co. Longford	188	4
Co. Louth	189	2, 5
Co. Meath	190-198	4, 5
Co. Offaly	199-200	4
Co. Westmeath	201-206	4
Co. Wexford	207-216	8
Co. Wicklow	217-219	5

Back

	Page
Getting around Ireland	261
Irish literature	264
Sawday's Travel Club	266
Ethical Collection	270
Feedback form	277
Quick reference indices	278
Wheelchair-accessible	278
On a budget?	278
Singles	278
Gardens	279
Riding	279
Travel without a car	280
Index by town	282
Index by property name	284
What's in each entry?	288

6 Our office & culture

The buildings

Beautiful as they were, our old offices leaked heat, used electricity to heat water and rooms, flooded spaces with light to illuminate one person, and were not ours to alter.

So in 2005 we created our own eco-offices by converting some old barns to create a low-emissions building. Heating and lighting the building, which houses over 30 employees, now produces only 0.28 tonnes of carbon dioxide per year. Not bad when you compare this with the 6 tonnes emitted by the average UK household. We achieved this through a variety of innovative and energy-saving building techniques, described below.

Insulation We went to great lengths to ensure that very little heat will escape, by:
- laying insulating board 90mm thick immediately under the roof tiles and on the floor
- lining the whole of the inside of the building with plastic sheeting to ensure air-tightness
- fixing further insulation underneath the roof and between the rafters
- fixing insulated plaster-board to add another layer of insulation.

All this means we are insulated for the Arctic, and almost totally air-tight.

Heating We installed a wood-pellet boiler from Austria, in order to be largely fossil-fuel free. The pellets are made from compressed sawdust, a waste product from timber mills that work only with sustainably managed forests. The heat is conveyed by water to all corners of the building via an under-floor system.

Water We installed a 6000-litre tank to collect rainwater from the roofs. This is pumped back, via an ultra-violet filter, to the lavatories, showers and basins. There are two solar thermal panels on the roof providing heat to the one (massively insulated) hot-water cylinder.

Lighting We have a carefully planned mix of low-energy lighting: task lighting and up-lighting. We also installed three sun-pipes – polished aluminium tubes that reflect the outside light down to chosen areas of the building.

Electricity All our electricity has long come from the Good Energy Company and is 100% renewable.

Materials Virtually all materials are non-toxic or natural. Our carpets, for example, are made from (80%) Herdwick sheep-wool from National Trust farms in the Lake District.

Doors and windows Outside doors and new windows are wooden, double-glazed, beautifully constructed in Norway. Old windows have been double-glazed.

We have a building we are proud of, and architects and designers are fascinated by. But best of all, we are now in a better position to encourage our owners and readers to take sustainability more seriously.

Photo: Tom Germain

What we do

Besides moving the business to a low-carbon building, the company works in a number of ways to reduce its overall environmental footprint:

- all office travel is logged as part of a carbon sequestration programme, and money for compensatory tree-planting is dispatched to SCAD in India for a tree-planting and development project
- we avoid flying and take the train for business trips wherever possible; when we have to fly, we 'double offset'
- car-sharing and the use of a company pool car are part of company policy; recycled cooking oil is used in one car and LPG in the other
- organic and Fair Trade basic provisions are used in the staff kitchen and organic food is provided by the company at all in-house events
- green cleaning products are used throughout the office
- all kitchen waste is composted and used on the office organic allotment.

Our total 'operational' carbon footprint (including travel to and from work, plus all our trips to visit our Special Places to Stay) is just over 17 tonnes per year. We have come a long way, but we would like to get this figure as close to zero as possible.

Alastair Sawday Publishing – a green company

For many years Alastair Sawday Publishing has been 'greening' the business in different ways. Our aim is to reduce our environmental footprint as far as possible – with almost everything we do we have the environmental implications in mind. (We once claimed to be the world's first carbon-neutral publishing company, but are now wary of such claims.) In recognition of our efforts we won a Business Commitment to the Environment Award in 2005, and in 2006 a Queen's Award for Enterprise in the Sustainable Development category. In that year Alastair was voted ITN's 'Eco Hero'.

We have created our own eco-offices by converting former barns to create a low-emissions building. Through a variety of innovative and energy-saving techniques this has reduced our carbon emissions by 35%.

Photo: Tom Germain

But becoming 'green' is a journey and, although we began long before most companies, we still have a long way to go.

In 2008 we won the Independent Publishers Guild Environmental Award. The judging panel were effusive in their praise, stating: "With green issues currently at the forefront of publishers' minds, Alastair Sawday Publishing was singled out in this category as a model for all independents to follow. Its efforts to reduce waste in its office and supply chain have reduced the company's environmental impact, and it works closely with staff to identify more areas of improvement. Here is a publisher who lives and breathes green. Alastair Sawday has all the right principles and is clearly committed to improving its practice further."

Our Fragile Earth series is a growing collection of campaigning books about the environment. Highlighting the perilous state of the world yet offering imaginative and radical solutions and some intriguing facts, these books will make you weep and smile. They will keep you up to date and well armed for the battle with apathy.

A word from Alastair Sawday

The changes take one's breath away. Years ago we honeymooned happily in Connemara, in a thatched cottage with no running water, no heating, no lighting – just a peat fire and candles. It is hard, now, to find an old thatched cottage in modern Ireland. I visited this summer and it is no more the Ireland of crumbling cottages, but it is still the Ireland of music and poetry, good talk, good humour and much much more – it exudes a new energy. Will the credit crunch change this? I doubt it. (And we did, by the way, find a beautiful thatched cottage for this book, though the open fire came with swish kitchen and roll-top bath.)

This year I found a B&B where the wind and sun combined at sunset to create a brooding, beautiful river backdrop to a simple house brought up-to-date with a handsome extension. I met people with gardens to linger in and enthusiasms to match. (There are now over 90 places in this book with fine gardens.) I was placed upon a horse by one owner and taken to the top of a hill to admire the vastness of the countryside. I met houses that were chaotic but irresistible. I met people whose passion for keeping the best of old Ireland's houses going, in spite of every difficulty, was inspiring. The sheer exuberance and character of the Irish owners appeared delightfully intact.

I never managed to see the places where you can learn how to sing and dance as

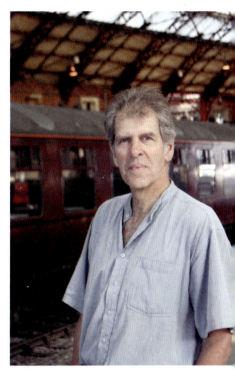

the Irish do. But they are here, in this lovely book. It seems that all of Ireland is here, for you can pick from a vast array of houses, people and types. You will also eat well in Ireland; they take their food seriously and most of these Special Places are proud to buy their food locally, many are growing their own vegetables and fruit.

And you don't have to take your car! Many owners – more than half, in fact – can pick you up from train or bus. That is a small blow for sustainability – and for sheer generosity.

Alastair Sawday

Photo: Tom Germain

Introduction

Could our beloved Emerald Isle become any greener? Well in one sense, no. My only visit there this year was during the wettest week in June; every day the rain pattered gently down, nourishing that magical bright green to the absolute max, soaking the already soaked hills and making tiny streams into huge, rushing torrents. Ah, I thought, that is why the place is so green and so beautiful. The cloud formations were the most wonderful I have ever seen, and in between bouts of rain the sun flooded out from behind the constantly shifting black and purple backdrop of the sky. It was hard not to leap out of the car every five minutes to take yet more photographs of the stunning landscape.

But green has another meaning too. It is defined nowadays as a desire to care for the environment, to take stock of how what we do affects the planet, to treat animals compassionately, and humans similarly. Take these ideas a step further and green meets the Slow Movement:

many environmentalists believe that our need to be connected with nature is very real and deep, and that it is only by slowing down and appreciating what is around us that we can connect with our own spirituality.

As my soggy visit progressed it occurred to me that the Irish are naturally, intrinsically green. Admittedly all of the owners I met lived in the countryside, but big cities anywhere in the world are now so homogenous that it is more difficult to find these indicators of a nation's character or real wealth. I met people who are keen to run their businesses in a more sustainable way, who are firmly steeped in their landscape and their community, who still have huge families all living near each other, who still know the names of all their neighbours, and many who are turning their backs on materialism and the spiritual poverty they feel it encourages.

My first visit was to County Galway. I was late and it was already dark by the time I found the house down a long remote lane in a tiny, working fishing village. I was tired, but I hardly had time to gather my bits of paper and open the car door before a lovely woman appeared like an angel and said "Come on in, I've supper waiting for you". Her house was an old mill, most ecologically converted into a beautiful upside-down space with an upstairs sitting room overlooking the sea. Toasty

Photo left: Newforge House, entry 7
Photo right: The Cahernane House Hotel, entry 123

with underfloor heating and thick-walled with insulation, on this dark night it was candlelit and a fire was burning in the grate. I was nurtured with wine, good bread and cheese and fruit, and by the time I was shown to a gorgeous comfy bed I felt like I was staying with an old friend.

And so it went on. I visited a fascinating community in a remote, wild landscape with owners who are passionate about the environment, committed to preserving Irish music and culture, welcoming to all. By the time I had tried several different vintages of their homemade hooch, been put in front of a roaring fire and fed scones warm from the oven, I could have just joined the community and stayed there forever, merely emailing my mother to post me my old school recorder!

Next stop was the Aran Islands and a young couple who, having gone off to university away from the island, had returned to open their own restaurant with rooms. A commitment to good, local food meant they grew loads of their own vegetables and were supporting local suppliers. They encourage folk to travel round the island by bicycle or on foot and are keen to cater for locals – all of whom they know – as well as guests and day visitors. Stuffed with a divine lunch and with two more lifelong friends under my belt I fell into a boat which I hoped would take me to my next stop. I just happened to say hello to the Captain on the way up the gangplank and suddenly I was in the engine room with him, drinking hot coffee and talking about life. He deposited me on another island where I was greeted warmly and tried Irish whiskey for the first time. And lovage soup. For some reason I left the next morning promising to return with a pig.

Back on the mainland, and I visit scores of seductively crumbling Georgian piles (some are installing solar panels, some using new woodchip boilers) with Connemara ponies flicking their tails on the lawn, or prancing past the dining room window at dinner time like a cabaret act. I stroke donkeys in a field with an artist, make best friends with a taxi driver, go for a long dog walk with somebody else's children, walk the land with land owners, chew the cud with seaside resort hoteliers, sit on the finest sand while the sun comes out briefly. I listen to the Irish radio and discover that I like fiddles and jigs and even the DJs are friendlier in Ireland.

So this is how I fell in love with the Irish and their landscape; a seductive mix of green fields, greener folk, lovely wholesome food, a lack of rush, zero cynicism and the kindest, most heart-warming friendliness. I hope you enjoy seeking out these places for yourself and I hope to go back soon with a pig under each arm.

Nicola Crosse

How we choose our Special Places

It's simple. There are no rules, no boxes to tick. We choose places that we like and are fiercely subjective in our choices. We also recognise that one person's idea of special is not necessarily someone else's so there is a huge variety of places, and prices, in the book. Those who are familiar with our Special Places series know that we look for comfort, originality, authenticity, and reject the insincere, the anonymous and the banal. The way guests are treated comes as high on our list as the setting, the architecture, the atmosphere and the food.

Inspections

We visit every place in the guide to get a feel for how both house and owner tick. We don't take a clipboard and we don't have a list of what is acceptable and what is not. Instead, we chat for an hour or so with the owner and look round. It's all very informal, but it gives us an excellent idea of who would enjoy staying there. If the visit happens to be the last of the day, we sometimes stay the night. Once in the book, properties are re-inspected every three to four years so that we can keep things fresh and accurate.

Feedback

In between inspections we rely on feedback from our army of readers, as well as from staff members who are encouraged to visit properties across the series. This feedback is invaluable to us and we always follow up on comments.

Photo: Picin, entry 125

So do tell us whether your stay has been a joy or not, if the atmosphere was great or stuffy, the owners cheery or bored. The accuracy of the book depends on what you, and our inspectors, tell us. A lot of the new entries in each edition are recommended by our readers, so keep telling us about new places you've discovered too. Please use the forms on our website at www.sawdays.co.uk, or later in this book (p. 277).

However, please do not tell us if the bedside light was broken, or the shower head was scummy. Tell the owner, immediately, and get them to do something about it. Most owners are

more than happy to correct problems and will bend over backwards to help. Far better than bottling it up and then writing to us a week later!

Subscriptions

Owners pay to appear in this guide. Their fee goes towards the high costs of inspecting, of producing an all-colour book and of maintaining our website. We only include places that we like and find special for one reason or another, so it is not possible for anyone to buy their way onto these pages. Nor is it possible for the owner to write their own description. We will say if the bedrooms are small, or if a main road is near. We do our best to avoid misleading people.

Disclaimer

We make no claims to pure objectivity in choosing these places. They are here simply because we like them. Our opinions and tastes are ours alone and this book is a statement of them; we hope you will share them. We have done our utmost to get our facts right but apologise unreservedly for any mistakes that may have crept in.

You should know that we don't check such things as fire regulations, swimming pool security or any other laws with which owners of properties receiving paying guests should comply. This is the responsibility of the owners.

Photo left: Clonalis House, entry 63
Photo right: The Schoolhouse, entry 68

Using this book

The places in this guide are arranged into the four historic provinces of Ulster (north), Connacht (west), Munster (south) and Leinster (east). Counties are listed alphabetically within the provinces and the type of place – B&B, hotel, inn, self-catering – is given on each entry.

Finding the right place for you

All these places are special in one way or another. All have been visited and then written about honestly so that you can decide for yourselves which will suit you. Those of you who swear by Sawday's books trust our write-ups precisely because we don't have a blanket standard; we include places simply because we like them. But we all have different priorities, so do read the descriptions carefully and pick out the places where you will be comfortable. If something is particularly important to you then check when you book: a simple question or two can avoid misunderstandings.

Maps

Each property is flagged with its entry number on the maps at the front. These maps are a great starting point for planning your trip, but please don't use them as anything other than a general guide – use a decent road map for real navigation. Most places will send you detailed instructions once you have booked your stay.

Ethical Collection

We're always keen to draw attention to owners who are striving to have a positive impact on the world, so you'll notice that some entries are flagged as being part of our "Ethical Collection". These places are working hard to reduce their environmental footprint, making significant contributions to their local community, or are passionate about serving local or organic food. Owners have had to fill in a very detailed questionnaire before becoming part of this Collection – read more on page 270. This doesn't mean that other places in the guide are not taking similar initiatives – many are – but we may not yet know about them.

Sawday's Travel Club

We've recently launched a Travel Club, based around the Special Places to Stay series; you'll see a symbol on those

Photo: The Merrion Mews & Stables, entry 170

places offering something extra to Club members, so to find out how to join see page 266.

Symbols

Below each entry you will see some symbols, which are explained at the very back of the book. They are based on the information given to us by the owners. However, things do change: bikes may be under repair or the owners have a new pet. Please use the symbols as a guide rather than an absolute statement of fact and double-check anything that is important to you — owners occasionally bend their own rules, so it's worth asking if you may take your child or dog even if they don't have the symbol.

Children – The symbol shows places which are happy to accept children of all ages. This does not mean that they will necessarily have cots, high chairs, etc. If an owner welcomes children but only those above a certain age, we have put these details at the end of their write-up. These houses do not have the child symbol, but even these folk may accept your younger child if you are the only guests. Many who say no to children do so not because they don't like them but because they may have a steep stair, an unfenced pond or they find balancing the needs of mixed age groups too challenging.

Pets – Our symbol shows places which are happy to accept pets. It means they can sleep in the bedroom with you, but not on the bed. Be realistic about your pet – if it is nervous or excitable or doesn't like the company of other dogs, people, chickens, or children, then say so.

Owners' pets – The symbol is given when the owners have their own pet on the premises. It may not be a cat! But it is there to warn you that you may be greeted by a dog, serenaded by a parrot, or indeed sat upon by a cat.

Quick reference indices

At the back of the book you'll find a number of quick-reference indices showing those places that offer a particular service, perhaps a room for under £70/€100 a night, or horse-riding nearby. They are worth flicking through if you are looking for something specific.

Photo: Rock Cottage, entry 87

Practical matters

Types of places
This book covers all types of places to stay in Ireland, as long as they are special. The type of place is indicated on each entry, and an outline of what we mean by each type is given below.

B&Bs – range from people's homes, where you can enjoy a glimpse of family life, through to guest houses with receptionists. And many B&Bs – in addition to the wonderful breakfasts – offer first-class food in the evenings. Some owners give you a front door key so you may come and go as you please; others like to have the house empty between, say, 10am and 4pm.

Hotels – come in all sorts too, from the country-house hotel with touches of luxury and lots of services, to the little modern place in town where the emphasis is on intimacy and hands-on attention. Food is nearly always a feature, often the best local produce.

Inns – also focus on the quality of their food and offer the well-fed guest a decent place to lay his head for the night. They will be busy in the evenings, often with live music and extended opening hours. This is part of their charm and those wanting peace and quiet should take it into account.

Self-catering – a good number of our entries are houses, gate houses, lodges and cottages that you can rent by the week. Unless otherwise stated, the price includes linen, heating and electricity but always check when booking. Owners may charge extra for fuel for the fire.

Rooms
Bedrooms – We tell you if a room is a double, twin/double (ie with zip and link beds), suite (with a sitting area), family or single. Owners will usually be flexible if they can, and juggle beds or bedrooms; talk to them about what you need before you book. It is rare to be given your own room key in a B&B. Where an entry reads '3 + 1' this means 3 B&B rooms plus 1 self-catering apartment/cottage.

Bathrooms – Most bedrooms in this book have an en suite bath or shower room; we only mention bathroom details when they do not. If these things are important to you, please check when booking.

Meals
Apart from at self-catering properties, a full cooked breakfast is included unless we say otherwise. Often you will feast on

Photo left: Inis Meáin Restaurant & Suites, entry 51
Photo right: Tankardstown House, entry 196

local sausage and bacon, eggs from resident hens, homemade breads and jams. Sometimes you may have organic yogurts and beautifully presented fruit compotes. Other places will give you a good continental breakfast instead. Some places are fairly unbending about breakfast times, others are happy to just wait until you want it, or even bring it to you in bed.

Do eat in if you can – this book is teeming with good cooks. And how much more relaxing after a day out to have to move no further than the dining room for an excellent dinner, and to eat and drink knowing there's only a flight of stairs between you and your bed.

Prices and minimum stays

The prices we quote are per night per room unless otherwise stated, breakfast included. For self-catering we specify if the price is per week; for half-board it may be per person (p.p.). Meal prices are always given per person.

Apart from breakfast, no meals should be expected unless you have arranged them in advance. Meal prices are quoted per person, and at B&Bs dinner is often a social occasion shared with your hosts and other guests.

Photo: Rathmullan House, entry 14

Price ranges cover seasonal differences and different types of rooms. Some owners charge more at certain times (during festivals, for example) and some charge less for stays of more than one night. Some ask for a two-night minimum stay at weekends or in high season, and we mention this where possible. Prices quoted are those given to us for 2009–2011 but are not guaranteed, so do double-check when booking. In Northern Ireland the prices are in sterling (£); in the Republic they are in euros (€). There's a conversion indicator (correct at time of going to press) at the back of the book.

Telephoning

The telephone code for the Republic is 353, for Northern Ireland it is 44. We have included the country code in the listings: dial your international access and the number as printed, ignoring the (0).

When telephoning from within the country just dial the national number including the (0).

Booking and cancellation

Requests for deposits vary; some are non-refundable, and some owners may charge you for the whole of the booked stay in advance.

Some cancellation policies are more stringent than others. It is also worth noting that some owners will take this deposit directly from your credit/debit card without contacting you to discuss it. So ask them to explain their cancellation policy clearly before booking so you understand exactly where you stand; it may well avoid a nasty surprise.

Payment

The majority of places take credit or debit cards, but do check in advance that your particular card is acceptable. Those places that do take cards are marked with the appropriate symbol.

Tipping

Owners do not expect tips. If you have been treated with extraordinary kindness, write to them, or leave a small gift. Please tell us, too – we love to hear, and we do note, all feedback.

Arrivals and departures

In hotels rooms are usually available by mid-afternoon; in B&Bs and self-catering places it may be a bit later, but do try and agree an arrival time with the owners in advance or you may find nobody there.

Closed

When given in months this means the whole of the month(s) stated. So, 'Closed: November–March' means closed from 1 November to 31 March.

Photo: Cuasnóg, entry 211

Key to general map

The regions of Ireland (colour-coded opposite)

Ulster • **Connacht** • Munster • **Leinster**

Ulster (entries 1–34)
Antrim
Armagh
Donegal
Down
Fermanagh
Londonderry
Monaghan
Tyrone

Connacht (entries 35–69)
Galway
Leitrim
Mayo
Roscommon
Sligo

Munster (entries 70–166)
Clare
Cork
Kerry
Limerick
Tipperary
Waterford

Leinster (entries 167–219)
Carlow
Dublin
Kildare
Kilkenny
Laois
Longford
Louth
Meath
Offaly
Westmeath
Wexfod
Wicklow

General map

Map 1

Map 2

26 Map 3

Map 4

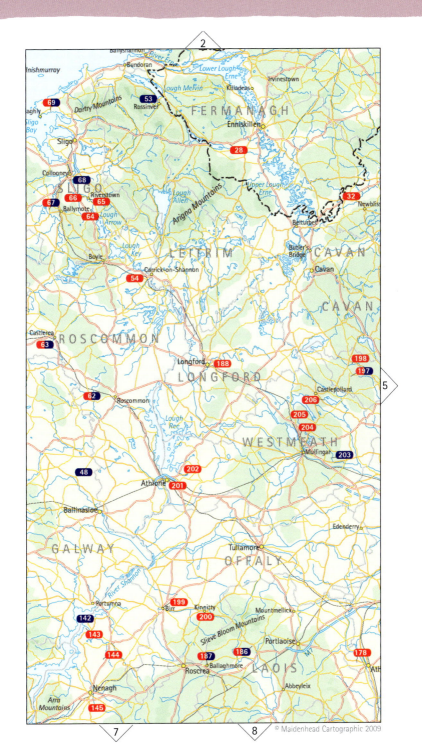

28 Map 5

Map 6

Map 7

Map 8

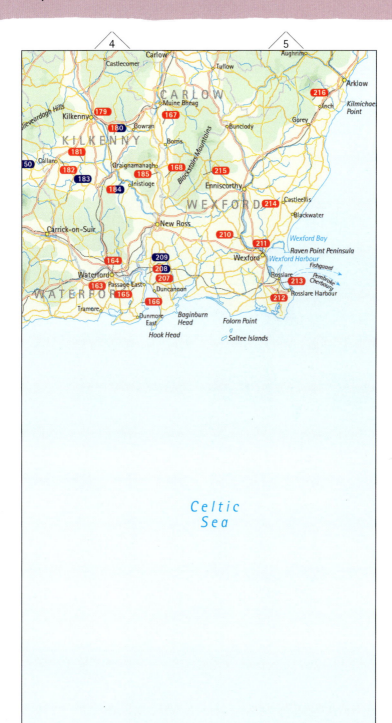

Ulster

Photo: istockphoto.com

Co. Antrim — Hotel

Bushmills Inn Hotel

The old coaching inn comes into its own at night, when the fires are all roaring and you are by one of them, perched on a rocking chair with a pint of Guinness to hand. Under new ownership, Bushmills has not lost its rustic appeal: there is much charm. Bedrooms are still divided between the old inn (small, comfortable, cottagey) and the ten-year-old extension, Mill House. Here, where rooms are spacious and quietly luxurious, the sense of settled age is surprising; there are distressed walls, dark wood and leather, space for a sofa or two. But the original warren-like 17th-century coaching inn lives on in masses of timber – panelling, partitions, beams, and, in the restaurant wooden booths ('snugs') where the stables once were. Expect multifarious sitting spaces, some with traditional gaslights, flagstones, oil lamps and rural bric-a-brac, and the delicious smell of turf fires. A warm atmosphere of relaxed indulgence prevails, ideal for small groups and couples. Most come for the golf, the Giant's Causeway coastline and the world's oldest distillery up the road. Raise your glass to Ireland!

Price	£178–£398. Singles from £68.
Rooms	41: 34 twins/doubles, 1 suite, 4 junior suites, 2 family rooms.
Meals	Dinner, à la carte, about £30. Day menu, until 6pm, £5–£25. Wine £14–£350.
Closed	Christmas Day.
Directions	From A26 at Ballymoney B66 then right B17 to Bushmills & Giant's Causeway. In town, hotel entrance before bridge near River Bush.

Alan Dunlop
9 Dunluce Road, Bushmills,
Co. Antrim BT57 8QG

Tel	+44 (0)28 2073 3000
Fax	+44 (0)28 2073 2048
Email	mail@bushmillsinn.com
Web	www.bushmillsinn.com

B&B	Co. Antrim

Whitepark House

Bob is amazing, the ultimate host, welcoming you as a friend, helping you plan your day, turning on your bedside light before you come home, conjuring up fabulous cakes. No wonder he was 'UK Landlady of the Year 2003'! The incongruously castellated frontage opens onto an eye-stretching gathering of beatific buddhas, prickly cacti, orderly elephants and manifold pictures among a mass of indoor vegetation. Bob and Siobhán created all this from trips to India, Sri Lanka and further east. Whitepark House, first built in 1735, is in a superb position looking right out to sea. On clear days you can see Rathlin lighthouse, Islay and Jura. Sun-streamed bedrooms ooze splendour, especially the big double at the top of the stairs, as do the bathrooms with their Laura Ashley wallpapers, big tubs and drenching showers. Mattresses are perfect, bed linen pristine. Breakfast by the window in the open-plan hall or in the luxurious conservatory and plot your walks along the coast – surely one of the reasons cameras were invented. *Children over 12 welcome.*

Price	£100. Singles £75.
Rooms	3: 2 doubles, 1 twin.
Meals	Restaurants within 5 miles.
Closed	Rarely.
Directions	From Bushmills A2 coast road to Whitepark Bay. Entrance on right, 300 yds past beach car park.

	Bob & Siobhán Isles Whitepark Bay, Ballintoy, Co. Antrim BT54 6NH
Tel	+44 (0)28 2073 1482
Email	bob@whiteparkhouse.com
Web	www.whiteparkhouse.com

Entry 2   Map 2

Co. Antrim

Self-catering

Bath Lodge

Perched at the end of half a mile of golden sand – waves lapping nearby, sea birds overhead, the heart-stopping view to Rathlin Island and Scotland all yours – Bath Lodge is a quaint, lovable family house, a warren of level changes, rambling staircase, corners, crannies and a comfortable mix of furniture. There's nothing posh or scary: bring the children, their friends and all the gear without fear for the ancient floorboards or well-worn rugs. The grown-ups will grab the deep-seated view-filled sitting room; the big downstairs 'dormitory' doubles as a fine playroom, the lawns are great for games, the walled garden for sheltered peace. Originally five 18th-century miners' cottages whose tiny attics were thrown up to create lofty ceilings, it has old bones and the essential modernities. In the large kitchen/breakfast room the Aga fights the huge refrigerator for centre stage, the scullery hides any mess. Bedrooms have the same old-style comfort of mixed antiques, good beds, space. Rabbits crop the clifftop of the wild garden in peace yet the town is just behind you. Brilliant for a family holiday.

Price	£400-£900 per week.
Rooms	House for 12. Also Garden Room: 1 double with child's bed & bath.
Meals	Restaurants 20-30 minute walk.
Closed	Rarely.
Directions	Directions given on booking.

Dr Sarah Mills
16 Carrickmore Road, Ballycastle,
Co. Antrim BT54 6QS
Tel   +44 (0)20 7834 5839
Email   sarah@mills158.co.uk

Self-catering   Co. Antrim

The Barnhouse at Drumkeerin

What a remarkable couple, gently retired into an early taste of paradise, strong-minded and active, both artists and art historians. Mary takes centre stage with her love of life and people, her sparkling talk of art and artists (original paintings and cartoons dot the walls), Ireland and the Irish. Joe quietly fills all the other roles with his strength, humour and wisdom. They chose their house for the heart-stopping view of hills and distant sea – "we are working with the scenery" they say – and you can only tear yourself away by walking out into it; now they have renovated the barn in the lower garden and opened it to self-catering guests. It has a pristine interior and a lovely garden view from its (narrow but very well-equipped) kitchen. The sitting room has a rust and green colour scheme and two sofas, the main bedroom has views across hills and the glens, the others are pleasantly plain with velux windows. A tamed garden and beautiful orchard leads to woodland and a rushing stream – a child's dream. The hens wander, the cats doze. A place of heart and humanity against an overawing backdrop of natural power and beauty.

Price	£500 per week.
Rooms	House for 6-7.
Meals	Restaurants in village.
Closed	Rarely.
Directions	From Larne A2, or from Ballymena A43, to Cushendall; continue A2 to Cushendun; continue to Torr Road junc.; right for 50 yds, left into lane, house signposted.

Joe & Mary McFadden
201a Torr Road, Cushendun,
Co. Antrim BT44 0PU
Tel   +44 (0)28 2176 1554
Email drumkeerin@zoom.co.uk
Web   www.drumkeeringuesthouse.com

Co. Antrim

B&B

Marlagh Lodge

A couple of young musicians take on a Victorian house, devote intense energy to saving and restoring it all: fine proportions, original fireplaces, "servants' quarters" (where they now live), the old garden… and declare themselves "Victorians at heart". Voracious readers, Rachel and Robert prefer long walks and good food to TV. Passionate about their house, they have treated it to stacks of books, antique pianos, prints, furniture and beautiful William Morris wallpapers, and shrouded it from the road with shrubs and trees. After strong colours and a certain formality downstairs, a lighter, quirkier touch informs the luxurious bedrooms: salvaged baths with character, imperfections and the view; lovely furniture, fabrics and linens. These delightful, energetic people did all the decorating themselves, invented Ballymarlagh Tummy Warmer porridge, among other breakfast marvels, and beyond the pretty courtyard, where the bell-tower still crowns the stables, have planted herbs at the foot of the monkey-puzzle tree. New are the hens, and the big patio at the back. It is a delight to stay.

Travel Club Offer. See page 266.

Price	£90. Singles £45.
Rooms	3: 1 double, 1 four-poster; 1 twin with separate bath.
Meals	Dinner £32.50, by arrangement. Wine from £14.50.
Closed	Rarely.
Directions	From Belfast A26 to Ballymena until signs for Larne; at 2nd r'bout, A36 for Larne 0.75 miles (end of crawler lane); right on to Rankinstown Road, drive immed. on left.

Rachel & Robert Thompson
71 Moorfields Road, Ballymena,
Co. Antrim BT42 3BU

Tel	+44 (0)28 2563 1505
Fax	+44 (0)28 2564 1590
Email	info@marlaghlodge.com
Web	www.marlaghlodge.com

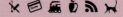

B&B   Co. Antrim

Ravenhill House

Belfast has a buoyant, contemporary cultural life and staying at Ravenhill will connect you to those vibes. The centre is 10 minutes by bus and there's lots of life within walking distance, the Real Music Club for example. Running this bright and well-loved B&B in a leafy district of smart Victorian houses, the Nicholsons are a young and enthusiastic couple. Roger, from the north of England, loves the buzz of his adopted city and is glad to share its sights and secrets. Olive, from Westmeath, is warm and friendly, faultlessly juggling the B&B and three energetic children. Ravenhill has a cheerful lived-in atmosphere, people come and go, kids play here and there, the city moves past the window. Good-sized bedrooms are done with soothing greens, crisp linen, the odd Barbara Allen print and locally-made ash and oak furniture with purple heart trim. There's a sitting room with books, a piano, log fire and internet connection. Entirely local or organic, breakfast is mouth-watering: Roger is proud of his authentic Ulster breakfasts with homemade bread and marmalade a speciality – not to be hurried.

Price	£75-£90. Singles £50-£60.
Rooms	5: 4 twins/doubles, 1 single.
Meals	Restaurants within walking distance.
Closed	Christmas & New Year.
Directions	From city centre, A24 Ormeau road for Newcastle & Downpatrick; over bridge; 500 yds further, left at r'bout; house 50 yds on right.

	Olive & Roger Nicholson 690 Ravenhill Road, Belfast, Co. Antrim BT6 0BZ
Tel	+44 (0)28 9020 7444
Fax	+44 (0)28 9028 2590
Email	relax@ravenhillhouse.com
Web	www.ravenhillhouse.com

Entry 6   Map 2 & 5

Co. Armagh

B&B

Newforge House

Beautifying, restoring, then inviting the world to share it is a splendid way to save an old family house. John's ancestors, who owned the local linen mill, built this elegantly generous mansion 200 years ago. After two years of deep and respectful restoration, he and Louise have hung up their tools, opened the door and put their creative talents at the service of people wanting gentle young style, lovely rooms and good fresh home-cooked food in season, be they independent travellers, wedding parties or business events. The Mathers love this house and its history, at every turn there's an old family photograph (don't miss the downstairs loo), a linen history memento, an original wall hanging. The blend of antique and modern gives the house easy charm, soft colours are mixed for serenity – peach, green, all the beiges – perfect foils for the lustrous furniture. Superb modern bathrooms and IT connections are unobtrusive extras. You won't easily forget Louise's lilting Scottish accent or John's fine food. Nor his father's tireless pursuit of perfection outside: the formal garden is deservedly listed.

Travel Club Offer. See page 266.

Price	£110-£165. Singles £75-£105. Discounts groups & over 2 nights.
Rooms	6: 3 twins/doubles, 2 doubles, 1 four-poster.
Meals	Dinner £32.50 (Tue-Sat). Wine from £14. By arrangement. Light supper Sun & Mon.
Closed	Christmas & New Year.
Directions	From Belfast M1 west, exit 9 for Lurgan 3 miles; in Magheralin left at Byrne's pub: Newforge Road 0.5 miles; 1st left after speed limit sign.

The Mathers Family
58 Newforge Road, Magheralin,
Craigavon, Co. Armagh BT67 0QL

Tel	+44 (0)28 9261 1255
Fax	+44 (0)28 9261 2823
Email	enquiries@newforgehouse.com
Web	www.newforgehouse.com

Entry 7   Map 2 & 5

B&B   Co. Donegal

Coxtown Manor

Relaxed, amiable and with a Donegal accent, Eduard came from Belgium to turn a Georgian manor into a popular and highly original Irish getaway. Owned by Hamiltons from 1750 until 'Miss Sheila' died in 1992, it oozes history. To avoid any intimations of grandeur, Eduard combines warm ochre colours with continental antiques, minimalist Belgian art with two tapestries and a sleek black piano. Also, lots of corners for chilling out in the main sitting room and a fine stone fireplace in the cosy bar. Bedrooms come in two styles: grand in the main house with old furniture, lots of space and open fires; contemporary in the coach house, also generous, with heavenly showers and more modern Belgian art. Luxury soaps for all and DVDs for the top rooms. But the restaurant is Coxtown's heart. A great chef, Eduard uses the freshest produce in a few beautifully cooked and presented dishes followed, for example, by a mousse made with real Belgian chocolate or his own ice cream. His free-range flock of hens fed on gourmet scraps give the most wonderful eggs: Belgian breakfast is a joy. Golf and beautiful beaches are close.

Price	€150-€210. Singles €100-€115.
Rooms	9: 3 doubles, 1 single. Coach House: 5 doubles.
Meals	Dinner €52 (not Mondays).
Closed	November-January.
Directions	From Donegal N15 for Ballyshannon 11km; left to Laghey and then on Old Ballintra Road 3km; house on right.

Eduard Dewael
Laghey, Co. Donegal

Tel	+353 (0)74 973 4575
Fax	+353 (0)74 973 4576
Email	coxtownmanor@oddpost.com
Web	www.coxtownmanor.com

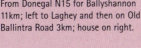

Entry 8   Map 1

Co. Donegal   B&B

Ard Na Breatha Guest House & Restaurant

It's a 15-minute stroll from here into Donegal where you can catch a water bus for a tour of the bay. Smiling, enterprising, hard-working Theresa loves what she does and she does it brilliantly; the restaurant and B&B are pristine and the food is delicious. This is a real farm-to-fork enterprise, with partner Albert both farmer and chef. They have 100 acres to rear their own beef and lamb and grow their own veg, and most of it is organic; real food is a passion. As for the house, it has an attractive stone front and a semi-urban view of Donegal town, with the Bluestack mountains rising majestically to the east. Reclaimed stone flag floors invite you in, a wall-hanging in Latin hangs beside an antique range, there are smart leather armchairs by the fire – cosy and convivial with an honesty bar – and white linen on the tables. The bedrooms are furnished with wrought-iron beds, the bathrooms have lovely soaps and towels, all is spotless and welcoming. A covered walkway links the B&B with the restaurant, which opens at weekends only; but if you stay here, you can eat in every night.

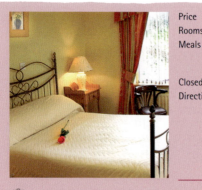

Price	€80-€110. Family €119-€139.
Rooms	6: 3 doubles, 2 twins, 1 family room.
Meals	Dinner €45. Wine from €18. Packed lunch €6.50. Restaurants in Donegal 1.5km.
Closed	November-January.
Directions	From Donegal Town N56; take first right signed for Ard Na Breatha. After 0.5km, take right at Vivo Store, straight ahead for 1km.

Travel Club Offer. See page 266.

Mrs Theresa Morrow
Drumrooske Middle, Donegal,
Co. Donegal

Tel	+353 (0)74 972 2288
Fax	+353 (0)74 974 0720
Email	info@ardnabreatha.com
Web	www.ardnabreatha.com

Entry 9   Map 1

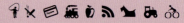

B&B & Self-catering   Co. Donegal

Bruckless House

Bruckless revels in peace and the subtlest sea light, the gardens bordering the estuary add charm and a sense of freedom: life is exceedingly mellow in this handsome old 'grange' farmhouse. It has a faded, lived-in Georgian elegance and Joan and Clive are a delightful couple to spend time with. They are the leading breeders of Connemara ponies in the north-west with 20 acres of stud farm. On good days, they harness a pony to their 1890 Limerick gig and trot off down to St John's Point. The tall graceful reception rooms are filled with lovely things from their years in the East: brush-stroke paintings from China, beautiful rugs, a gorgeous rosewood table. Some finds are more local, such as the Irish oak sideboard, deeply carved with fish and gargoyles, that Joan restored after discovering it in a peat store. Comparatively unadorned family-feel bedrooms overlook the original cobbled courtyard. Joan's pride is the garden, a neat-wild mixture of lawn, flower bed, rockery and woodland where paths meander through mossy glades past bluebells and montbretia to the quayside by a tiny sea inlet.

Price	€110-€130. Singles €55-€65. Cottage €255-€550 per week.
Rooms	4 + 1: 1 double, 1 twin; 2 singles, sharing bathroom. Cottage for 4.
Meals	Restaurant 1.6km.
Closed	October-March.
Directions	From Donegal N56 for Killybegs 19km & through Dunkineely. House signposted on left after 3km.

Joan & Clive Evans
Bruckless, Dunkineely,
Co. Donegal
Tel   +353 (0)74 973 7071
Email   bruc@bruckless.com
Web   www.bruckless.com

Entry 10   Map 1

Co. Donegal

B&B

The Green Gate

Rabbits mow the lawn, a rusting Citroen decorates the garden, the sea pounds at the cliffs below (glory) and Paul revels in his windswept eyrie. He is the most un-Parisian of exiles, the most unlikely of adopted Irishmen, but his bookish leanings and many travels are revealed by his fireside when he tells the journey of a city intellectual into deepest Donegal. The compact cottage is big enough for Paul, his few treasures, his many friends and his all-ears guests – as well as an incredible number of homemade preserves and the lampshades made from mother-of-pearl that his son dived for off Corsica. Bedrooms are in low-slung converted cowsheds clustered round the cottage: stone, thatch and slate keep the elements out, beams and pine slatting, warm rugs and tweed curtains, woven bedcovers, the odd country antique or unexpected French piece, brown water in the taps, hangers on hooks for a few clothes, stiff (but clean) towels… all create a unique effect, a million miles from the American way of life. Dutch guests love his 'Swiss' coffee: go with an open mind, and layers of jumpers. *Smokers welcome.*

Price	€90-€110. Singles from €70.
Rooms	4 doubles.
Meals	Pubs & restaurants in Ardara, 5-minute drive.
Closed	Never.
Directions	N56 from Ardara to Killybegs; 1st left up winding road, just after Texaco garage on your right. Follow Green Gate signs for 1.5km on narrow road.

Paul Chatenoud
Ardvally, Ardara, Co. Donegal
Tel +353 (0)74 954 1546
Web www.thegreengate.eu

Entry 11   Map 1

B&B Co. Donegal

The Mill Restaurant

The jewel in the crown of many an Irish culinary tour. Susan and Derek have breathed new life into The Mill, creating both B&B and well-loved restaurant. Derek cut his teeth on the prestige of Gleneagles in Scotland then returned happily to his native Donegal to cook – beautifully – with the ingredients: Donegal lamb, oysters, duck, salmon, mussels… and the Guinness bread is divine. Susan, young, modest and wise, makes sure that guests and diners are well looked after. Pleasant carpeted bedrooms, some with sleigh beds and tapestries or watercolours on the walls, have pretty tiled bathroom floors and lake views. Exposed to the mercurial Atlantic and enclosed by the Derryveagh mountains, the hostile beauty of north-west Donegal is manna to the artist – and that includes Susan's grandfather, watercolourist Frank Egginton, who bought the 19th-century mill on New Lake's shores in 1949; his antiques and paintings flow from room to room. Walk up Muckish Mountain or take a ferry to Tory Island where fishermen artists produce well-reputed works – or get your own paintbox out. Quietly special.

Price	€105. Singles €75.
Rooms	6: 4 doubles, 2 twins.
Meals	Dinner from €42. Wine €18. Restaurant closed Mon.
Closed	Mid-Dec to mid-Mar. Open weekends only Nov to mid-Dec & Mar.
Directions	From Dunfanaghy N56 for Falcarragh past gallery on right, down small hill; entrance on right; house overlooks lake.

Susan & Derek Alcorn
Figart, Dunfanaghy, Co. Donegal
Tel   +353 (0)74 913 6985
Fax   +353 (0)74 913 6985
Email info@themillrestaurant.com
Web   www.themillrestaurant.com

Entry 12   Map 1

Co. Donegal   Self-catering

Ardroe Cottage

Not only does it look like beloved great-granny's storybook cottage, it actually is Michael's 300-year-old ancestral home, and its renovation shows how much he and Margaret love it. The deep-country approach, the cobbled yard, half door and thatch outside, the amazing flagged floor inside, the open fire with its old cooking utensils (for you to use…) will transport you to never-neverland. Both living rooms are properly furnished with rustic antiques and old pottery pieces, red and white gingham giving the final cottagey flourish. It's a lesson in conservation: even light switches are hidden in old shelves in old walls. Upstairs, the enchantment is contained beneath pine-clad attic ceilings. One bedroom, on a raised wooden floor, has tiny eyes to the outside world, little windows dug deep in the gable ends, and soft cotton fabrics. The other has an old iron bedstead and larger windows. Through their arched doors, they are simple and inviting. Add a lovely tree-sheltered garden, Portsalon's fine beach, endless wonderful walks and Rathmullan House for an evening treat and you have perfect seclusion and rest.

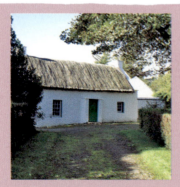

Price	€395-€595 per week.
Rooms	Cottage for 4.
Meals	Restaurants in Portsalon, 3km.
Closed	Rarely.
Directions	Directions given on booking.

Michael & Margaret McElwee
Portsalon, Fanad, Co. Donegal
Tel   +353 (0)74 912 2267
Email enquiries@donegalholiday.com
Web   www.donegalholiday.com

Hotel   Co. Donegal

Rathmullan House

Elegant, professional, ever-friendly – Rathmullan is impossible to fault. Despite (seamless) expansion the Wheelers work to maintain the warm feel that their parents created and there are so many lovely drawing rooms inside, such gorgeous grounds to roam outside, that numbers may only be evident at breakfast. Rathmullan already had its fine Georgian looks, its gardens that roll gently down to the shores of Lough Swilly and its comforting fires. Richly furnished bedrooms overlook the garden through superb tall windows onto balconies or little terraces and have big panelled bathrooms; the family rooms in the old house are veritable suites; there's even a room for your dog. The Wheelers are members of Ireland's Slow Food movement and the canopied restaurant is the backdrop to some wonderful food. Work up an appetite at tennis or croquet, in the indoor heated swimming pool or the steam room, stroll across the lawn and through the dunes to a long empty beach, sally forth to explore the rocky coves of the Fanad Peninsula or Rathmullan village: it has bags of seaside charm.

Price	€170-€330. Singles €85-€140.
Rooms	32 twins/doubles.
Meals	Dinner €55. Wine from €20.
Closed	Christmas; mid-January to mid-February.
Directions	From Letterkenny R245 through Ra(th)melton to Rathmullan. Left in village at sign to hotel; gates on right, through holiday park to house.

Travel Club Offer. See page 266.

	The Wheeler Family Rathmullan, Co. Donegal
Tel	+353 (0)74 915 8188
Fax	+353 (0)74 915 8200
Email	info@rathmullanhouse.com
Web	www.rathmullanhouse.com

Entry 14   Map 1

Co. Donegal

B&B & Self-catering

Frewin

Charming, amusing, Thomas and Regina have taken Irish hospitality to a new level in their relaxed, historic home. The Victorian part was a rectory but the fortified annexe dates from 1698 when landowners needed protection from the odd uprising. Thomas, an antiques collector and restorer of historic buildings, uncovered a curious family link: his great-aunt, a servant girl here before the Great War, had carved her name on the back of a bedroom cupboard. The bedrooms, white-walled, fresh, uncluttered, with great bathrooms and woodland views, are the kind you never want to leave; the small green suite has its own library, a perfect writer's retreat. Regina will cook dinner for groups, served in the elegant buxom dining room – old crockery and silver beneath a chandelier of real candles. Nod off over a nightcap by the fire in the snug, lined with antique lithographs and books. There's a lovely sitting room too, and sweet nooks in the garden. As for the cottage, it's warm and characterful, filled with books and perfect for two. All who leave feel better for having stayed. Special.

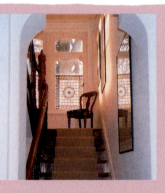

Price	€140-€190. Singles €80-€100. Cottage €500-€575 per week.
Rooms	4 + 1: 3 suites; 1 double with separate bath. Cottage for 2.
Meals	Dinner €50, by arrangement. Restaurant within walking distance.
Closed	Christmas.
Directions	From Letterkenny R245 to Ramelton 13km. Approaching Ramelton, right at speed limits; house 300m on right.

Thomas & Regina Coyle
Ramelton, Co. Donegal
Tel +353 (0)74 915 1246
Fax +353 (0)74 915 1246
Email frewin.ramelton@gmail.com
Web www.frewinhouse.com

B&B   Co. Donegal

Mount Royd Country House

Jo's is an open, comfortable and friendly house. She will gather you in, pour you tea by the fire and entertain you with all you might want to know about the village, the area (Agatha Christie wrote thrillers on the hill opposite), the country past and present: she has won acres of awards for her landladying talents. Her cluttered living room juggles mementoes of the many visitors and every available space has a knick or a knack. The house was built as a farmhouse by one man in the 1940s, it took him four years. Today, creeper softens the edges and curious garden ornaments decorate the front. Don't be alarmed when you enter your boudoir bedroom: the teddy bears will not rush out to hug you nor the porcelain dolls seize you in a crazy waltz; they are simply part of the homely atmosphere, along with Jo's personal mixture of red swirly carpets, lilac bathrooms and fresh flowers. Her Jacob sheep graze happily in the field, her breakfasts flourish everything delicious and the village church is one of the oldest in Ireland. Jo is unusual in particularly welcoming single guests and readers are full of praise.

Price	From €70. Singles €40.
Rooms	4: 2 doubles, 1 twin, 1 triple. Extra bath.
Meals	Roadside diner 1 mile; restaurants 5 miles.
Closed	Rarely.
Directions	From Letterkenny N13 & N14 16km; left R236 to St Johnson/Carrigans then A40 for Londonderry. House signposted on right on leaving village.

	Josephine Martin Carrigans, Co. Donegal
Tel	+353 (0)74 914 0163
Fax	+353 (0)74 914 0400
Email	jmartin@mountroyd.com
Web	www.mountroyd.com

Entry 16   Map 1

Co. Donegal   Self-catering

Johnny's Cottage

Standing on a hill in six acres of glorious country-house gardens, the cottage is a shining gem in the glittering crown of Donegal. After years of renovating for others, Chris seized the chance to convert a derelict 1820s stone cottage near his childhood home – and left the exterior, squat against the elements, deliberately low-key. The inside is an unexpected treat. Space, colour, tradition and contemporary design blend deliciously, in coral walls and slate floors, old pine and new oak, fine woven blankets, a tiled open-plan shower, interesting books, prints and paintings and two open fires. A wall of windows frames the spectacular view of the sandy arc of Culdaff Bay; the informal gardens and the sun-drenched terrace are magical in summer. Your kitchen is an ultra-modern mix of Muji and stainless steel, with sign-rolls from old buses for local history; the 'old kitchen' is totally authentic with turf fire, flagstones, an old Irish settle bed (suitable for one adult or two kids). Hear the sea in summer through open doors, or the blatter of rain in winter snug by a wood stove. Wonderful.

Price	From €1,400 per week.
Rooms	Cottage for 8 (2 doubles, 2 twins, 2 bathrooms).
Meals	Pubs and restaurant in Culdaff, 1.6km.
Closed	Rarely.
Directions	Directions given on booking.

Chris Tinne
Dunowen, Culdaff, Co. Donegal
Tel   +353 (0)74 937 9510
Email   christinne@dunowen.net
Web   www.dunowen.net

Entry 17   Map 2

Clanmurry

Long before the age of steam, John's ancestors carried Irish emigrants to America in square-rigged clippers. Clanmurry celebrates the brave beauty of these ships and their crews and John is a mine of enthralling historical fact. The tumult of the handy Dublin/Belfast A1 fades at the gates as the gentle air of this fine garden and 1820s house takes over. Inside, friendly country pieces sit well among original marble fireplaces, gracious arches and moulded ceilings. Bedrooms, traditionally furnished like the rest of the house, are full of light and garden views; two can connect for families; their daughter's old room is fresh yellow and still shelters a tribe of fluffy friends. Your warm and kindly hosts delight in telling those seafaring tales, helping guests plan their Irish travels or talking gardening. They have put their own stamp on the marvellous mature garden, laid out in the 1960s by a passionate gardener – it deserves more than a passing saunter. And their speciality is coddling eggs for breakfast: they had their first coddled egg on their African honeymoon and have been coddling ever since.

Price	£70. Singles £50.
Rooms	3: 1 twin; 2 twins with separate bathrooms.
Meals	Restaurant 3 miles.
Closed	Christmas & New Year.
Directions	From Belfast M1 south then A1 south to Dromore for exactly 8 miles; 1st right after only road bridge over Dromore bypass; entrance 1st on right.

Sara & John McCorkell
16 Lower Quilly Road, Dromore,
Co. Down BT25 1NL

Tel	+44 (0)28 9269 3760
Fax	+44 (0)28 9269 8106
Email	clanmurry@btinternet.com
Web	www.clanmurry.com

Co. Down   B&B

Sylvan Hill House

One of the most enjoyable couples you could hope to meet. Elise travels, adventurously, intelligently, to wild places in wild ways (huskies to ice hotels in the Arctic, horses round Patagonia, legs in the Himalaya) – not bad for a grandmother. Jimmy prefers his home comforts and is happy seeking adventure over dinner with friends while Elise is away. Horses are a shared passion, they are involved in the annual Balmoral Show in Belfast and have lots of remarkable racing memorabilia. It is a harmonious, human old house of calm character which they have extended over the years and dressed in good plain fabrics plus many colourful touches: Andean shawls rather than chintz, good furniture, hundreds of pictures. The bedrooms are soft, pretty, individual and deeply restful (note the twin's shower cubicle is in the corner). Your hosts almost always dine with their guests, in summer in the little conservatory overlooking the rolling hills, in winter in the deliciously cosy living room – huge fun. Elise is a self-trained chef and loves cooking. Breakfast is a treat, too. *Pets by arrangement.*

Price	£64. Singles £32.
Rooms	3: 1 double; 1 twin with shower & separate wc; 1 triple sharing bath.
Meals	Dinner with wine, £20.
Closed	Rarely.
Directions	From Dromore B2 to Lurgan; 0.5 mile after red houses, right Kilntown Rd for Moira 1.5 miles; house at top of hill on right.

Elise & Jimmy Coburn
76 Kilntown Road, Dromore,
Co. Down BT25 1HS
Tel   +44 (0)28 9269 2321
Email   coburns@sylvanhillhouse.freeserve.co.uk

B&B   Co. Down

Fortwilliam Country House

Eggs from the garden at breakfast and a gorgeous Irish welcome. Tall, friendly, ever-elegant, Mavis loves chatting with you over tea and homemade cakes or the most generous breakfast round a comfortable table in her country-style Aga kitchen where baskets hang from oak beams. Four-square Fortwilliam is 300 years old with 1930s bay windows. Cool colours underfoot, hunting prints on the wall, glass ornaments and antique furniture of great character: fine 1930s coordinates in the Garden bedroom where a window seat looks over the daisy-strewn lawn, gleaming mahogany in the Victorian room, fabulous Irish carved beds in the Primrose room. Each bed is topped by a stylish patchwork throw, bed linen is crisp and white, cosy bathrooms have delicious extras, Terry is a busy farmer tending a suckling herd on 70 acres with help from two friendly dogs; plus his hobby, the thoroughbred brood mares. Curl up beside the fire in the snug drawing room or relax in the tranquil walled garden and enjoy the view of the hills. Nothing is too much trouble here and the Dunlops have won awards – rightly so.

Price	£70. Singles £50.
Rooms	3: 1 double; 1 double, 1 twin each with separate bathroom.
Meals	Restaurant in Hillsborough 3.5 miles.
Closed	Rarely.
Directions	From Hillsborough B177 for Ballynahinch 3.5 miles. House on hill on right, up steep drive.

Terry & Mavis Dunlop
210 Ballynahinch Road, Hillsborough,
Co. Down BT26 6BH
Tel   +44 (0)28 9268 2255
Fax   +44 (0)28 9268 9608
Email info@fortwilliamcountryhouse.com
Web   www.fortwilliamcountryhouse.com

Entry 20   Map 2 & 5

Co. Down   Inn

Dufferin Coaching Inn

The new owners of the Dufferin Inn, a well-travelled sister team, run it with fresh and friendly enthusiasm: they both love meeting new people. Rooms have been brightened up and the big new lounge is a summery festival of leaf-green, yellow and wine-red round the wood-burning stove; breakfast is now prettily arranged in the light of the ground floor. Lush patchwork quilts on four-posters in wrought iron and wood make for colourful, tempting bedrooms, some big, others snugger. The light flows in through floral-framed windows over walls decked in William Morris onto superior pine furniture. The spotless bathrooms are big and square and… different, be it spriggy wallpaper, blood-red panelling or, in one case, the bath in the bedroom. This solid old former bank has a banqueting hall with licensed bar down below (the gents is in the old strongroom) and, as well as tailored receptions, Leontine and Sabina are planning casinos nights, Oktoberfest, murder mystery and private dinner parties. The Dufferin Arms next door has a lovely timeworn atmosphere, excellent food and live music at weekends.

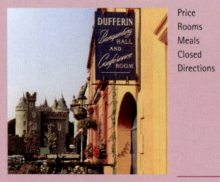

Price	£50-£90. Singles £35-£55.
Rooms	7: 2 doubles, 1 twin, 4 four-posters.
Meals	Dinner at Dufferin Arms next door.
Closed	Rarely.
Directions	From Belfast A22 for Downpatrick to Saintfield; bear left to Killyleagh 18 miles; Killyleagh Castle on your right follow around to the right then left down Hight Street, Inn on left 100 yds.

Leontine Haines
33 High Street, Killyleagh,
Co. Down BT30 9QF
Tel   +44 (0)28 4482 1134
Fax   +44 (0)28 4482 1102
Email   info@dufferincoachinginn.com
Web   www.dufferincoachinginn.com

Entry 21   Map 2 & 5

B&B   Co. Down

The Carriage House

Maureen is the perfect host and her new-old house will charm you with its eclectic interiors and its tranquillity. Delicate antique wardrobes mix easily with retro and modern pieces; lovely oils, prints, tapestries, carvings and, unforgettably, the metal horse sculpture in the yard, decorate the uncluttered open space; a gang of quirky wooden parrots perches in the rubber plants trying to talk to the fat cat and the patient labrador as he strolls around Maureen's long walled garden, delighting her grandchildren. She has a good eye, a feel for colour, a huge heart, tends her guests as carefully as her window boxes and gives her modestly luxurious rooms some special little extras, like fresh rosemary in a vase and home-sewn tapestry cushions. The gorgeously plump bed was made with the finest cotton sheets, its pillows piled high and soft, rather like the local mountains, all designed to counter any slight traffic nuisance (one room is at the back). And next morning, prepare for as dainty or as hearty a feast as you choose: spiced plums, delicious (organic) porridge, herby sausages, homemade scones.

Price	£70. Singles £40-£45.
Rooms	3: 1 double, 2 twins/doubles.
Meals	Buck's Head restaurant next door.
Closed	Rarely.
Directions	From Belfast A24 through Ballynahinch & Clough to Dundrum. House in village centre, painted rich blue, name etched in fanlight.

	Maureen Griffith
	71 Main Street, Dundrum,
	Co. Down BT33 0LU
Tel	+44 (0)28 4375 1635
Email	inbox@carriagehousedundrum.com
Web	www.carriagehousedundrum.com

Travel Club Offer. See page 266.

Ethical Collection: Food.
See page 270.

Entry 22   Map 2 & 5

Co. Down   B&B

Ballymote House

You may feel you have entered a whirlwind: let yourself be swept up by this vibrant young family. Nicola runs the place with gusto and seemingly boundless energy, poaching nectarines for breakfast one moment, conversing with great erudition the next, then out to feed the horses, dogs in tow. They run an insurance business here, too. A genuine no-frills, intelligent and organised family. Neither grand nor lowly, Ballymote stands in an undisturbed pocket of historic monuments, deserted beaches and rolling countryside. A short drive or bike ride leads to the dolmens, castles, healing wells and 10th-century churches left by earlier inhabitants. One of the area's first unfortified houses, this place has wonderful charm, its graceful 1730s Georgian looks framed by a fine park laid out by 19th-century plantsman George Carter. The sight of mature ash and sycamore lifts any morning. The house has natural style, hugely comfortable, easy country-house bedrooms, and there's an odd Landseer glass sculpture of two polar bears. Killough village is near, walks in the Mourne Mountains are stupendous.

Price	From £75. Singles from £40.
Rooms	3: 1 double, 1 single; 1 double with separate bath.
Meals	Meals by arrangement. Pubs & restaurants 2 miles.
Closed	23-30 December.
Directions	From Downpatrick B176 for Killough; house 1 mile on left after town.

James & Nicola Manningham-Buller
Killough Road, Downpatrick,
Co. Down BT30 8BJ
Tel   +44 (0)28 4461 5500
Fax   +44 (0)28 4461 2111
Email bandb@ballymotehouse.com
Web   www.ballymotehouse.com

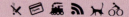

Self-catering   Co. Down

Barr Hall Barns

If you drive along this shore when the tide is out you can watch the grey seals basking on the rocks like fat lazy bananas. It's a magical area, the rolling hills on one side of the water, the dark Mournes rising above the mist on the other, mostly owned by the National Trust. And Barr Hall Barns fit perfectly: stone and brick for the Barn and Cottage, limewash for the haybarn Loft with its floor-to-ceiling window and wow-provoking interior. The gracious, talented owners have converted these once tumbledown outhouses brilliantly and Maureen's creative flair and needlework skills are obvious: vibrant colours, a set of Russian dolls here, a quilt hanging over an internal balcony there. Quality counts too: open-plan kitchens with oil-fired Esse stoves, Le Creuset pots and sharp knives; soft-cushioned sitting areas warmed by cast-iron gas fires. Light pours in through well-placed windows onto original timbers and stonework, pale walls and good furniture. It is all clean-cut, vivid and welcoming, the communal garden, laundry and barbecues making the ideal final flourish.

Price	From £250 per week.
Rooms	Barn for 6-8. Cottage for 4. Loft for 2.
Meals	Restaurants 3.5 miles.
Closed	Rarely.
Directions	Directions on booking.

Dr Maureen Edmondson
31 Barr Hall Road, Portaferry,
Co. Down BT22 1RQ
Tel   +44 (0)28 4272 9895
Fax   +44 (0)28 4272 8053
Email edmondson.barrhall@btinternet.com
Web   www.barrhallbarns.com

Entry 24   Map 2 & 5

Co. Down   B&B

Edenvale House

Up from the main road by the lapping waters of Strangford Lough, the long narrow lane brings you to Edenvale, a very fine, very well-kept Georgian house, steeped in rural peace. Diane welcomes you with tea, cakes and friendly exuberance in the beautiful drawing room (polished mahogany, colourful rugs, gleaming silver) or in the bright sunroom with its views of the brooding Mourne mountains. Gordon has a quick humour, too, and is quite prepared to take over welcome duties as the occasion requires. Large, immaculate bedrooms are well proportioned with luxuriously big beds, pelmets and hangings. There are some unusual pieces of furniture: old 'Flemish' bedheads, an inlaid dressing table, a fine oval-mirrored wardrobe. A lot of effort goes into each aspect of the Edenvale experience, and that includes the well-stocked honesty bar and the superb and varied breakfasts. The garden, as well as happy flourishing roses, has a jungle full of trees for climbing, shrubberies for hiding, a run-around lawn, and hens – a paradise for children. Gentle, playful dogs, too. *20 minutes from Belfast City Airport.*

Price	£90-£100. Singles £60. Child (over 8 years) £15.
Rooms	3: 1 double, 1 twin, 1 family.
Meals	Restaurants in Bangor & Newtownards.
Closed	Christmas & New Year.
Directions	From Newtownards A20 for Portaferry 2 miles; entrance on left through stone pillars. Edenvale 400 yds up lane.

Diane & Gordon Whyte
130 Portaferry Road, Newtownards,
Co. Down BT22 2AH
Tel   +44 (0)28 9181 4881
Email   info@edenvalehouse.com
Web   www.edenvalehouse.com

Entry 25   Map 2 & 5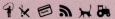

B&B Co. Down

Anna's House

A peaceful house just 14 miles from the city. Anna's love are the gardens beyond Ken's workshop: pine wood with hammock, secret lily pond, orchard, organic veg patch with gazebo, voluptuous borders, all risen to maturity in 30 years, her son's terracotta characters giving the finishing touch. Ken the steel-builder and music-lover has designed a soaring 'concert hall' extension to their old farmhouse: actually a new 30-foot-high living space with a musician's gallery and acoustics for oratorios… steel struts, polished granite floor, a wall of glass to tip you into the serenity of unlandscaped natural beauty and the lake. It is an unmitigated success, a real pleasure to be in, be it for a quiet read or the magic of music. Gently cosmopolitan, hugely kind, Anna loves cooking and baking: one guest told of "breakfasts like wedding feasts". Bedrooms, one on the ground floor, two off the new gallery, are simply pretty with white and pine backgrounds, beautiful linen, mahogany doors, good showers and private balconies; two have leather massaging chairs! Rural seclusion, the freshest food, the loveliest people.

Price	£80–£90. Singles £50.
Rooms	4: 1 double, 1 twin, 2 suites.
Meals	Pub-restaurant 0.8km (free taxi service).
Closed	Christmas & New Year.
Directions	From Belfast A20; A22 for Downpatrick; 3 miles after Comber, pass petrol station & pub on right; right Lisbarnett Rd 0.5 miles; right into private lane to end.

Ken & Anna Johnson
Tullynagee, 35 Lisbarnett Road,
Comber, Co. Down BT23 6AW
Tel +44 (0)28 9754 1566
Email anna@annashouse.com
Web www.annashouse.com

Travel Club Offer. See page 266.

Ethical Collection: Environment; Food.
See page 270.

Entry 26 Map 2 & 5

Co. Down

B&B & Self-catering

Beech Hill Country House

If you don't believe in ground-hugging grandeur, be converted. In this pastoral setting, Victoria's grandmother built a memory of the house she grew up in: Georgian proportions and family elegance, all on one floor. The drawing room is pure landed gentry with Grandmother's cameos, paintings and antiques, lightened by Victoria's superb strong colour touches on the fireside armchairs and cushions; breakfast is a magnificent scene, fine fruits among the silverware, mahogany, walnut and Crown Derby. After years in the catering trade, Victoria is a natural host with lots of local knowledge who clearly enjoys chatting to visitors. You will be greeted by a clutch of happy dogs and offered tea and delicious cakes, possibly in the marvellously floral conservatory between old terracotta tiles and floods of sky. Bedrooms are eminently, seductively comfortable in gently-defined colours, well-chosen fabrics and good furniture. All rooms have French windows onto the peaceful garden and bathrooms are both pretty and immaculate. A most gracious house. *Children over ten welcome.*

Price	£90-£100. Singles £55-£60. Cottage £400-£480 per week.
Rooms	3 + 1: 2 doubles, 1 twin. Cottage for 2-3.
Meals	Restaurants in Holywood & Belfast 4 miles.
Closed	Rarely.
Directions	From Belfast A2 for Bangor. Bypass Holywood; right up Ballymoney Rd at sign to Craigantlet; house 1.75 miles on left.

Victoria Brann
23 Ballymoney Road, Craigantlet,
Holywood, Co. Down BT23 4TG

Tel	+44 (0)28 9042 5892
Fax	+44 (0)28 9042 5892
Email	info@beech-hill.net
Web	www.beech-hill.net

B&B Co. Fermanagh

Abocurragh

You will like them immediately: Bernie, Gerry and the lovely golden lab. The Mullallys have built onto and over their original basic bungalow to produce this house, including the sitting room with its delightful window seats and views... and two extra rooms. Gerry runs the dairy farm, Bernie does a bit of midwifery, and, after 16 years of B&B, they're brilliant at it. Pretty bedrooms are warm, comfortable, immaculate – the cushions just so, the water on the tray, the high-class showers sparkling. Good lighting is another detail, modern pine furniture adds to the clean-cut feel, an old chest of drawers reminds you this is the country. Gerry dashes on his quad bike from yard to field, occasionally dropping by to say a cheery hello and grab a coffee: Abocurragh is busy living its productive life. The front 'pleasure garden' with its tinkling pond and prettiness is as carefully manicured as the house. Breakfast is at one table in the flowery conservatory, or on the terrace: organic oats, free-range eggs from a friend, bacon from happy pigs on an island in Lough Erne. Great value.

Price	£60-£65. Singles £40-£50.
Rooms	3: 1 double, 2 family.
Meals	Restaurants in Belcoo, 4 miles.
Closed	Rarely.
Directions	From Enniskillen A4 for Sligo; through Letterbreen; 2 miles on, left at sign to end of road.

The Mullally Family
Letterbreen, Enniskillen,
Co. Fermanagh BT74 9AG
Tel   +44 (0)28 6634 8484
Fax   +44 (0)28 6634 8288
Email abocurragh@yahoo.com
Web   www.abocurragh.com

Travel Club Offer. See page 266.

Entry 28   Map 1 & 4

Co. Londonderry
Self-catering

Drumcovitt House Cottages

No wonder poets and writers love Drumcovitt, its atmosphere is like no other: hands-on hard work combines with landed grandeur. The original workaday farmhouse on the hill shrank from sight in 1796 when a lofty declaration of Georgian wealth was stretched across its face but the useful parts remained, stalwart as ever, hidden behind the makeover. Here, in the solid old stone barns beneath the towering trees, are three sweet little cottages, each with its own stretch of terrace, two with open fires… and a child's timber trail planned for the garden. With excellent materials and workmanship and lots of colour, they have been converted into welcoming, family-friendly spaces. There's nothing luxurious or fragile, just old-fashioned armchairs, easy wooden floors and simple spotless kitchens. The view will gather you up, on misty mornings, when only the Sperrin peaks and the spire of Banagher church are visible. Walks in the glens may bring sightings of rare birds; back 'home' are three dogs and a lovely young family should you need anything – and that includes a decorated tree at Christmas. *Games room & toys.*

Price	£305-£425 per week.
Rooms	3 cottages for 4.
Meals	Restaurant 20-minute drive.
Closed	Rarely.
Directions	From Derry A6 for Belfast 10 miles; right B74 to Feeny. Through village, house 0.5 miles on left.

The Sloan Family
704 Feeny Road, Feeny,
Co. Londonderry BT47 4SU

Tel	+44 (0)28 7778 1224
Fax	+44 (0)28 7778 1224
Email	drumcovitt.feeny@btinternet.com
Web	www.drumcovitt.com

Self-catering   Co. Londonderry

Derry Farm Cottages

Views to the Donegal hills, Sperrin mountains, a weave of hedgerow-patterned fields – yet Derry's urban buzz only ten minutes away. This sturdy one-storey cottage is in an enviable position. Tucked up a quiet country road, it's a two-minute drive from the main farmyard – and its elegant and effervescent owners. A farmer and former teacher, they've thrown their energy into willow-growing (for bio-energy) and countryside management. They'll point you towards fishing, golf, Derry's historic sights and the north-coast beaches. This is a bright, purpose-built cottage, crisp and airy rather than cosy and twee. In the open-plan living area, a Rayburn sparkles at one end (electric cooker if you prefer), an open fireplace at the other. With white walls, creamy tiled floor, pine furnishings and colourful sofas, it's fresh, welcoming and gleams with modern comforts: smart crockery, dishwasher, entertainment gizmos, even WiFi. Bedrooms are similarly spare yet comfortable, with heaps of goodies in the bathrooms. An excellent food hamper includes wine; this is classy self-catering in tranquil countryside.

Price	£450-£695 per week.
Rooms	Cottage for 4-6.
Meals	Pub/restaurant 2.5 miles.
Closed	Never.
Directions	A6 Londonderry-Belfast; through Drumahoe village. 1st left signed Derry Farm Cottages & Tirbracken Road. 2nd left onto Gortree Rd. 1.5 miles to no. 74.

David & Mary Hunter
74 Gortree Road, Drumahoe,
Londonderry, Co. Londonderry BT47 3LL
Tel   +44 (0)28 7130 1214
Email   info@derryfarmcottages.com
Web   www.derryfarmcottages.com

Entry 30   Map 1

Co. Londonderry

B&B & Self-catering

The Merchant's House

Do visit Derry, Ireland's best-preserved walled city. Fascinating because of its position at the core of Northern Ireland's turbulent 20th century, it also has St Columb's Cathedral in the Planter gothic style to blow its trumpet, and the Verbal Arts Centre to celebrate the Irish oral tradition. The real find, though, is the Merchant's House, an 1868 townhouse built in the Georgian style on a quiet street and lovingly, simply, naturally restored by Joan and Peter, two of the most unusual and civilised people you are likely to meet. Now they live a few streets away but join a colourful list of previous owners who include a Justice of the Peace, a grocer, two rectors and a butcher. Edward VII is said to have had tea in the dining room where breakfast is now served round a large wooden table. The bedrooms are full of period furniture, including a gorgeous half-tester bed; note that one shower room is down a short flight of stairs. The rich-red, first-floor living room has the glorious generosity of the Georgian ideal; the self-catering apartments stand within sight of the cathedral. *Handy for Derry airport.*

Price	£55–£65. Singles £35–£50. Aparments £350–£550 per week.
Rooms	4 + 2: 1 double with sep. bath; 1 twin with sep. shower; 1 double, 1 twin, sharing bath. 2 apts for 4 & 8.
Meals	Restaurants in Derry.
Closed	January.
Directions	A2 to Derry over Craigavon Bridge, right for centre. Over 2 r'bouts, past Tesco, left Lower Clarendon St, 1st right after lights. Ask about parking.

Joan & Peter Pyne
16 Queen Street, Derry,
Co. Londonderry BT48 7EQ

Tel	+44 (0)28 7126 9691
Fax	+44 (0)28 7126 6913
Email	saddlershouse@btinternet.com
Web	www.thesaddlershouse.com

B&B   Co. Monaghan

Hilton Park

Hilton Park is a stunning one-off, a majestic building in beautiful grounds that has been in the same family since it was built in 1734. The setting has something of an 18th-century Gainsborough and since this most imposing country house lies in a less-visited part of Ireland its original spirit remains intact. Johnny deserves much of the credit for this, steadfastly refusing to turn the family pile into a theme park and taking huge care of wildlife habitats and woodland (pine martens and red squirrels have even returned). Walk the estate and see why he's holding on. Explore the biodynamic kitchen garden where Lucy grows for the table – and maybe for her next book. She already has *Potatoes* and *Squashes* on the shelves. They are a strong intelligent couple. Dine before an incomparable view that stretches across formal gardens and mature parkland to a lake where the evening sun glints. The two master bedrooms are fabulous, the odd heirloom lends charm to the others, and refurbishment is ongoing. Lounge in splendid decadence and let Hilton Park cast its spell. *Children over seven welcome.*

Price	€250-€300. Singles €165-€190.
Rooms	6: 3 doubles, 2 twins, 1 family.
Meals	Dinner from €55. Wine from €20.
Closed	November-February, except to groups.
Directions	From Clones for Scotshouse 3 miles: gates on right. Airport bus to Monaghan: pick-up can be arranged.

Travel Club Offer. See page 266.

Johnny & Lucy Madden
Clones, Co. Monaghan
Tel   +353 (0)47 56007
Email mail@hiltonpark.ie
Web   www.hiltonpark.ie

Entry 32   Map 1 & 4

Co. Monaghan

Hotel & Self-catering

Castle Leslie

It is informal, grand, slick, tasteful, enchanting. Sammy, strong and fearless with a huge sense of fun – like all the artistic, eccentric Leslies – runs the family home. Castle Leslie is a professional operation set in magnificent grounds, like a small village that has seen big changes, especially last year. The new riding centre will challenge you, the cookery school will entertain you, the refurbished Hunting Lodge will charm you. The castle itself is a private members club but come for a 'tester' night and discover… the drawing room where a million cameos, fine antiques and heaps of Churchilliana live in grandeur with yards of extravagant sofas and the vast lake view; the theatrical, inimitable dining room; the bedrooms up the great stairs: big or small, sumptuous all, bursting with individuality – one has the oldest bath in Ireland. For upmarket self-caterers, the cottages – swish new builds – lie just outside the grounds; those in the converted stables lie within. Thanks to Sammy's staff – warm, down-to-earth, professional – a sense of purposeful joy hovers over all.

Travel Club Offer. See page 266.

Price	Castle €300–€500 p.p. Lodge €190–€230 per room. Cottages €700–€800 per wk. Stable Mews €610 per wk.
Rooms	Castle: 19 doubles, 1 twin. Lodge: 28 twins/doubles, 2 triples. Cottages: 4 for 10; 8 for 8. Stable Mews: 12 cottages for 5.
Meals	Dinner, 7 courses, with wine €135 (Castle); 3 courses from €45 (Lodge). Bar food option.
Closed	Rarely.
Directions	From Monaghan N12 to Armagh, left on R185 to Glaslough. At end of village.

Samantha Leslie
Glaslough, Monaghan, Co. Monaghan

Tel	+353 (0)47 88100
Fax	+353 (0)47 88256
Email	info@castleleslie.com
Web	www.castleleslie.com

Entry 33 Map 2 & 5

B&B Co. Tyrone

Grange Lodge Country House

People come a long way for Norah's cooking: she is actively involved in promoting Irish food and holds 'Cook with Norah' classes — hugely popular. She and Ralph are friendly, open people, with Ralph front of house spinning yarns as he serves and Norah in the kitchen producing memorable food and winning hatfuls of awards. Many of her vegetables, herbs and soft fruits are home-grown and served in season. After a dinner that would satisfy most folk, coffee may be taken in the antique- and trinket-filled pale green and pink drawing room — an Aladdin's cave! — or, on wet, wintry evenings, around an open fire in the cosy 'den'. The bedrooms are all different with thick carpets, feminine frills, pot-pourri, more trinkets and ivy-clad windows. On its round knoll of manicured lawns beneath the giant chestnut tree, this proud old house has been extended ever since it was built in 1698; the result is a harmonious whole, although telltale floorboard creaks and ceilings that vary in height point to different eras. The breakfast special of porridge and Irish whiskey is astounding. *Children over 12 welcome.*

Price	£89. Singles £69.
Rooms	5: 3 doubles, 1 twin, 1 single.
Meals	Dinner from £33. Wine from £12. By arrangement only.
Closed	Mid-December to 1 February.
Directions	From M1 junc. 15, A29 for Armagh & Moy 1 mile; left at Grange Lodge sign then 1st right. House on right through white-walled entrance.

Norah & Ralph Brown
7 Grange Road, Dungannon,
Co. Tyrone BT71 7EJ
Tel   +44 (0)28 8778 4212
Fax   +44 (0)28 8778 4313
Email stay@grangelodgecountryhouse.com
Web   www.grangelodgecountryhouse.com

Travel Club Offer. See page 266.

Entry 34 Map 2 & 5

Connacht

Photo: istockphoto.com

Hotel & Self-catering　　　　　　　　　　　　　　　　　　　　　　　　Co. Galway

Delphi Lodge

No money can buy such bleak and mighty beauty: surrounded by the tallest mountains in Connemara, the estate's 1,000 acres of mountain, water and bog are kept alive by buckets of lovely Irish rain. The Marquis of Sligo built the house in the mid-1830s as his fishing lodge in the wilds of Connemara. Fly-fishing is still popular with guests, but there's far more to Delphi than fish. Long walks in unspoilt country; friendly outgoing company and a warming whiskey in front of a roaring fire on your return; delicious dinner with the other guests at one long table with gentle, kind Peter often at the helm: the lively conversation, local ingredients and superb house-party atmosphere make these occasions hard to beat and just as hard to leave. Simple, uncluttered bedrooms have good pine beds, plain ticking-type fabrics, proper bathrooms, the odd stuffed trout; front rooms have a heart-stopping view of Fin Lough; and the cottages have been excellently restored. A home not a hotel, Delphi does it well whatever the season, whatever the reason, and most guests know it's only a matter of time before they return.

Price	€200–€266. Singles €133–€166. Cottages €800–€1,250 per week.
Rooms	12 + 5: 12 doubles. 5 cottages for 4–6.
Meals	Lunch €16. Dinner €50. Wine €25–€250.
Closed	Groups only mid-October to mid-February. Cottages open all year.
Directions	From Westport N59 for Leenane & Clifden. 3km before Leenane, right onto Louisburgh/Delphi road for 9km; lodge on left in woods 1km after Delphi Spa.

Peter Mantle
Leenane, Co. Galway

Tel	+353 (0)95 42222
Fax	+353 (0)95 42296
Email	info@delphilodge.ie
Web	www.delphilodge.ie

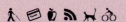 Travel Club Offer. See page 266.

Entry 35　Map 3

Co. Galway   Hotel

Rosleague Manor Hotel

From the moment you see the Twelve Pins of Connemara National Park across the front lawn and over Bearnaderg Bay, you know you've made a good choice. This delightful 200-year-old Regency manor looks, feels, even smells just as a country-house hotel should: where others fall short of expectations, Rosleague delivers. It doesn't feel impersonal, either. Snug drawing rooms have unstuffy elegance: open fires, comfortable seats, private cubbyholes. The grand dining room draws in the view – ideal for a leisurely breakfast by the window. In the evening, it has the buzz of a dinner party despite the separate tables. Friendly staff orchestrate each course with little fuss, serving much-lauded dishes, and the bar overlooking the courtyard feels friendly and somehow colonial. Front bedrooms with the view are the best but the other few compensate by being absolutely enormous. A double room may have a giant bed and a palatial bathroom that make it feel more like a suite. If you can pull yourself away from all this laid-back luxury, visit Inishboffin Island, play tennis, take a sauna, or climb a Pin. *Pets by arrangement.*

Price	€140-€240. Singles from €85.
Rooms	22: 15 twins/doubles & triples, 4 suites, 3 four-posters.
Meals	Dinner from €50.
Closed	Mid-November to mid-March.
Directions	From Clifden N59 for Westport 11km; through Moyard. Hotel entrance sign on left as road dips into Letterfrack.

Mark & Edmund Foyle
Letterfrack, Co. Galway
Tel   +353 (0)95 41101
Fax   +353 (0)95 41168
Email info@rosleague.com
Web   www.rosleague.com

B&B   Co. Galway

Crocnaraw Country House

Prepare to leave this century, detach from material cares, and join Lucy on the 'hill of the fairy fort' (Crocnaraw means just that). Both place and owner have an untroubled, almost ethereal quality so you may sit talking to Lucy for hours in the comforting Aga country kitchen. She took over her mother's Georgian country-house B&B in 1985 and has stamped her own character on it without changing much: bedrooms are old-fashioned and homely; bathrooms are pure 60s in ointment pink or baby blue, jazzed up with a bright red seat or some scented treats. There are lovely antiques before the log fire in the big airy drawing room, a unique bamboo wardrobe made by a local craftsman and black and white painted hall tiles. Take your time, ask Lucy to walk you round the garden and explain its history and development. It was planted by her mother in 1960, Lucy looks after it now, and decorates the house with beautifully arranged fresh flowers. She also cares for special donkeys in a field next door, who are very friendly. Here in the heart of Connemara the magic of Ireland is alive and well.

Price	€100-€150. Singles from €50.
Rooms	4: 2 doubles, 2 twins.
Meals	Dinner €35. By arrangement. BYO wine.
Closed	November-February.
Directions	From Clifden N59 for Westport 9.5km; small sign on left 200m before entrance on left; drive slowly or you'll miss it.

| | Lucy Fretwell
Moyard, Co. Galway |
|---|---|
| Tel | +353 (0)95 41068 |
| Fax | +353 (0)95 41068 |
| Email | rooms@crocnaraw.co.uk |
| Web | www.crocnaraw.co.uk |

Entry 37   Map 3

Co. Galway

B&B

Dolphin Beach House

Imagine lying in a mahogany sleigh bed watching dolphins play in the bay (if you're lucky), then walking through a magical garden to a private cove for a swim. Youthful, vibrant, Dolphin Beach is no ordinary place. Extended and modernised, the 200-year-old farmhouse lies at the windswept edge of Europe among wild fuchsia and the light of the Atlantic. Big bedrooms are full of luxurious fun and eccentric detail: Billy's fabulous handmade headboards, mosaic tiles, wooden ceilings, portholes, warm floors and patio doors that open with smooth precision onto quiet courtyards full or colourful pots or staggering views. The whole family are involved here and they will organise just about any activity you want – riding, deep-sea fishing, hikes, bikes. Barbara cooks with inspiration and fresh produce from the farm and the local area – Connemara lamb, organic veg grown in her neat-as-a-pin plot, wild salmon, fresh lobster. Savour it in the raised dining room overlooking Clifden Bay. After dinner, visit the bustling town by taxi, or lounge in leather in the dark sitting room. Finally, let the sea lull you to sleep.

Price	€140–€190. Singles €80–€110.
Rooms	8: 4 doubles, 3 twins/doubles, 1 single.
Meals	Dinner €43. Wine from €24.30.
Closed	Mid-November to mid-February.
Directions	From Clifden, Sky Rd for 3km to Y-junction; left on Lower Sky Rd. On left after 2.5km, overlooking bay.

The Foyle Family
Lower Sky Road, Clifden, Co. Galway

Tel   +353 (0)95 21204
Fax   +353 (0)95 22935
Email   stay@dolphinbeachhouse.com
Web   www.dolphinbeachhouse.com

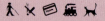

Sea Mist House

Ah, the flowers! Sheila is new to gardening but she's clearly a natural and the garden that leans up the hill behind her house, past the old stables and the suntrap terrace, is a flurry of berries, flowers and scented herbs – they all come into the house for your greater pleasure – with the prettiest little church peering over the wall. Sheila loves having guests in her old family home, you can feel it has always been a happy house. Her auctioneer grandfather furnished it well: a fine sideboard is set with cut-glass wine glasses and a corkscrew for your use in the sitting room, the dining-room paintings hover proudly over a huge old dresser, bought from the Maharajah of Ballinahinch, and some gleaming silver. The effect is welcoming, country, not at all pretentious. There are more paintings, each with a story of its own, in the 'gothic' conservatory which frames the garden so lovingly and keeps the geraniums and ferns warm. Husband Rod gardens at weekends, too. Comfortable bedrooms are generous, simple and fresh, breakfast is delicious, you are in a quiet street bang in the town centre.

Price	€80–€130. Singles €50–€80.
Rooms	4: 3 doubles, 1 twin. (Also 2 overflow rooms for 4.)
Meals	Restaurants within walking distance.
Closed	Midweek in winter; Christmas.
Directions	Follow one-way system round town to square; turn left at square: house down on right.

Sheila Griffin
Seaview, Clifden, Co. Galway
Tel +353 (0)95 21441
Email sgriffin@eircom.net
Web www.seamisthouse.com

Co. Galway

B&B

The Quay House

Everyone should visit the Quay House at least once. Paddy is a hugely generous, big-hearted man, with an enormous talent for mixing antiques, ancestral portraits and ornate mirrors with African shields, tiger skins, sculpture and stuffed anything. And Julia has a great eye for colour. Yes, it's quirky, but it is also steeped in sybaritic luxury and style: big bedrooms are all different, perhaps with a four-poster, a grand view, a working fireplace, and there's not a whiff of meanness. All have soundproofed walls, deep mattresses, thick curtains, large fluffy towels, piping hot water and proper bathrooms with windows. Sleep soundly to the clinking of boats in the harbour, breakfast slowly on home-baked bread, full Irish, devilled kidneys, even oysters, in a sunny conservatory. Step out to discover bustling Clifden with its chic shops, or head for golden sands, fishing, golf, walking – it's all here in glorious Connemara. Return to a beautifully furnished drawing room, a comfy sofa by a roaring fire, homemade brac and a restorative chat with this charismatic and humorous couple. Marvellous.

Travel Club Offer. See page 266.

Price	€140-€170. Singles from €95.
Rooms	14: 9 twins/doubles, 2 triples, 3 four-posters.
Meals	Restaurants within walking distance.
Closed	November to mid-March.
Directions	In Clifden, Beach Road down hill from centre of town. House 500m on right, on quayside.

Julia & Patrick Foyle
Beach Road, Clifden, Co. Galway

Tel	+353 (0)95 21369
Fax	+353 (0)95 21608
Email	thequay@iol.ie
Web	www.thequayhouse.com

Entry 40   Map 3

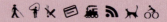

B&B Co. Galway

The Anglers Return

Warm, funny, self-deprecating, Lynn adores her gorgeous garden and her guests equally, giving you her undivided attention. In her highly personal house, lavender-blue woodwork sets off a stunning runner carpet by Millar's of Clifden, odd chairs full of personality stand on the red sitting-room tiles, the whole effect is fresh, simple, thoroughly country. She is an artist, has lived here all her life, knows the best fishing and walking spots. She sings, too, and listens to classical music while making her bread and scones to go with the organic cereals and homemade jams next morning. In the peace of whitewashed walls, the house breathes through wooden floors, old maps, antiques, fresh wild flowers, log fires. Lynn's pretty mixed-size bedrooms have enchanting river views and robes for the corridor run to the bathroom, the walls of the huge dining room carry musical instruments, seascapes, boats and baskets. An impossibly cute courtyard leads to three acres of natural garden; paths wind past azaleas, an organic veg patch, wild rocky outcrops to bluebell woods and a well-earned hammock.

Price	From €95.
Rooms	4: 1 double; 1 double, 1 twin, 1 triple each with separate bathroom.
Meals	Dinner for groups by arrangement. Restaurants 3-7km.
Closed	December-January.
Directions	From Galway N59 for Clifden through Recess & continue 7km; left R341 for Roundstone; house on left, 6km after R341 turn off.

Ethical Collection: Environment; Food. See page 270.

Lynn Hill
Toombeola, Roundstone, Co. Galway
Tel +353 (0)95 31091
Email info@anglersreturn.com
Web www.anglersreturn.com

Entry 41 Map 3

Co. Galway

B&B & Self-catering

Emlaghmore Lodge

The Tinne family's holiday house for over 80 years is now Nick's home. Emlaghmore still has the air of an 1860s fishing lodge: near the wild Atlantic coast, surrounded by the only trees for miles, it looks across its own little river and oceans of lake-strewn moorland to the mountains. Otters, badgers, birds of prey and unusual plants abound in this nature-lover's paradise. In simple country-house style, gilt-framed ancestors look down from faded pink walls in an elegant dining room and uncluttered bedrooms have that old-world charm of rooms just waiting for the family to arrive. Climb the nearby mountain to see as far as County Kerry, fish on private lakes, walk on sandy beaches where seals may be sprawling on the rocks and fishermen bring in their catch (lobster sometimes finds its way to the kitchen). Dine in candlelit style with Nick and Janet: they create suburb, imaginative dinners using the finest ingredients; Connemara lamb, fillet of Irish beef... You will sleep deeply in this utterly secluded house – and wake to the sun streaming through the windows, and views over lake, river or mountain.

Travel Club Offer. See page 266.

Price	€130–€170. Singles €65. Cottage €400–€950 per week.
Rooms	4 + 1: 1 double, 1 single, each with separate bathroom; 1 double, 1 twin. Cottage for 8.
Meals	Dinner €50. Wine €15.50. Book 24 hrs ahead.
Closed	November–Easter.
Directions	On R341 9.5km from Roundstone, 4km from Ballyconneely. 100m on Roundstone side of Callow bridge, take narrow lane inland (no sign) 100m; sign on gate.

Nick Tinne
Ballyconneely, Co. Galway
Tel   +353 (0)95 23529
Fax   +353 (0)95 23860
Email info@emlaghmore.com
Web   www.emlaghmore.com

Entry 42   Map 3

Hotel   Co. Galway

Currarevagh House

A peaceful, family-run place in magnificent countryside on the banks of vast Lough Corrib, Currarevagh is surrounded by 150 acres of woodland with rhododendrons brought back from India by the generation of Hodgsons who built the house in 1842. Although much has stayed the same there are moves to be more eco-friendly: grey water collected on the roof, their own spring water for drinking and self-sufficiency in wood for burning. Graceful June will usually greet you with afternoon tea in the drawing room or in the garden on sunny days; sandwiches, cakes, scones with jam… leave some room for supper! Henry's wife Lucy is a Leith trained cook and has the best of local ingredients to show off her modern Irish cooking. Bright welcoming bedrooms, three with great lake views, have big Victorian beds, old-style décor, space and excellent bathrooms. After dinner beneath the Old Masters, guests come together for coffee by the drawing room fire. You can boat and fish from their own jetty, a picnic and a ghillie can be arranged; nature lovers and birdwatchers will adore it here – you may spot a great crested grebe.

Price	€160-€210. Singles from €85. Half-board (min. 3 nights) €130 p.p.
Rooms	13: 12 twins/doubles, 1 single.
Meals	Dinner, 5 courses, €52 (8pm). Wine €19.50-€50. Afternoon tea included.
Closed	End-October to March. Winter house parties available.
Directions	From Oughterard, Glann Lakeshore road for 6.5km; entrance on right.

The Hodgson Family
Oughterard, Co. Galway
Tel   +353 (0)91 552312
Fax   +353 (0)91 552731
Email mail@currarevagh.com
Web   www.currarevagh.com

Ethical Collection: Food.
See page 270.

Entry 43   Map 3

Co. Galway

B&B & Self-catering

Railway Lodge

You are treated as a friend here – no flying TVs or tea trays – and Carmel is natural, easy, unfussy; you'll find it hard not to yield to her charm. This is a new house, painted a lively red, but Carmel is determined to make it look old; and she succeeds. She collects lovely bone china, beautiful linen, Irish pottery, faded old pine and good antiques. She makes superb, thick curtains too. Bedrooms are wooden-floored, comfortable and filled with books; generous bathrooms are neat as a pin. There's quite a bit of railway memorabilia too, and lots of interesting bits and pieces to admire. You will be given freshly squeezed orange juice and a vast Irish breakfast in the dining room, there are comfy places to sit by the fire – or watch TV – in the snug, and the conservatory is a good spot for an evening glass of wine: lounge in a wicker chair as the sunlight floods in and admire the Cloosh Hills. For those who prefer a bit of privacy there's a rocking love-nest of a cottage in the garden, filled with good things too. No excuse for hanging around though. Connemara beckons, with ponies and wild beaches.

Travel Club Offer. See page 266.

Price	€100–€110. Singles €70. Cottage €650 per week.
Rooms	4 + 1: 3 doubles, 1 twin. Cottage for 2.
Meals	Restaurants within walking distance.
Closed	Rarely.
Directions	From Galway N59 for Clifden to Oughterard; through town; left after Corrib House Hotel and immed'ly right; follow signs to house.

Carmel Geoghegan
Canrower, Oughterard, Co. Galway
Tel   +353 (0)91 552945
Email   railwaylodge@eircom.net
Web   www.railwaylodge.net

Entry 44   Map 3

B&B   Co. Galway

Camillaun

It is so quiet and peaceful down here by the river Owenriff; no wonder Greg and Deirdre choose the site to build their cosy new family house. Walkers, nature lovers, fishers and birdwatchers will be in their element. Deirdre's breakfasts set you up for a hearty day out in this beautiful countryside; return to a roaring fire in a comfy sitting room or a game of pool on the full-sized table. Dinners are scrumptious and impeccably delivered by Deirdre in a proper chef's outfit, including hat! Bedrooms look out over the neat garden and are simply, attractively furnished with some good antiques; bathrooms have plenty of towels and piping hot water. You can fish straight from the house – a ghillie can be arranged and Greg is an expert so can give advice. Should you prefer to swing a racket, there's a tennis court in the garden; for less active souls there's a hot tub in a gazebo. Try Galway for shopping, take a boat trip to Inchagoill Island and its two monasteries; Deirdre can provide a picnic so you can make a day of it. This is an easy-going place where you'll feel at home.

Price	€90–€100. Singles €55–€62.
Rooms	4: 1 twin, 3 family.
Meals	Dinner from €35. BYO wine. Packed lunch from €8.
Closed	November–February.
Directions	From Galway N59 to Oughterard; in centre of village right into Glann Rd, 1st right after bridge; house signed 200m on right down side road.

Travel Club Offer. See page 266.

	Deirdre & Greg Forde Oughterard, Co. Galway
Tel	+353 (0)91 552678
Fax	+353 (0)91 552439
Email	camillaun@eircom.net
Web	www.camillaun.com

Entry 45   Map 3

Co. Galway
Self-catering

Cnoc Suain

While the rest of us plod on (some with dreams, others more jaded) Charlie and Dearbhaill are busy smashing the paradigm on this remote, beautiful homestead. Their patch is vast and open-skied, a silent slab of bog, heather and birdsong overlooking Spiddal's coastline, guarded by an ancient standing stone, soaked in history. Residential or half-day courses here range from herbal cures to painting and music; Dearbhaill is a professional musician. Or you could just come to rest and walk, explore the Aran Islands and the Burren. Wildlife is abundant and Charlie grows organic herbs; he is starting a physic garden and is infectiously excited about everything they have achieved so far. You stay in tiny dry-stone-wall cottages, fabulously unfussy, toasty with underfloor heating and with walk-in showers. Brightly coloured kitchens have all you need to cook, beds are cosy, window sills deep and whitewashed. The main house is warmed with a wood fire around which music rings, stories are told, evenings grow long; there's a library and even a little pub for a warming tot before bed. Sleep deeply in the peace.

Price	€520–€1,200.
Rooms	3 cottages: 1 for 2, 1 for 4, 1 for 6-7.
Meals	Pubs/restaurants 3.5 miles.
Closed	Rarely.
Directions	From Galway, take Clifden Rd (N59) to Moycullen. Left at village crossroads; 5 miles, signed Cnoc Suain.

Travel Club Offer. See page 266.

Ethical Collection: Environment; Community; Food.
See page 270.

Dearbhaill Standun & Charlie Troy
An Spideal, Spiddal, Co. Galway
Tel +353 (0)91 555703
Fax +353 (0)91 555703
Email info@cnocsuain.com
Web www.cnocsuain.com

Entry 46   Map 3

B&B & Self-catering   Co. Galway

Lisdonagh House

Deep in glorious 'Quiet Man' countryside, this 1720 Georgian house has been restored with style. Eighteenth-century trompe l'œil murals of the four virtues greet you in the oval hall, whose shape is mirrored in a lovely bedroom above. Bedrooms are upstairs, uncluttered and luxurious with antique furniture and lake views from huge beds. In a former rent house, the pavilion suite with its pyramid roof and Venetian window is brilliant. Enjoy delicious food in the formal dining room; face the window and you will see the Connemara ponies frolicking and flicking in the field. Peace and quiet predominate, so fish from your own boat on the lough, walk through acres of woodland, or snaffle a picnic from Finola and head for the 'crannog' (small island). Perfect for private house parties, intimate weddings and big family reunions; all is as flexible as you want, from fully looked-after to left to your own devices with a cracking big kitchen and a huge Aga – great fun. There are two drawing rooms to slump in and plenty of quiet places to escape with a book. Lovely. *Self-catering in courtyard villas & gate lodge.*

Price	€160-€280. Singles from €120. Villas €790-€980 per week. Lodge €620-€680 per week. Main house available for rent.
Rooms	9 + 3: 9 twins/doubles. 2 villas for 4, 1 lodge for 4.
Meals	Dinner €49 (from 7.30pm). Wine €25. Packed lunch for fisherfolk from €12.
Closed	November-May.
Directions	From Galway N17 for Sligo 25km; left R333 to Caherlistrane. Right at Queally's pub 3km; left down narrow lane: house signposted.

	John & Finola Cooke Caherlistrane, Co. Galway
Tel	+353 (0)93 31163
Fax	+353 (0)93 31532
Email	cooke@lisdonagh.com
Web	www.lisdonagh.com

Entry 47   Map 3

Co. Galway   Self-catering

Castlegar Stables

Just out of the village, a mile down its private drive, Castlegar stands in fifty acres of beautiful grounds with two lovely wooded paths looping the house. The conversion of the stables and the pretty stable yard is smart and luxurious and the American and French owners have taken great care over every detail: bathrooms have the latest fittings and you will want for nothing in the way of furnishings, linen or cutlery. Both houses are the same, only the number of bedrooms changes. The front door opens onto an attractively furnished kitchen/diner where you will be happy to cook and eat. Upstairs is the enormous sitting room with pretty little windows looking out. Douglas has helped the air flow over the heavy, dark, sink-or-swim sofas with big black ceiling fans. Bedrooms are in the same vein of luxurious modern comfort. This strong masculine atmosphere is deeply restful. Moreover, guests are welcome to use the gym, hot tub, sauna, table tennis, boules set, internet and lots of other toys in the main basement. And the walking here is rich. *The two houses can connect.*

Price	€1,300–€2,000. Together €3,000. Prices per week.
Rooms	2 stables: 1 for 6; 1 for 4.
Meals	Restaurants in Ballinasloe.
Closed	Rarely.
Directions	Provided on booking.

Douglas Woessner
Castlegar House, Ahascragh,
Ballinasloe, Co. Galway
Tel   +353 (0)90 968 8653
Fax   +353 (0)90 968 8689
Email castlegarhouse@eircom.net

Entry 48 Map 4

Self-catering   Co. Galway

The Humble Daisy

A deep relief to arrive at The Humble Daisy, for you may have given up hope of seeing one of Ireland's whitewashed and thatched cottages. But here it is, polished to within an inch of perfection. Mary Rose's grandfather lived here and her family farm is next door. Oliver is a horticulturalist and part-time farmer, managing this farm. So the contact with the house is authentic and nostalgic. A rare quantity of love and determination has gone into transforming the simple cottage into a very sophisticated home for guests, able to look any house anywhere right in the eye. Floors are of slate or coir, furniture is wooden and solid, and much of it modern. The big kitchen-dining room is equipped with everything to make anyone happy, including space. The sitting room has an open fire, the bedrooms and the bathrooms are immaculate and there are more rooms upstairs. Outside there is a little barn where you can play table tennis. A big reason for being here is the great lough only a hundred yards down the road. Upon it, and upon the piano, you can play to your heart's content.

Price	€350-€750 per week.
Rooms	Cottage for 6-8.
Meals	Restaurant 11 miles.
Closed	Never.
Directions	From Portumna, R352 towards Ennis. After approx. 8 miles turn left at Looscaun church. Take 1st right after church; follow signs.

Mrs Mary Rose Donnelly
Old Village, Douras, Woodford,
Co. Galway
Tel   +353 (0)90 974 9859
Email satchmo2@eircom.net

Travel Club Offer. See page 266.

Entry 49   Map 3

Co. Galway   Self-catering

Kinvara Suites

One of the most picturesque villages in Ireland, with a quiet harbour overlooking bobbing boats and grandly green views. Walk off the main street through a pretty garden and climb the outdoor steps (this was once a hayloft) to two beautifully designed spaces. The top suite has a higher ceiling but both are stunning and clever: everything you need here in one large light room with high, quirky windows, pale wooden floors and white walls. A hub in the middle separates living area from sleeping and contains on one side a super modern shower room and on the other a dazzling kitchen – fully equipped for cooking everything! Loll on a broad leather sofa with creamy cushions, turn the gas-fuelled stove on, lower the chrome lighting and settle down to relax – there's a peaceful, uncluttered atmosphere here. More active souls have much on the doorstep to explore: walk the Burren and discover Mediterranean and Arctic flowers growing side by side, take a picnic to the beach, spot otters in the bay, birdwatch, snaffle some local oysters, mussels, crab or smoked salmon. The perfect place to chill – or be creative.

Price	€500-€700 per week. €390 for 3 days.
Rooms	2 suites for 2.
Meals	Breakfast ingredients & basic provisions provided.
Closed	Rarely.
Directions	From Shannon N18 North. From Galway, N18 south to Kilcolgan; N67 to Kinvara. Kinvara suites are visible from main street on left-hand side.

Travel Club Offer: see page 266.

Ethical Collection: Community.
See page 270.

	Elizabeth Murphy
	The Courtyard, Lower Main Street, Kinvara, Co. Galway
Tel	+353 (0)91 637760
Fax	+353 (0)91 637760
Email	murphystore@kinvara.com
Web	www.kinvarasuites.com

Entry 50   Map 3

B&B   Co. Galway

Inis Meáin Restaurant & Suites

The quietest and most beautiful of the Aran Islands is now the perfect place to stay – for total immersion in a slower way of life. Arrive by boat, or plane if you must; you will be delivered to your suite along roads with no signs, no lines and always the brooding sea in view. Perched on the hill is the whale-shaped restaurant: stunning, modern, perfectly designed to bring the surrounding landscape in. Eat good, local or homegrown food, cooked by handsome, charismatic Ruairi in the open-plan kitchen, and presented without fuss (drizzling is thankfully banned). Enjoy ambrosial puddings cooked by stylish Marie-Thérèse. The suites are very special: each a light open space with long views, a living area, a sleeping area with huge bed overlooking island and sea, great lighting and a fridge crammed with delicious cold meats, cheeses and wines. Bicycles and fishing rods are by the door, breakfast is delivered each morning and is generous enough to make a picnic for lunch, and if you want to watch a DVD just ask and all will appear. Peace seekers, nature lovers and each-other lovers will adore it here.

Price	€200-€250. Singles €150-€200.
Rooms	3 suites for 2.
Meals	Dinner, 3 courses, €40. Wine from €20. Packed lunch available.
Closed	October-April.
Directions	Take ferry from Rossaveal or 10-seater plane from Inverin, Co. Galway. Staying guests will be collected from pier or airport.

Travel Club Offer. See page 266.

Ruairi & Marie-Thérèse de Blacam
Inis Meáin, Aran Islands, Co. Galway
Tel   +353 (0)86 826 6026
Email post@inismeain.com
Web   www.inismeain.com

Entry 51 Map 3

Co. Galway   B&B

Man of Aran Cottage

The perfect little hideaway. You'll unwind the minute you stoop through the door into the cosy little restaurant and the seductive whiff of home cooking: delicious soups, stews, omelettes and puddings. Maura (a gorgeous powerhouse) and Joe (tall, handsome and calm) are the warmest souls. Built right by the ocean in the 1930s for Robert Flaherty's documentary on the islands, *Man of Aran*, the house is surrounded by wild roses, gentian, maidenhair fern, saxifrage and Joe's splendid hydroponic garden; leaves from here are mixed into fabulous, imaginative salads or tasty soups. Thick, white-painted stone walls enclose bedrooms that are sweet and cosy, with deep window sills, thick duvets and spotless bathrooms… sleep deeply in the peace, the only sound the odd gust of wind. The Aran Islands get very popular in summer so it's best to visit in spring or autumn, or even a wild winter's day; there's a roaring fire in the low-ceilinged sitting room, plenty of books to read and sofa space to curl up in. You could be inspired to write your first novel here.

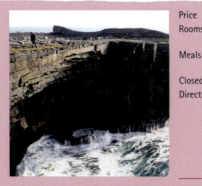

Price	€80–€90. Singles €55–€70.
Rooms	3: 1 double with separate bathroom; 1 double, 1 twin, sharing bathroom.
Meals	Dinner €35. Wine €20. Packed lunch on request.
Closed	November–February.
Directions	From Galway R336 through Spiddal 36km; left to Roseaveal Ferry. On island, hire a minibus or bike.

	Maura & Joe Wolfe
	Inishmor, Aran Islands, Co. Galway
Tel	+353 (0)99 61301
Email	manofaran@eircom.net
Web	www.manofarancottage.com

Self-catering   Co. Leitrim

Roosky Cottage

The prettiest Irish cottage in thoroughly rural surroundings: low stone walls to hug you in, rustling thatch to soothe, birdsung moorlands all around, the neighbour's cattle crossing the lane (so look before you leap). And Lough Melvin, peaceful yet exciting for nature-lovers and sportsmen: rent a boat and try your luck. Just inside Co. Leitrim, Roosky Cottage is a stone's throw from Donegal and 15 minutes from lovely seaside Bundoran. The interior is *au naturel*: the Bradleys have left the bare stone walls to tell the memories of the farmers who lived here for 100 years. Rooms are cosy, mildly colourful and rustic: simple holiday furniture sits peacefully, there are three open turf fireplaces – yes, each bedroom has a fire and a bathroom. To rub shoulders with so much ancientness is precious indeed yet the kitchen has all the necessary modernities as well as a fine old Irish dresser. The area is stuffed with things to do and see: the stunning Donegal coast, prehistoric sites, medieval monuments, mind-stretching walks, golf, riding, marvellous food. *Linen, heating, electricity included.*

Price	€450–€600 per week.
Rooms	Cottage for 4-5.
Meals	Restaurants 15-minute drive.
Closed	Rarely.
Directions	Directions given on booking.

Mary & Paul Bradley
Rossinver, Co. Leitrim
Tel   +1 773 528 1192 (USA)
Email   mbradboo@aol.com
Web   www.irishcottagerental.com

Entry 53   Map 1 & 4

Co. Leitrim

B&B

Hollywell

A gorgeous surprise to leave the busy road and the town's tumult and two seconds later be driving quietly up to elegant country-house life. Gracious Georgian with 1850s add-ons, Hollywell is decorated with impeccable taste that never overpowers. Although Tom and Rosaleen live in the annexe, it has the feel of a real house. Former hoteliers, charming, helpful and easy to get on with (*maher* means hospitable in Gaelic), they know what guests like. No helter-skelter of children or dogs here, all is peace, the creeper peeks in at the windows, you may watch the ever-changing Shannon scene for hours from the front rooms, lounge in a living room stuffed with pictures, portraits and antiques, glory in the sofas and the view on the landing, retire to deeply welcoming (TV-free) bedrooms. For lunch or dinner, sons Conor and Ronan run the excellent Oarsmen pub and restaurant in Carrick, which is a pretty town, popular with Dubliners at the weekend, offering boat trips, megaliths, arts and crafts. Then retire to seclusion: soon breakfast will arrive on the beautiful burr walnut table. *Children over 12 welcome.*

Price	€110-€140. Singles €70-€90.
Rooms	4: 3 doubles, 1 twin/double.
Meals	Restaurants in Carrick-on-Shannon.
Closed	Mid-November to late February.
Directions	From Dublin N4 to Carrick; over River Shannon; keep left at Ging's Pub up lane. Entrance 1st left, signposted.

Rosaleen & Tom Maher
Liberty Hill, Carrick-on-Shannon,
Co. Leitrim
Tel   +353 (0)71 962 1124
Fax   +353 (0)71 962 1124
Email   hollywell@esatbiz.com

B&B & Self-catering   Co. Mayo

Drom Caoin

Way out at the tip of North West Mayo, only just attached to the mainland, Belmullet town bustles on market day, welcoming eager anglers, twitchers, golfers (Carne Golf Links are ranked 28th in the world), sculpture vultures (Tir Saile Scultpure Trail), walkers and watersporters. Drom Caoin, a modern, practical house on a rise, brims with light from the sea and family photographs, stripped pine, pale colours and simplicity. No frills in the bedrooms, but much cosiness in those tucked under the roof, and a TV and a welcoming fire in the sitting room. As for the family, Máirín is passionate about Ireland ancient and modern, the Irish language, her tribe of nine (grown) children, the courses she takes and gives (rural tourism, food and wine), her B&B guests… How does she do it? You could listen to her for weeks. Gerry is the perfect foil, a quiet crinkly man with a tender smile who speaks little and well. They give you maps to off-the-beaten-track places, and cater (deliciously) for special dietary requirements. A friendly, genuine, laid-back place to stay, full of positive energy.

Price	€76-€85. Singles €47-€51. Apartment available.
Rooms	4 + 1: 2 twins/doubles, 1 family, 1 single. Apartment for 4.
Meals	Dinner €25-€35, BYO wine, by arrangement.
Closed	Mid-December to mid-January.
Directions	In Belmullet, at central roundabout with granite pillars, take Church Road; up hill, past church, on left.

Máirín Maguire-Murphy
Church Road, Belmullet, Co. Mayo
Tel   +353 (0)97 81195
Fax   +353 (0)97 81195
Email stay@dromcaoin.ie
Web   www.belmullet-accommodation.com

Travel Club Offer. See page 266.

Co. Mayo

B&B

The Bervie

Elizabeth runs the Bervie wearing a contented smile. Who wouldn't? Achill Island feels like the end of the world and is a favourite haunt of poets and painters: the setting is majestic and you can smell the sea. Once a coastguard station, it became a salmon centre, then a guest house, a three-generation tradition that Elizabeth and John keep alive with love and gusto. More like a terrace of interconnected cottages than a guest house, the place looks so spotless and welcoming after a journey: a fire burns in the hearth, antimacassars cover sofas and chairs, there's local art on the walls and spectacular cliff and ocean views from the dining room windows. Bedrooms have big pine beds piled with fluffy blankets and those at the back give directly onto the Atlantic – it comes to within 30 metres of your window at high tide. The garden is that endless, fabulous beach, reached through a little wooden gate. Elizabeth takes pride in making all her visitors happy, from families and surfers to artists and writers. An unhurried place where humanity and delicious food nourish soul and body.

Price	€110–€140. Singles €60–€90.
Rooms	14: 7 doubles, 1 suite. Outbuildings: 6 doubles.
Meals	Dinner from €40. Wine €19. Afternoon tea.
Closed	November–March.
Directions	From Westport N59 to Achill Island then R319 across island to Keel. Bervie well signposted in village.

Elizabeth & John Barrett
Keel, Achill Island, Co. Mayo

Tel	+353 (0)98 43114
Fax	+353 (0)98 43407
Email	bervie@esatclear.ie
Web	www.bervieachill.com

Entry 56 Map 3

Self-catering Co. Mayo

Rosturk Woods

You wander through these woods, weaving your way through the undergrowth – until suddenly you arrive at the shore. The magical bay will steal your heart away. Along the headland, castle turrets peer over trees: Alan's birthplace. At high tide, the sea laps the garden; take the boat, spot a seal. At low tide, walk to an island, spot an otter. The Stoneys are a warm, humorous young family. The Wing, at one end of their superb modern house, has space, light, old fireplaces, a green and yellow kitchen with matching china and, upstairs, a deeply comfortable master bedroom. The Waterfall House stands alone, spreading its generous windows before a south-facing terrace, all in spanking new quality and, again, decorated for comfort and æsthetics with modern sofas and country antiques, thick rugs and good pictures. In the natural garden you will discover a little stream and an extraordinarily rare Chinese Fern Tree. The games room is for all, so is the tennis gear. Turf for fires is provided within reason; hot water is solar. An exceptional place... for fishing, boating, birding or just being.

Price	€800-€1,400 per week.
Rooms	The Wing for 6. Waterfall House for 8.
Meals	Pub 1km.
Closed	Never.
Directions	From Newport N59 for Mulranny & Achill 11km; blue sign on left.

	Louisa & Alan Stoney
	Rosturk, Mulranny, Westport,
	Co. Mayo
Tel	+353 (0)98 36264
Fax	+353 (0)98 36264
Email	stoney@iol.ie
Web	www.rosturk-woods.com

Co. Mayo

B&B & Self-catering

Enniscoe House

History and good taste are the pillars of Enniscoe, a splendid house set beneath the towering presence of Mount Nephin in parkland surrounding Lough Conn. If the sitting room's exquisitely restored ceiling and cornices seduce you, the rarer, grander drawing room will bowl you over: 1790s marble fireplace, 1850s wallpapers, curvaceous antiques. Susan is a descendant of the original family who arrived here in the 1660s and runs it all beautifully, aided by her son DJ. A fabulous pink-carpeted staircase winds up from floor to floor, to grand, tall-windowed rooms softly decorated with plush beds, paintings by Susan's mother and the spectacular lake view – or to lower, cosier farmhouse rooms with sprigged florals. Four simple but comfortable self-catering houses, with books, beams, patios and woody views, lie off the courtyard. The grounds are a dream, and open to the public: five acres of restored Victorian gardens, trails through woodland, boats to fish the lake, a tea shop for light lunches, a Heritage Centre that traces family trees. Cows in the pasture, dogs by the fire, divine dinners. Special!

Price	€190–€240. Singles €96–€120. Apts €450–€800 per week.
Rooms	6 + 3: 1 double, 1 twin, 2 triples, 2 family suites. 3 apartments for 4-6.
Meals	Dinner €50. Wine from €22. Packed lunch from €10.
Closed	November-March. Groups in January by arrangement.
Directions	From Ballina N59 to Crossmolina; left R315 for Castlebar 3km. House entrance 1st of two on left.

Susan Kellett
Castlehill, Crossmolina, Co. Mayo
Tel   +353 (0)96 31112
Fax   +353 (0)96 31773
Email mail@enniscoe.com
Web www.enniscoe.com

Self-catering   Co. Mayo

Laragan Lodge

Wild, rugged, beautiful. The views from these windows make you itch to be out – or relaxing, dreamily, over a book in a window seat. At the top of a lane, the long, traditionally built, whitewashed cottage gazes down over famous, fish-rich Lough Conn and across stone-walled fields to Nephin Mountain. Inside, all is brisk and bright. A large, open-plan living area is crisp with light pine floor and furnishings, a modern, well-equipped kitchen, a family-friendly dining table, comfy cherry-red sofas and open stone fireplace. Three large bedrooms plus bathroom are on the other side of the entrance hall with just one bedroom upstairs. Two have showers – no queues for the bathroom here. Light and uncluttered with modest furnishings, this is a sensible, well-ordered house: clean and functional, not flouncy and frilly. But who wants extras with those gorgeous views? Outside decking means you can chase the sun and the views; landscaping is afoot. There's fishing, walking and horse riding for sporty days, and the pub's two miles; this is a decent, solid bolthole for an away-from-it-all break.

Price	€600-€1,500 per week.
Rooms	House for 8-9.
Meals	Pub 3km.
Closed	Rarely.
Directions	Exit Foxford on the Ballina road R318; after 3km, left on R310 to Pontoon. At Pontoon (Healys Hotel), right on R315 for 2km. Left up lane; Laragan Lodge is last house.

	Susie Lyddon
	Bofeenaun, Pontoon, Co. Mayo
Tel	+32 (0)2 647 38 93 (Belgium)
Email	lyddon@skynet.be
Web	www.laragan.com

Entry 59   Map 3

Co. Mayo

Self-catering

The Crooked Cottage

Could this be the perfect retreat? Once here, you are alone in a rural idyll, a little huddle of buildings in 10 acres, surrounded by trees, old walls and gorgeous views to lovely Lough Conn. The cottage is furiously ancient, not a right-angle in sight, the windows furiously modern, the interior appealingly personal with books and painted floorboards, old stones and white walls, old-fashioned bedcovers on pine beds and a comforting lived-in feel. The main bedroom under the rafters has space and a huge bed. Along the passage where the friendly wellies are kept you find the simple white bathroom and the smaller bedroom. The galley-like kitchen has all you need to prepare a good spread for the big old table in the easy, open living room. 100 years ago, the then owner did a roaring trade in poteen, an illegal potato alcohol. The fierce brew was made on an island in the lake then stored in a secret place in the thatch – never discovered. Stock up before you arrive, the nearest village is five miles away, but a nearby hotel serves good dinners. *Noel also owns Dublin hotel Number 31.*

Price	€500-€750 per week.
Rooms	Cottage for 4.
Meals	Restaurants 8km.
Closed	Rarely.
Directions	Directions given on booking.

Noel Comer
Terrybawn, Pontoon, Co. Mayo

Tel	+353 (0)1 676 5011
Fax	+353 (0)1 676 2929
Email	info@number31.ie
Web	www.number31.ie

B&B   Co. Mayo

Ballywarren House

Crunch up the driveway to Ballywarren House – no ancient pile but a handsome new build. Inside is a rich décor and lovely hosts for whom nothing is too much trouble. English David and Diane decided to follow three (of five) daughters to Ireland, built their house as they like it and have poured energy and passion into the whole gorgeous place. Sash windows and plaster mouldings, fireplaces and staircases have been worked by craftsmen in the Georgian style, then embellished with bright curtains and decorative hangings, gilt mirrors and fresh flowers. The sitting room, sheathed in green with a polished wood floor, has deep sofas, a real fire and glossy magazines – a heady mix; in the pink and sage dining room you can be as intimate or as convivial as you wish. Each bedroom is different, each a treat: big beds, bold colours, snowy linen, cut-glass decanters, Crabtree & Evelyn by the baths. At the back are views to pastures where sheep munch. There's music and art in the family, cooking is a passion and they make all their own bread, biscuits, puddings and jams. There's even a ghillie if you like to fish.

Price	€136-€148. Singles €98-€136.
Rooms	3: 2 doubles, 1 four-poster.
Meals	Dinner, 4-5 courses, €42. Wine €4 per glass. Pub/restaurant 3-4 miles.
Closed	Never.
Directions	From Galway on N84 to Headford then R334 to Cross; at Cross church, left onto R345 to Cong; house 0.75 miles on right.

David & Diane Skelton
Cross, Cong, Co. Mayo
Tel   +353 (0)94 954 6989
Email ballywarrenhouse@gmail.com
Web   www.ballywarrenhouse.com

Entry 61   Map 3

Co. Roscommon

B&B & Self-catering

Castlecoote House

Apple jams and juices from the orchard, garden flowers in every room. In ten pastoral acres, surrounded by stunning gardens, stands this Palladian mansion where you will be welcomed, usually by a housekeeper with an easy Irish charm. Built in the 1700s with wonderful medieval castle ruins dotted around like Victorian follies (and the lovely river flowing past the ice house), it has been brilliantly restored by Ireland's best: woodwork, moulding, stucco and hand-crafted sash windows. Duchesses grew up here: loved by George II, set in oils by Sir Joshua Reynolds; copies hang in the hall. Browse through rare tomes in the library, take tea in the kitchen, sit down to succulent dinners, warm your toes before the drawing-room fire. Bedrooms are magnificent: antiques, rich rugs, bucolic views… a shimmering chandelier; the master bathroom is a… masterpiece to delight a sybarite. Lower ground-floor bedrooms are less spectacular but supremely comfortable; deluxe bathrooms and heated floors bow to modernity. A romantic slice of real old Ireland, in a small village. *Minimum stay two nights.*

Price	€180.
Rooms	4 doubles. Whole house available.
Meals	Dinner €49. Wine from €20.
Closed	October-January.
Directions	From Athlone N61 to Roscommon; there, take R366 to Castlecoote & follow signs to house.

Kevin Finnerty
Castlecoote, Co. Roscommon
Tel   +353 (0)90 666 3794
Email info@castlecootehouse.com
Web   www.castlecootehouse.com

Entry 62   Map 4

B&B & Self-catering　　　　　　　　　　　　　　　　Co. Roscommon

Clonalis House

Standing in 700 acres, aloof up a mile-long drive, Clonalis is a précis of Irish history. The O'Conor clan has been connected to this land for 2,000 years; Charles Owen O'Conor Don built the house in 1878 as a proud 45-room fanfare in the Victorian Italianate style and Pyers, your engaging, down-to-earth host, is the expert on its all-Irish history. Marguerite, relaxed and informative, will show you up the portrait-lined stairs to some of the loveliest bedrooms we have seen in Ireland, each generous and luxurious, each decorated with just the right family pieces, each surveying the gardens. Bathrooms are huge, with armchairs and fireplaces. Wake to breakfast with palm-tree silver in a dining room fit for a lord, take a book to the dell on fine days; in the very fine park, gardens, woods and trout rivers call. As evening falls, enter the glorious library, lined top-to-toe with ancient tomes of the family's and others' tales; here a fire is lit daily and pre-dinner sherry awaits. Four sturdy self-catering cottages lie off the courtyard – as excellent all the rest. *House open to the public.*

Price	€190-€220. Singles €115. Discount for 3 nights or more. Cottages €300-€480 p.w.
Rooms	4 + 4: 1 double, 1 twin, 2 four-posters. 4 cottages.
Meals	Dinner €46 (Tues-Sat). 24 hours' notice required.
Closed	October to mid-April. Groups by arrangement in winter.
Directions	From Athlone N60 west to Roscommon; house on edge of town just past Golf House. Entrance on right.

Pyers & Marguerite O'Conor Nash
Castlerea, Co. Roscommon
Tel　　+353 (0)94 962 0014
Fax　　+353 (0)94 962 0014
Email　clonalis@iol.ie
Web　　www.clonalis.com

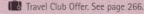
Travel Club Offer. See page 266.

Entry 63　Map 4

Co. Sligo   Hotel

Cromleach Lodge

Nothing is restrained here: the welcome is fulsome, the décor plusher than plush, the views spectacular and the food unforgettably epicurean. You have stylish uniformed staff at the marble counter, stitched quilts as thick as your thumbs, brocades and acres of carpet and, Nature's gift, views of Lough Arrow and beyond to Carrowkeel that can only be described as knock-out, framed by lavish ruched pelmets over huge windows. Better to be on the inside looking out. Bedrooms are pretty big and have some stunning decorative elements: loads of pictures (Victorian girls with velvet puppies…), bits of brass, glass and china, and plump frilly hearts on the doors. But let's not forget that people come a long way just for Moira's cooking. Locally-born and bred, easy, friendly and highly professional, she and Christy are turning Cromleach Lodge into a serious eating and meeting centre. A huge new restaurant with a keen new chef is under way, plus bars for all-day service and a vast reception room. There's a woodland walk, the lakeside is beautiful and don't miss the megalithic cairn tombs at Carrowkeel.

Price	€158–€338.
Rooms	68 twins/doubles.
Meals	Dinner, à la carte, about €50. Tasting menu (8 dishes) €65. Wine €25.
Closed	Christmas.
Directions	From Sligo N4 27km to Castlebaldwin; left at sign & follow signs 6km.

	Christy & Moira Tighe
	Lough Arrow, Castlebaldwin, Co. Sligo
Tel	+353 (0)71 916 5155
Fax	+353 (0)71 916 5455
Email	info@cromleach.com
Web	www.cromleach.com

Entry 64   Map 1 & 4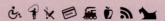

B&B   Co. Sligo

Ross House

Genuine working farmers who finally decided to retire, Nicholas and Oriel are as natural and relaxed as their surroundings of cow pastures and the mellifluous sounds of nature. Both are infectious smilers who rejoice in life, obviously fascinated by the people with whom they travel the world from their plain snug little sitting room. "One day we had a Tongan, a St Lucian and two Indians," said Nicholas with amazement. They were made for B&B, it's hard to believe they only planned to do one year when they started… over 30 years ago. Their 1890s farmhouse has always been in Oriel's family, it feels warm, lived-in, loved-in. Enter through the flower-decked porch to discover a down-to-earth, unpretentious interior. Bedrooms upstairs are simple and old-fashioned with the occasional antique piece; some are in the ground-floor extension – Nicholas's own work. Nearby lies the unsung archæological site of Carrowkeel with its elaborate passage tombs and the history of farm life in Sligo Folk Park. Unaffected peace on a proper Irish farm, run by very dear people. *Dogs welcome in car or kennel.*

Price	€120. Singles €60.
Rooms	6: 2 doubles, 1 twin, 1 family; 1 single, 1 family sharing bathroom.
Meals	Dinner €35. Wine from €15 or BYO. Packed lunch on request.
Closed	Christmas & New Year.
Directions	From Sligo N4 for Dublin to Drumfin 17km; left to Riverstown; follow signs in village for about 1.5km; on left.

	Oriel & Nicholas Hill-Wilkinson Ross, Riverstown, Co. Sligo
Tel	+353 (0)71 916 5140
Fax	+353 (0)71 916 5140
Email	rossfarmhouse@eircom.net
Web	www.rossfarmhouse.com

Entry 65   Map 1 & 4

Co. Sligo   Inn

Coopershill House

Coopershill is out of this world. The long drive winds through beautiful parkland to formal gardens where a muster of peacocks roams resplendent and you may glimpse Brian mowing in baggy corduroys. The house is one of the most handsome and distinguished examples of Irish Georgian. Despite these fine looks, the welcome couldn't be warmer: this is a well-loved home buzzing with activity, not a grand hotel. Simon and Alice the spaniel greet you with friendly smiles before inviting you into the awesome stone-floored hall. Pause a moment and look up at the flags, the stags, the marble figurines, the old parchment map of Ireland. That's just the hall! There are ancestors, antlers and antiques everywhere, fresh flowers and a chaise longue in every room, amazing high old beds with oh-so-fitting sheets, blankets and eiderdowns. Top-floor bedrooms look over copper beech and croquet lawn to the River Unsin and the four-poster room with huge corner windows is stunning. Great bathrooms, too: the 1900s canopied bath in its green-tiled grotto will knock your socks off. Penny Parrott roams around but only talks when alone.

Price	€228-€284. Singles €149-€177.
Rooms	8: 4 doubles, 1 twin, 2 four-posters; 1 double with separate bathroom.
Meals	Dinner, 5 courses, €63. Wine from €23.
Closed	November-March (except for house parties).
Directions	N4 17km east of Sligo take signs for Riverstown, after 2km take left for Coopershill.

Travel Club Offer. See page 266.

Ethical Collection: Environment; Food. See page 270.

Brian, Lindy & Simon O'Hara
Riverstown, Co. Sligo

Tel	+353 (0)71 916 5108
Fax	+353 (0)71 916 5466
Email	ohara@coopershill.com
Web	www.coopershill.com

Entry 66   Map 1 & 4

B&B & Self-catering   Co. Sligo

Temple House

The gardens rolling down to the lake past some very special trees and the ruins of three earlier Temple Houses – medieval, Tudor, Jacobean – announce rich history. The present house, built in 1864 by the 'Chinaman' ancestor (he made fortunes out east), reveals grandeurs galore in the most welcoming family atmosphere you can imagine, aristocratic relations gazing down on wellies and tricycles in the monumental hall, tall morning-room windows sporting gorgeous pink velvet against cream furnishings. After that echoing hall where a hundred could waltz, the 'Half-Acre' bedroom confirms the scale: 50 more could shimmy among the antique beds. Other rooms, though less vast, all exude an old-fashioned ease; bathrooms have been revamped and retiled. Roderick and Helena, natural, unpretentious people, full of enthusiasm for house, farm and estate – a huge on-going project – wear their treasures lightly. The 1,200 acres are shared with sheep and the lake is full of pike; boats and kit are for borrowing, so wander where you will. Meet fellow guests over drinks or dinner – or bring your own house party.

Price	€160-€190. Singles from €105.
Rooms	6: 2 doubles, 1 twin, 2 family suites; 1 family with separate shower.
Meals	Dinner by arrangement. Wine from €18. High tea for under 10s at 6pm.
Closed	December-March.
Directions	From Sligo N4 for Dublin then N17 for Galway. House signposted left 0.5km south of Ballinacarrow.

Roderick & Helena Perceval
Ballinacarrow, Ballymote, Co. Sligo
Tel   +353 (0)71 918 3329
Fax   +353 (0)71 918 3808
Email enquiry@templehouse.ie
Web   www.templehouse.ie

Travel Club Offer. See page 266.

Entry 67   Map 1 & 4

Co. Sligo   Self-catering

The Schoolhouse

You might hear the whispers of children past as they sit in rows listening to the birdsong outside, but unable to peer over the high windows – can you smell the chalk? Or perhaps you can imagine the teacher making a grand entrance through the solid wood double doors. Happily, the austerity of the former 1860s schoolroom has gone, to be replaced by a cosy, comfortable sitting-dining room adorned with unusual bird watercolours; yet the old fire grate, coat hooks and chalk boards still survive. No longer is Master's permission needed to run down to the banks of the wide Owenmore river, crossed by a lovely old stone bridge, and gaze back at this careful restoration of Tudor revival, tucked into lush beech and chestnut woodland. Lattice windows, quarry tiles, lime-plastered walls: the original features remain and everything is new where it matters, including a charming, Shaker-blue kitchen. Antique mahogany and wrought-iron bedsteads promise a good night's sleep and an oriel window seat in the upstairs bedroom is the perfect place from which to contemplate the island lakes of Sligo.

Price	€400–€994 per week.
Rooms	House for 4.
Meals	Restaurants 5km.
Closed	Never.
Directions	From Corrick on Shannon, N4 for 30km. At r'bout, N17 for Galway. After 5km, right, opposite yellow road sign 'end of hard shoulder'. Drive over bridge; Schoolhouse straight ahead.

Travel Club Offer. See page 266.

The Irish Landmark Trust
Annaghmore, Colloney, Co. Sligo

Tel	+353 (0)1 670 4733
Fax	+353 (0)1 670 4887
Email	bookings@irishlandmark.com
Web	www.irishlandmark.com

Entry 68   Map 1 & 4

B&B & Self-catering   Co. Sligo

Ardtarmon House

In the middle of nowhere, and the views are magnetic. On a clear day the eye travels 60 miles out to sea; pebble, sand and crashing surf are a short walk. (The dogs will take you there – down through the wood and the grassy paths.) Amazingly, Ardtarmon started as a thatched cottage. The Henry family's home since an ancestor bought it in 1852, it grew to country house stature a century ago, the 'cloud-shrouded' top being familiarly known as the cosmos, and you sense venerability as you walk through the door. Floors are painted, rugs faded, family oils hang on muted walls, breakfast tables are laid with Denby crockery. Stairs wind up to big spotless bedrooms with views – of tangled orchards and a giant cedar with a treehouse. Charles and Christa, gentle, charming, are bringing up their young family in this place of peace and environmental friendship. Hearty meals are served in the dining room as it ripples with sunset gold; or step out to a great little pub/restaurant in Carney. The cottages are small and simply furnished, as is reflected in the price, but warmed to perfection by a new woodchip boiler.

Price	€90-€120. Singles €65-€80. Cottages €200-€600 per week.
Rooms	4 + 5: 3 doubles, 1 family. 5 cottages for 2-6.
Meals	Dinner €30. Wine €15. Restaurant 7km.
Closed	Christmas & New Year.
Directions	From Sligo N15 for Donegal 8km to Drumcliffe; left for Carney 1.5km. In village, follow signs to Raghley 7km; left at Dunleavy's shop 2.5km; gate lodge & drive on left.

Charles & Christa Henry
Ballinfull, Co. Sligo

Tel	+353 (0)71 916 3156
Fax	+353 (0)71 916 3156
Email	enquiries@ardtarmon.com
Web	www.ardtarmon.com

Ethical Collection: Environment.
See page 270.

Entry 69   Map 1 & 4

Munster

Photo: istockphoto.com

B&B   Co. Clare

Mount Vernon

Gazing across cornflowers and poppies to the dancing bay, the house flows, airy and gentle, like one of the Impressionist paintings famously collected by Hugh Lane when he lived here. Then came Lady Augusta Gregory, bringing Yeats, Synge, Shaw and the Celtic literary revival in her wake. There are three Augustus John fireplaces – and more. The place oozes artistic temperament. Ally, the bright Mercury, and Mark, the laid-back Epicurus, both talented and interesting, fit it perfectly. They have added some astounding and exotic travel mementoes to the lovely pieces left by Mark's mother – Kalahari bushmen's baskets, vast green birds from Bali, great kites in the kitchen, elephants everywhere (their 'thing'). It's not a shrine to the past, rather a vibrant evolving home where dining and drawing rooms are stunning in their mix of soft colours, antiques and quirky modern pieces and bedrooms are a delight. They work as a team in the kitchen, Mark creating imaginative wonders with whatever he finds, straight from the sea, Ally baking breads and making puddings. An exceptional place.

Price	From €198.
Rooms	5: 4 doubles, 1 single with separate bathroom.
Meals	Dinner €55. Wine €22-€70. By arrangement.
Closed	January-March.
Directions	From Dublin N6 then N18 south 19km to Kilcolgan; right N67 through Kinvarra 7km; right to New Quay; 1st right after Linnanes Lobster Bar: 3rd house on shore.

Mark Helmore & Ally Raftery
New Quay, The Burren, Co. Clare

Tel	+353 (0)65 707 8126
Fax	+353 (0)65 707 8118
Email	info@mountvernon.ie
Web	www.mountvernon.ie

Travel Club Offer. See page 266.

Entry 70   Map 3

Co. Clare

B&B

Drumcreehy House *a small family hotel!*

At the front, the shimmer of Galway Bay, at the back, the Burren strangeness: this fabulous spot was what Armin and Bernadette were after. She used to come here as a child, he fell under the spell when they moved from Germany with their dream of running an old country guest house in Ireland. In the end they built a new one – in solid old style. Its lemony façade and white dormers blend well into the surroundings, whitethorn and fuchsia hedges now make a colourful border and, beyond the reception desk, they have created a handsome guest house and home for their young family. Rich colours, varnished floors, old walnut furniture and an ever-lit open fire make for a cosy atmosphere, while the breakfast rooms is filled with morning sun. The honesty bar is inviting with its woodburner and exceptional view. Breakfast is a mouthwatering spread of stewed and fresh fruits, local meats, cheeses and fish, home-baked breads, pastries… Generous bedrooms, each with a hand-painted local wild flower nameplate, are spick and span in their mixture of old and new pine furniture; bathrobes, too. The sunsets are spectacular.

Travel Club Offer. See page 266.

Price	€80–€110. Singles €56–€90.
Rooms	12: 5 doubles, 7 twins/doubles.
Meals	Choice in village.
Closed	Rarely.
Directions	From Ennis R476 to Corofin; through village, right R480 to Ballyvaughan; right in village at Hylands Hotel. 1.5km on right past blue cottage.

Bernadette & Armin Moloney-Grefkes
Ballyvaughan, Co. Clare

Tel	+353 (0)65 707 7377
Fax	+353 (0)65 707 7379
Email	info@drumcreehyhouse.com
Web	www.drumcreehyhouse.com

Entry 71   Map 3

Hotel   Co. Clare

Gregans Castle Hotel

In overwhelming scenery, Gregans' darkly imposing look belies the gentle open-doored open-armed welcome of the aromatic turf fire, the quirky antiques and the jug of unpretentious country flowers on the hall mantelpiece. Simon and Frederieke, a particularly charming, outgoing, no-nonsense couple with buckets of energy, have taken over from his parents and are bringing Gregans into the 21st century – slowly. So there's a bit of everything in this rabbit warren at present, an endearing confusion of country house traditional and clean-limbed 1930s elegance: old botanical prints and modern art in the drawing room, horse brasses on the hefty beams and super soft Bennison bird fabric at the windows in the bar, dated florals falling from pelmets to the superb new pale green carpet in the huge Galway Bay suite (stunning great Victorian antiques set off its fine bones), new tiles on bathroom floors, old on walls. A fascinating work in progress complemented by lovingly-made 50% organic food, a beautiful garden and an annual Burren rubbish removal commando.

Price	€195-€235. Singles €152-€192.
Rooms	21: 15 twins/doubles, 6 suites.
Meals	Lunch €10-€30. Dinner €30-€60. Wine €25.
Closed	December-13 February.
Directions	From Ballyvaughan N67 south 5km then follow signs.

Simon & Frederieke Haden
Ballyvaughan, Co. Clare

Tel	+353 (0)65 707 7005
Fax	+353 (0)65 707 7111
Email	stay@gregans.ie
Web	www.gregans.ie

Entry 72   Map 3

Co. Clare

B&B & Self-catering

Fergus View

Declan, a school principal, is the latest in a long line of country teachers: this house was built as a teacher's residence and his great-grandfather was the first occupant – out here on the edge of the moon. A short walk through the Burren wilderness, with its weathered limestone, prehistoric dolmens and rare flowers, is said to be great therapy for mind and body. Declan can guide you to the best parts. Everything is done well here, both owners are eager to make you welcome and communicate their love of the Irish language and music, while the sitting room is awash with books on the Burren. Mary's breakfasts, with her own sodabread, are acclaimed by guests from all over the world. The small, tidy, brightly coloured bedrooms are compact and cosy with orthopædic beds, elegant bedcovers and timber windows that keep the cold out. The garden stretches down towards the river Fergus which disappears behind a welter of colour in summer. You can walk to the ruins of an Elizabethan fortress or a medieval churchyard, then out into the moonscape. Genuine Irish hospitality in a lovely family home.

Price	€78-€80. Singles €53-€55. Cottage €400-€640 per week.
Rooms	6 + 1: 3 doubles, 1 twin/double, 1 family; 1 double with separate bathroom. Cottage for 5.
Meals	Restaurants 3km.
Closed	Mid-October to February. Cottage open all year.
Directions	From Shannon N18 through Ennis to r'bout for Ennistymon 3km; right R476 to Corofin then Kilnaboy. House on left after ruined church.

Mary & Declan Kelleher
Kilnaboy, Corofin, Co. Clare
Tel +353 (0)65 683 7606
Fax +353 (0)65 683 7083
Email deckell@indigo.ie
Web www.fergusview.com

Self-catering   Co. Clare

Ballyportry Castle

Walk into this Gaelic tower house and step back in time. It was built in the late 15th century, occupied for 200 years, left to decline, and saved in the Sixties by an American; history vibrates beneath your feet. The present owners let the original dynamic of Ballyportry guide them in their brilliant conservation project: its ancient fabric demands deep respect (hence the damages deposit). Four floors pile room upon room – vaulted ceilings, massive fireplaces – up to the roof where hammocks are slung between battlements for sunbathing, stargazing, Burren poetry. First you encounter the kitchen: giant fireplace, range and pans, stone coffee table, mod cons hidden away, and a bathroom. Next, two great bedrooms, one with a huge waterbed the other a four-poster. Off the tall winding stone stairs are small bedrooms, then the top floor that explodes in atmosphere with its double-height living room (and another small kitchen). Stay in winter, when open fires are ablaze and candles throw shadows on uneven walls. Ballyportry is a unique experience.

Price	€1,600-€3,200 per week.
	2-4 day break €1,100-€1,900.
	€500 damages deposit.
Rooms	Castle for 4-8.
Meals	Dinner €30. Breakfast from €10.
	By arrangement only.
Closed	Never.
Directions	Directions given on booking.

	Siobhán Cuffe & Patrick Wallace
	Corofin, Co. Clare
Tel	+353 (0)1 660 9038
Fax	+353 (0)1 663 0011
Email	info@ballyportry.ie
Web	www.ballyportry.ie

Entry 74   Map 3

Co. Clare   Hotel

Vaughan Lodge Hotel

Michael can't help himself: a fourth-generation hotelier, he wants things to be perfect for his guests and is putting his heart and soul into his new hotel. He has a charming, twinkling presence, clever ideas (big drying room, extendable bedside reading lights), an eye for detail and is an interesting photographer. Lovely people, he and Maria chose a modern-classic interior designer and are still adding their essential personal touches to the low-key high-luxury result. Everything that comes to them has a story attached. The family's 1850s mahogany sideboard presides over the hexagonal dining room, an eclectic collection of old china smiles out of an antique cabinet on the way to the bedrooms, generous friends leave great paintings, a piano, a plant,… The Vaughans and chef Philippe Farineau care hugely about local produce and traceability, their butcher and fishmonger are named, their food is of the highest quality. You will lounge in leather to read Michael's invaluable local guides or Golfing Ireland, dine excellently under his convivial guidance, sleep in smooth/crisp white and plum comfort.

Price	€140-€300.
Rooms	22: 21 doubles, 1 suite.
Meals	Dinner €45-€65.
Closed	November-March.
Directions	From Ennis N67 to Lahinch. Hotel just inside 50km zone.

	Michael & Maria Vaughan
	Ennistymon Road, Lahinch, Co. Clare
Tel	+353 (0)65 708 1111
Fax	+353 (0)65 708 1011
Email	info@vaughanlodge.ie
Web	www.vaughanlodge.ie

Hotel   Co. Clare

Moy House

Moy House is different: it looks not landwards but out to sea, to the mercurial Atlantic whose raging grey tempests and deliriously pink sunsets can hold you, recharging your soul, for hours. There's a sandy beach at the bottom of the garden and the awesome Cliffs of Moher rise from the sea in the distance. Built on 9,000 acres in the 1820s as a summer house for Augustine Fitzgerald, Moy now stands on just 15 well-kept acres that include an ever-developing organic vegetable garden and orchard: good news for dinner. The incomparable O'Looney family, funny, intelligent, imaginative, have restored it into unintimidating formal splendour. In clear good taste, the feel is friendly and welcoming: exquisite antiques, original art, sumptuous bedrooms, even pop-up TVs in wooden cabinets. A glass-panelled floor in one of the stunning bathrooms looks down into the old well; a spiral wooden staircase leads up the tower for quiet contemplation at the summit. Dinner is superb and you will retire to find chocolates and slippers waiting for you: Brid O'Meara sees to that. Wonderful, worth every cent.

Price	€185–€280. Singles €145–€175. Suite €270–€360.
Rooms	9: 3 doubles, 2 twins, 3 singles, 1 suite.
Meals	Dinner, 4 courses, €55. Wine from €28.50.
Closed	January to mid-February.
Directions	From Lahinch, N67 south for Milltown Malbay 1.5km. Entrance on right in wooded dip.

Brid O'Meara
Lahinch, Co. Clare

Tel   +353 (0)65 708 2800
Fax   +353 (0)65 708 2500
Email moyhouse@eircom.net
Web   www.moyhouse.com

Travel Club Offer. See page 266.

Ethical Collection: Food.
See page 270.

Entry 76   Map 3

Co. Clare   B&B

Berry Lodge & Cookery School

An amazing cook, Rita sources the best of what is locally available on the basis that "it would be a crime not to use all the lovely fish we have on our doorstep". She used to have a popular radio show on cookery and still teaches here, with verve, including a course for Men in the Kitchen. The whole team are smiley, helpful, efficient and flexible, the place has a relaxed feel, dinner in the rustic cottage-style restaurant or the big light conservatory is fun and pleasurable (sizzling garlicky tiger prawns with pilpil then lavender crême brulée, for example). The locals love it. The modernised Victorian house, sheltered from the Atlantic blasts by its walled garden where patio chairs await you on balmier evenings (or there's the breakfast/sitting room), has been sweetly furnished with solid pine and thick rugs on wooden floors. Pretty bedrooms have window-seats, firm beds, warm colours, patchwork quilts, tied-back curtains, original fireplaces and, on generous days, views of the sea. Ask for an upstairs room. Breakfast absorbs the taste buds and seaside walks are ideal for rebuilding the appetite.

Price	From €90. Singles from €55.
Rooms	5: 2 doubles, 1 twin, 2 triples.
Meals	Dinner, 4 courses, €40. By arrangement.
Closed	December-March.
Directions	From Ennis N85 to Inagh; left R460 for Milltown Malbay. In village, N67 for Killimer car ferry road, past Bellbridge Hotel, over bridge, 2nd left; house 1st on right.

Rita Meade
Annagh, Milltown Malbay, Co. Clare
Tel   +353 (0)65 708 7022
Fax   +353 (0)65 708 7011
Email info@berrylodge.com
Web   www.berrylodge.com

Self-catering Co. Clare

Old Parochial House Cottages

West Clare is steeped in culture, has pubs that swing to traditional music, fabulous countryside, deserted sandy beaches, cliff walks – and friendly easy-going people. None more so than Alyson and Seán in their 1872 former parish priest's house. The main house stands on four acres overlooking the sleepy village of Cooraclare. The old stables, coach house and shibeen have been converted and two stone cottages built in traditional Irish style. All the O'Neills' work is a labour of love expressed in turf fires, stone floors, exposed beams, old artefacts and bags of character. It would be hard to pick a favourite but the open-plan living room in the stables is beautiful, with views over rolling countryside. Lean on your half-door, breathe the heavy gorse-scented air, chat to whomever goes by, take your time. Insects hum, birds sing, goats and pony graze – and there are three pubs in the village with good beer and music, a five-minute stroll. The Cliffs of Moher and the magical Burren are not that far. Come and live the slow life. Just being here will do you a power of good. *50km from Shannon airport.*

Price	€350–€650 per week.
Rooms	6 cottages: 1 for 5; 4 for 2-3; 1 for 3-4.
Meals	Restaurants 1km.
Closed	Rarely.
Directions	From Ennis N68 for Kilrush 29km; right to Cooraclare, following signs. In village, right at petrol station R483 for coast; 3rd house on left.

Alyson & Sean O'Neill
Old Parochial House, Cooraclare,
Kilrush, Co. Clare
Tel +353 (0)65 905 9059
Email oldparochialhouse@eircom.net
Web www.oldparochialhouse.com

Entry 78 Map 3

Co. Clare

Self-catering

Mount Cashel Lodge

Lawns run down to the lake, a path leads up to the woods; beyond is a garden for veg and a paddock with two donkeys. Pat and Annette so love this place that you cannot conceivably leave unconverted: the view raises your spirit, the peace restores your soul. The two pretty 18th-century stone lodges stand creeper-clung round a courtyard, the stables stand apart. Renovated with a light, sensitive hand, they feel unassuming and genuine, the interiors done in a straightforward modern country style for comfort and practicality: pine kitchens with all the bits, pretty iron beds with excellent bedding, proper armchairs before open fires, French doors to private terraces stretching out to the limpid lake and moorland. All you need, and more: barbecues, babysitting (book ahead), free broadband, satellite TV. The beautiful lakeside position, its paths, boats and rich fishing, are yours for the duration… Pat has built a jetty, provides safety equipment and is ever willing to guide and advise. Amazingly close to Shannon, Limerick, Ennis – and famous Dromoland Castle is just down the road.

Price	€660-€1,750 per week.
Rooms	2 lodges for 5 (1 double, 1 single, 2 bathrooms). Stables for 9 (3 doubles, 1 triple, 4 bathrooms).
Meals	Restaurants within 3km.
Closed	Never.
Directions	From Limerick N18 for Ennis 15km; exit Cratloe onto R462 through Sixmilebridge 2.5km; right after castle, follow signs for Mt Cashel Lodge: lane 1km by stone wall on left, long drive through black gates.

Travel Club Offer. See page 266.

Pat & Annette Shanahan
Kilmurry, Sixmilebridge, Co. Clare

Tel	+353 (0)61 369142
Fax	+353 (0)61 369142
Email	pat@mtcashel.com
Web	www.mtcashel.com

Entry 79   Map 3

Hotel   Co. Claire

Charnel Castle

After a day toiling moiling digging dodging from dawn till dusk with never a sight of joy or sport, what better place to enjoy a stony sleep than the charming Charnel Castle. Standing lonely on a windswept hillside the great turrets and battlements rear to the sky. Things may indeed fall apart, but at least you can lie in the gutter and look at the stars, for here midnight's all a-glimmer. The remoteness of the location means there's truly nothing to be done. Indeed, the jung may well be freudened here, for under skies black as the hour of night, bedevilled by rats and rotten floors, echoes of grogochs, banshees and even the feared pooka may still be heard within the castle's crumbling walls. Fear not – the genial host, stately, plump Mick Bulligan, a quare fellow indeed, and his wife, the wild Swansa Coole, will make sure everyone enjoys happiness down all the days, with their wilde synging and rejoycing. Relax, maybe spend time digging in their bee-loud glade, green and heavy handed, and you too will marvel at the power of a loy.

Price	Ask a cynic.
Rooms	Just the one, with stunning sky views.
Meals	Morning dew is a delicacy.
Closed	Never.
Directions	Ask the old blind couple at the well.

	Mick Bulligan
	Coomclochancoolcullen,
	Coomclochancoolcullencullencool,
	Coom, Co. Cool C00 0C0
Tel	1606 1904
Email	bulligan@blooming.co.nn
Web	www.irishmist.co.nn

Entry 80   Map 355

Co. Cork

B&B

Ulusker House

Up a winding lane, snug inside its own special privacy, Ulusker House has a beautifully crafted interior, magical views over Bantry Bay and warm artistic owners. David and Lorna's is a tale of hard work and talent. They came from Bath, found a ruin, rebuilt every bit with extraordinary skill and heaps of reclaimed materials — ~~David~~ is an architectural salvage expert, Lorna has a love of texture, perfection and food — and summoned the world to eat and sleep in it. Communal rooms lead off one another like an open invitation; a warm yellow sitting room is alive with fresh flowers and open fire, opulent bedrooms are like poems where unusual antiques rhyme with soft colours, perfect details with luscious bathing. Lorna created the garden from scratch, grows her own veg and herbs and does the cooking; eggs from their own hens appear at breakfast. Dinner happens in the elegant dining room or the flagstoned conservatory or on the summer terrace: in the flickering light of candles and three fantastic Victorian cast-iron gas lamps, you will want to linger for hours. Lovely people and tremendous value.

Price	€90–€150. Singles €55–€85.
Rooms	4: 3 doubles, 1 twin.
Meals	Dinner, 3 courses, €40. Wine from €19. Lunch on request.
Closed	Rarely.
Directions	From Glengariff for Castletownbere to Adrigole. Entering Adrigole, right at sign; 1km down lane.

David & Lorna Ramshaw
Adrigole, Beara, Co. Cork

Tel	+353 (0)27 60606
Fax	+353 (0)27 60606
Email	mossies@eircom.net
Web	mossiesrestaurant.com

B&B   Co. Cork

Ballylickey House

The lawns of Ballylickey roll down to Bantry Bay, Whiddy Island looms across the water, the Caha Mountains rise beyond: in this incomparable setting, four generations of the Graves family have nurtured their house and gardens into glory. Don't miss the lily pond and the two myrtle trees, indigenous to Bantry. Reached by a granite path curling through rhododendrons and azaleas, the cottages sprawl round the gardens down to the road. Paco has taken the B&B over from his parents and is gradually refurbishing. The cottages vary in size – the larger have their own drawing room and fireplace – and décor: old-fashioned florals, some with pine clad walls, and fabrics in midnight blue and gold; bathrooms are adequate if not the latest design. The best big suite has a stupendous view. You breakfast in the elegant old mansion house at separate tables. Come for the peace of the garden, the majesty of Bantry Bay, Bantry's excellent restaurants and bars, and Francine's friendly helpful welcome. *Pets by arrangement. Vegetarian meals available.*

Price	€100-€180.
Rooms	6: 5 doubles, 1 suite.
Meals	Choice in Bantry, 3-minute drive.
Closed	November to mid-March.
Directions	From Bantry N71 for Ballylickey; house signposted on right in village.

	The Graves Family
	Ballylickey, Bantry Bay, Co. Cork
Tel	+353 (0)27 50071
Email	ballymh@eircom.net
Web	www.ballylickeymanorhouse.com

Entry 82   Map 6

Co. Cork   B&B

Hagal Healing Farm

Be greeted by homemade scones – and Fred, a spring of lavender behind one ear, a twinkle in his eye. Hagal is different, marvellously different. It always was: the farmhouse was built 150 years ago by one man in 40 days. At its heart is a tree trunk around which chunky polished oak steps spiral, with similarly polished branches acting as grab rails on the walls. Rooms flow from conservatory to kitchen to large, low living area: simple, neat, unfrilly. Take lemon balm tea under the huge old vine in the conservatory among candles, jingling buddha chimes and lots of harmony, retreat into a secluded corner of the beautiful garden, left natural like everything here; insects hum, birds trill. Seating is low, ethnic and tempting; the chill-out room with white sofas has breathtaking views of Bantry Bay. Hagal is New Age heaven, run by gentle Dutch folk – Fred the garden-lover, Janny the yoga teacher, both deeply involved in the boundless natural energy of this land. Eat subtly spiced organic vegetarian food, or learn to cook it yourself. Wonderful. *Ask about weekend courses & week-long healings.*

Ethical Collection: Environment; Food. See page 270.

Price	€70. Singles €50–€60. Full-board €150 per room (singles €90–€100).
Rooms	4 doubles.
Meals	Lunch €17. Dinner, 3 courses, €28. BYO wine. Book ahead.
Closed	Rarely.
Directions	From Bantry for Glengariff; right after Esso petrol station at Donemark; 12km of winding road; left at Hagal Farm sign.

Janny & Fred Wieler
Coomleigh, Bantry, Co. Cork
Tel   +353 (0)27 66179
Fax   +353 (0)27 66179
Email hagalhealingfarm@eircom.net
Web   www.hagalholistichealth.com

Entry 83   Map 6

B&B　　　　　　　　　　　　　　　　　　　　　　　　　　　Co. Cork

Bantry House

Wreathed in history, basking in its famous Italianate gardens (the house stands on the third of seven grand terraces) and spectacular view over The Bay, this is one of Ireland's finest stately homes. Egerton, the earnest and knowledgeable trombone-player, will serve your breakfast kippers with fine old cutlery. His family are the ninth generation of Whites to live here since 1739. His staff are competent and charming, too. The vast drawing room, dining room, library and halls are open to the public. Go one better: after visiting hours sit by the blazing hearth, the 1st Earl's coronet and the grand piano in the incredible library. The racing-green billiard room has the hugest table, great family portraits hang everywhere, there are books, an honesty bar, sitting spaces, generosity. Refurbished east-wing bedrooms (two with bay view) now have super bathrooms. West-wing family-friendly rooms look over the wisteria-hung water feature of those fabulous restored gardens. A flight of 100 stone steps, the Stairway to the Sky, leads to awesome views of islands and distant mountains. Staying here is a rare treat.

Price	€220-€240. Singles €130. Children under 10 free, 11s-15s half price.
Rooms	7: 4 doubles, 2 twins, 1 family.
Meals	Snack lunch in tea room €5-€15. Restaurants within easy walking distance.
Closed	November-February. End of June.
Directions	From Cork, N71 to Bantry. Big entrance on right just before village.

	Egerton & Brigitte Shelswell-White Bantry, Co. Cork
Tel	+353 (0)27 50047
Fax	+353 (0)27 50795
Email	info@bantryhouse.com
Web	www.bantryhouse.com

Entry 84　　Map 6

Co. Cork   B&B

Ballyroon Mountain

Spectacularly remote, in one of the last inhabited spots before Europe sinks into the Atlantic, Ballyroon ('secret place' in Irish) lives in the drama of plunging ocean and mountainous peninsulas. Friendly and sophisticated, Roger and Sue – ex-cameraman and garden designer – came to this rugged hillside to farm and breathe clearer air. The little stone bothy beyond the main house is your cosy mountain cabin: one large bed-sitting room, simply, thoughtfully furnished with stone, timber and a thick woolly rug, the bed raised to catch the view, and your own garden where stylish recliners invite you to contemplation as choughs wheel above, or laze with a book from the well-stacked shelves in your room. Breakfast in the conservatory next door includes home-produced bacon, sausages and honey; Roger and Sue will talk about the lovely walks they have opened up, the waterfall, and their farming and conservation efforts. Take all day to explore their 36 varied acres, walk the Sheep's Head and Poet's Ways, feel how every minute counts. You will come to love this retreat from urban frazzle as much as they do.

Price	€80–€100.
Rooms	1 double.
Meals	Dinner €25. BYO wine. 24hrs notice required.
Closed	Rarely.
Directions	Directions given on booking.

Travel Club Offer. See page 266.

Ethical Collection: Environment; Food. See page 270.

Roger & Sue Goss
Kilcrohane, Bantry, Co. Cork
Tel   +353 (0)27 67940
Email   info@ballyroonmountain.com
Web   www.ballyroonmountain.com

B&B & Self-catering   Co. Cork

Blairs Cove House

The picture can tell the brilliant setting but not the charm and atmosphere on the ground, the embrace of the cobbled courtyard where modern sculpture stands by an old lily pond. Outbuildings have been converted into one lofty yet intimate stone-walled restaurant and four beautiful two-storey suites, each with its own kitchen. Be charmed by stripped furniture and country antiques, brushed aluminium and boldly striped seating, each space joyously filled with contemporary art. The studio apartment above the restaurant is just as funky, with sensational bay views. Philippe (from Belgium) and Sabine (from Germany) are a cosmopolitan couple who believe in fabulous food and sophisticated comfort. Breakfast is delivered to you, a healthy spread ordered the night before. The atmospheric restaurant serves seafood in season, laid out like sculpture in the middle of the room; meat is grilled over logs, a pianist plays on Saturdays: a feast for all senses. In summer, you eat in the conservatory overlooking the courtyard. The De Meys are thoroughly professional, good at detail and know how to spoil you.

Price	Apts €150-€260 per night. Cottage for 8, €875-€1300 per week. Cottage for 4, €585-€950 per week.
Rooms	1 apt for 4; 1 family cottage for 8; 1 cottage for 4 (8 miles away).
Meals	Breakfast included. Dinner €58. Wine €22. Restaurant closed Sun/Mon.
Closed	February to mid-March.
Directions	From Cork N71 west; just before Bantry, left R591 to Durrus; left for Goleen 2.5km. Entrance on right before sharp right bend (caution).

Philippe & Sabine De Mey
Durrus, Co. Cork
Tel   +353 (0)27 61127
Fax   +353 (0)27 61487
Email blairscove@eircom.net
Web   www.blairscove.ie

Entry 86   Map 6

Co. Cork   B&B & Self-catering

Rock Cottage

Barbara excels at B&B in a region where she spent many a happy holiday as a child. She particularly likes having animal lovers to stay – the animals are "part of the place"; sheep roam, dogs, cats and donkey must be introduced, all as friendly and down-to-earth as she. Her eco credentials include protecting habitats on her left-to-the-wilds land; with humour she tells, in a wonderful mix of German and Cork accents, how she fought to restore this property. An 1826 hunting lodge, it is built on a huge slab of rock, hence the split levels on the ground floor. It looks irresistible when you arrive; then Barbara's cooking, joyously local, much of it organic, and her fresh, contemporary and enticing bedrooms cast their spell. Barbara's talents include a delightful sense of colour. Rooms, each with its own personality, are stylishly simple with timber floors, country-house beds and views over lightly wooded paddocks. A great sense of privacy here, surrounded by green wilds… behind, a path through gorse bushes leads up a small hill where you can sit and gaze on the glorious view over Dunmanus Bay.

Price	€140. Singles €100. Cottage €380–€600 per week.
Rooms	3 + 1: 1 double, 2 triples. Cottage for 2-3.
Meals	Dinner from €50. BYO wine. Supper on request.
Closed	Rarely.
Directions	From Cork N71 west. Just before Bantry, left R591 to Durrus; left for Goleen 13km. Entrance on right after small cemetery.

Barbara Klötzer
Barnatonicane, Schull, Co. Cork
Tel   +353 (0)28 35538
Fax   +353 (0)28 35538
Email rockcottage@eircom.net
Web   www.rockcottage.ie

B&B   Co. Cork

Grove House

Katarina is Swedish and quite a woman. Not only talented – she teaches the piano, rides in events, cooks inventively – she is also full of zest and fun, loving her new life as B&B and restaurant owner. Looking across to the living picture that is Schull harbour, the charming old house, where Bernard Shaw once stayed, has kept its former riches of warm cranberry hall, racing green library/piano room and fudge-cream dining room, now an atmospheric restaurant. The food, prepared by Katarina and son Nico, served by son Max in candlelight, has already attracted attention. Guests may play the piano and impromptu sing-songs are frequent. Comfortably worn bedrooms have the odd quirk: a funny Edwardian fireplace, interesting oddments, an original Victorian loo with a square wooden seat. Excellent bathrooms have careful tile patterns. Katarina has planted trees and bushes to hide the new houses next door; her next project is to restore the garden. There are seats for admiring the superb harbour view, a croquet lawn and a great welcome for children to this friendliest of houses. *Pets by arrangement.*

Price	€90-€120. Singles €60-€90.
Rooms	5: 4 doubles, 1 twin.
Meals	Dinner €30-€35. Lunch €10-€15.
Closed	Never.
Directions	From Cork N71 to Ballydehob; R592 to Schull; left opp. AIB bank. House 500m on right.

	Katarina Runske
	Colla Road, Schull, Co. Cork
Tel	+353 (0)28 28067
Fax	+353 (0)28 28069
Email	katarinarunske@eircom.net

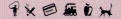

Entry 88   Map 6

Co. Cork

Self-catering

Fortview & Elacampane Cottages

Welcome to Connell country. Richard has cattle and this land has been in his family for four generations. Wander around and you'll find reed beds, hedgerows and a small lake for wildlife, all of which are part of a rural environment protection scheme and have made his 70 hectares a Department of Agriculture demonstration farm for West Cork. He also built these imperious stone cottages – single-handedly. A couple of miles apart, they are pretty much identical and offer the very lap of countryside luxury: brass chandeliers above polished tables, dressers full of crockery, bright galley-style kitchens with every mod con. There are timber floors, heavy beams, mezzanines for extra beds and two bathrooms apiece – it is elegant yet cottage cosy. Light floods onto the yellow rendered walls giving the place a smart rustic feel. Wood everywhere, slate patios outside, and Richard's Friesians for company in the fields. Alternatively, climb the ridge that leads up to Mount Gabriel for huge panoramic views, walk up to Dunmanus Bay to watch the seals or visit Mizen Head, Ireland's most southerly point.

Price	€400-€950 per week.
Rooms	2 cottages for 6
Meals	Restaurants 9km.
Closed	Never.
Directions	From Skibbereen N71/R592 to Toormore. There, R591 for Bantry & Durrus 2km.

Violet & Richard Connell
Gurtyowen, Toormore, Goleen,
Co. Cork

Tel	+353 (0)28 35324
Email	fortviewhousegoleen@eircom.net
Web	www.fortviewhousegoleen.com

Hotel   Co. Cork

The Heron's Cove

This is a spectacular part of Ireland with its deep inlets, steepling cliffs, scintillating or thundering seas; roads dip, twist, clamber round the hills, then peter out or land you at a beach or village – an explorer's heaven. Choose The Heron's Cove and belong here for a spell. Sue has been part of the village for 45 years, launched and still carries the Mizen Head Signal Station Visitor Centre (don't miss it), and knows all the lore – just ask. She is also deeply eco-aware. Sitting on its own bay, this modern restaurant with rooms has comfortable, carpeted bedrooms, all but one with limpid bay views, and sliding glass doors to balconies with wide-armed wooden chairs, wonderful for soft days. But the heart of the house is the airy restaurant with a fire at each end, wicker chairs and, miracle, a Slow Food ethos: that organic search for local, seasonal goodness that requires taking proper time to prepare, to cook – and to consume. A warm-hearted, no-nonsense woman, backed by a wonderful staff, Sue enjoys having guests stay. The constant ebb of the tide results in glorious wildlife, birdsong and... herons.

Price	€70-€110.
Rooms	5: 3 doubles, 1 twin, 1 family room for 4.
Meals	Dinner from €30 à la carte. Wine from €17.50. Lunch for special occasions. Restaurant closed Nov-Apr except for residents and bookings.
Closed	Christmas & New Year.
Directions	From Skibbereen N71 to Ballydehob; left R592 to Toormore; left R591 to Goleen; there, left opp. Green Kettle to harbour. 75 miles from Cork.

Ethical Collection: Food.
See page 270.

	Sue Hill
	The Harbour, Goleen, Co. Cork
Tel	+353 (0)28 35225
Fax	+353 (0)28 35422
Email	suehill@eircom.net
Web	www.heronscove.com

Entry 90   Map 6

Co. Cork   B&B & Self-catering

Grove House & Courtyard Cottages

No-one could be more helpful than these two and, despite its formal chequered hall, Grove House is neither immaculate nor super-smart but the most relaxed place you could hope for. Peter, whose passion is old buildings, will point out the best local secrets, the beaches without ice cream vans, the special walks; he also serves in the red, antique-furnished dining room, stopping to chat if you want. Anna does the cooking. She trained with a former chef at the Ritz but fear not, it won't be over-sophisticated: she decides what to cook when she goes shopping each day, just the freshest local ingredients done simply to reveal their innate goodness. Then she too will emerge to chat with her guests. Good-sized rooms have canopied beds, the best ones have three windows to the front lawns, one is super-French in pink Jouy prints; much attention to detail has gone into refurbishing the big bathrooms. Should you stay in one of the cottages, you will relax in a clear modern interior with private hot tubs or jacuzzi baths. Remarkable value for unfussy folk.

Travel Club Offer. See page 266.

Price	€118–€136. Singles €89–€99. Cottages €99–€169.
Rooms	4 + 2: 4 four-posters. 2 cottages for 2.
Meals	Dinner with wine, €29.
Closed	Christmas.
Directions	From Cork N71 to Skibbereen; at Skibbereen r'bout follow signs to Hospital. House 1km past Hospital on right.

Peter & Anna Warburton
Skibbereen, Co. Cork
Tel   +353 (0)28 22957
Fax   +353 (0)28 22958
Email relax@grovehouse.net
Web   www.grovehouse.net

Entry 91   Map 6

B&B   Co. Cork

Horseshoe Cottage

Joe and Fiona, the happy owners of little old Horseshoe, are wonderfully warm fun characters who have achieved much, including raising unnumbered goats and nine children. Joe, a retired commercial fishing skipper, has sailed the Atlantic, can take you whale or dolphin watching, show you his film on humpback whales near the Cap Verde Islands or his book of sea-faring yarns. Fiona, a registered homeopath and massage therapist, expends her exuberant energy re-vamping the garden, collecting eggs from her hens for your delicious breakfast, baking bread and flapjacks and cooking delicious, mostly organic, dinners – maybe mackerel caught that day and sizzled on the garden barbecue. This is three, 400 year old cottages, now rolled into one. The bedrooms are small and cosy, newly painted with colourful soft rugs on wooden floors, views are dizzying, the corridor is lined with books – but linger not, you are here to walk, swim, sail, discover. After breakfast sally forth to experience the peace and solitude of this beautiful little island (pop. 120): the Franciscans thoughtfully left a ruined friary to explore.

Price	€80-€95. Singles €40-€50.
Rooms	3: 1 double, 1 twin/double, 1 single.
Meals	Dinner from €25. By arrangement only. Pubs within short walking distance. Packed lunch.
Closed	Rarely.
Directions	Ferry from Baltimore (all year) or Schull (summer only). Up hill past friary ruins; left at telephone box; cottage on right.

Fiona & Joe Aston
Horseshoe Harbour, Sherkin Island,
Co. Cork
Tel   +353 (0)28 20598
Email   joe@gannetsway.com
Web   www.gannetsway.com

Travel Club Offer. See page 266.

Ethical Collection: Environment; Community; Food. See page 270.

Entry 92   Map 6

Co. Cork   B&B & Self-catering

Lis-ardagh Lodge

Carol is utterly genuine and gentle, her lovely big smile just says "come on in" and you'd never guess she used to be in the police. Jim, a Cork man, gardens, professionally and passionately. He's also a keen road bowler... They left London with their two children to build this house in local stone, lay soft pine floors and live in peace. The children now help in the house, as does lovely labrador Megan. Carol's rich, generous breakfast, served in the bright and cheery dining room or on the flagstoned patio, includes her own brown sodabread and possibly kippers from the local smokery. The odd teddy bear fits easily into the big floral-friendly sitting room. Jim's garden meanders slowly, revealing quirks among its various levels: an old curragh boat turned into a sheltered seaview seat with creeper growing up the 'roof', a hot tub on the south-facing deck, a sauna, a stone stable (horses will come), fabulous birdlife. Two rooms look over this marvellous spread and out to sea (you can go whale watching here), all are pine-clad, homely, comfy and fresh blue in colour. Tremendous value.

Price	€70-€80. Singles €45-€50. Apartments €300-€500 per week.
Rooms	3 + 2: 1 triple, 1 suite for 5, 1 family for 5. 2 apartments for 4.
Meals	Pubs 5-minute walk. Restaurants 3-8km.
Closed	Christmas & New Year.
Directions	From Cork N71 to Leap (75km); 1.5km outside leap, left at sign for Union Hall Fishing Village 2km; stone house on right.

	Carol & Jim Kearney Union Hall, Co. Cork
Tel	+353 (0)28 34951
Email	info@lis-ardaghlodge.com
Web	www.lis-ardaghlodge.com

Entry 93   Map 6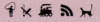

B&B   Co. Cork

The Glen Country House

They grow everything here from sea kale to raspberries to asparagus; stroll in the walled vegetable garden, sit on the lawn, gaze past the cows, soak up the peace. Guy is an easy, laid-back farmer, Diana as friendly and helpful as you could wish; both love doing B&B. The family has farmed this land between rolling pastures and the Atlantic for 350 years and lived in the house for 100 years. Diana hasn't hesitated to use good strong colours to tremendous effect and turn her main rooms into perfect backdrops for antique coffee cups, oriental teak dining chairs and old family photographs. Bedrooms are paler in their smart stripey or soft floral wallpapers, all beautifully finished and furnished, antique wardrobes sharing the wall space with flat-screen televisions, big beds firm beneath fluffy linen-covered duvets and the modern little bathrooms fitting perfectly without destroying the harmony of these old rooms. Old class, new comforts, the ever-inspiring ocean light and a young family – the Scotts are all that.

Price	€120-€130. Suite €200.
Rooms	5: 4 twins/doubles, 1 family suite.
Meals	Pub within walking distance, 3 restaurants within 5km.
Closed	November-March.
Directions	Midway between Kinsale & Clonakilty: signs on R600.

Guy & Diana Scott
The Glen, Kilbrittain, Co. Cork
Tel   +353 (0)23 884 9862
Fax   +353 (0)23 884 9862
Email guyscott@eircom.net
Web   www.glencountryhouse.com

Entry 94 Map 7

Co. Cork

Self-catering

The Cottage

Allow yourself a sigh of pleasure as you arrive: with its sash windows, slate roof and sensitive extension, this charming seaside cottage on a beautiful part of the coast is all you hope for and seldom find. Set below the road in its own simple, private garden, it comes with long soft views of the beach and Courtmacsherry Bay. You go through the traditional half door straight into the sitting room to be greeted by an open fire, simple, well-chosen country furniture and plenty of space for four in Elizabeth's hallmark cosy-comfy décor. The new part is an accurate reflection of the old, walls are painted white or done with attractive limed tongue-and-groove timber, original watercolours and decent prints alongside check and gingham fabrics all emphasise the cottagey look, the neat little bedrooms have new beds, the bathrooms (one in a heated outhouse) have new showers, the traditionally furnished dining/kitchen area has good natural light – indeed the whole cottage is exceptionally well-lit. Ideal for a couple or a family with young children looking for a classic seaside holiday.

Price	€300–€650 per week.
Rooms	Cottage for 4-6.
Meals	Pubs/restaurants 0.5km & 5km.
Closed	Never.
Directions	12 miles west of Kinsale on R600, 14 miles east of Clonakilty. Directions on booking.

Elizabeth Connolly
Harbour View, Kilbrittain, Co. Cork

Tel	+353 (0)87 261 8418
Fax	+353 (0)59 972 2332
Email	kente@eircom.net

Entry 95   Map 7

Self-catering   Co. Cork

Casino Cottage

A sunlit bay just down the hill, a charming restaurant a stroll up the road. Casino Cottage was once the gate lodge to Casino House, now a great place to dine. Kerrin is from the island of Sylt in Friesland, which she says is remarkably similar to this delightful rural backwater. Michael is the chef, born in Croatia, brought up in Germany. They stumbled upon the 200-year-old farmhouse 13 years ago, decided to open a restaurant and raise a family; soon after they converted the cottage, hunkered down beside the green-verged road (busy in daytime), into a cosy little nest for two. Done with flagstones, tiles and plain colours, the living area is rustic-modern with a welcoming brick fireplace, logs on the house, books, radio, no TV. The kitchen has chunky wood worktops, the bed is simple wrought iron, the blue shower room done with shells; it is stripped down but very pleasing. As for the restaurant, it's in the family's lovely old farmhouse and has a continental décor — worn leather sofas, inspirational Irish art. Michael's food (just try the lobster risotto) is sublime. *Min. stay one week July/August.*

Price	€85 per night. €210-€350 per week.
Rooms	Cottage for 2.
Meals	Casino House Restaurant (closed January to mid-March). Wine €30-€40.
Closed	Never.
Directions	R600 between Kinsale and Timoleague.

Kerrin & Michael Relja
Casino House, Coolmain Bay,
Kilbrittain, Co. Cork
Tel   +353 (0)23 884 9944
Fax   +353 (0)23 884 9945
Email chouse@eircom.net

Co. Cork   B&B

Kilbrogan House

In the heart of Bandon, a big Georgian house. The list of Kilbrogan's owners over the years reads like a summary of Irish upper-class history: a duke, a land agent, a merchant, an electricity maker, a miller and, fame at last, Joseph Brennan, whose signature appeared on Irish bank notes after the war. Catherine escaped from bond-trading four years ago and did a brilliant renovation job, giving the house that Georgian vibration of glowing antique beneath delicate cornice, rich dark curtains by tall windows, wooden floors spread with thick decorative rugs hand-made by Catherine's father, flashes of tangerine and egg-yolk yellow, beautiful art and gilt mirrors. Further interest in the drawing room is created by a piano and a delightful tubby Dutch cabinet. Beds are modern brass or timber with top-class mattresses, soft duvets, starched sheets. A fine double-glazed conservatory graces the first floor, where armies of geraniums thrive and the garden's serenity pours in. Add her brother's breakfast mastery – another testimony to this family's talented eye and hand – and you have a triumph of taste and humanity.

Price	€100-€110. Singles €60-€70.
Rooms	5: 4 doubles, 1 twin.
Meals	Restaurants within walking distance.
Closed	November-March.
Directions	From Cork N71 to Bandon; right at Methodist church, cross river, bear left at statue and Post Office; next right up Kilbrogan Hill; at top, entrance opposite Kays Flowers.

Catherine FitzMaurice
Bandon, Co. Cork

Tel	+353 (0)23 884 4935
Email	kilbrogan.house@gmail.com
Web	www.kilbrogan.com

Self-catering   Co. Cork

Kilbrogan Coachhouse

Renovating this fine Georgian stone coachhouse was a huge job and, with her practical sense and eye for detail, Catherine has done the three apartments beautifully, treasuring all the original features. Two apartments are one above the other, the Circles being windows above the Arches. Up steep iron steps you enter an open-plan garden-view living space: white walls, brown leather sofas, a great mix of modern and old with pristine white and chrome kitchen ware, an intimate pull-out table; then a big pretty bedroom, a high bright bathroom and, oh luxury, a separate shower room. Arches is similar but on the ground floor, with French doors onto the front garden and just one bathroom. Pretty flower boxes deck the Gardener's House window sills, florals abound inside where there's space, a wood-burner in the sitting room, cosy comfort in the darkish bedrooms. Three clear, uncluttered places to stay with lots of clean whiteness – crockery, tiling, walls –, wooden floors, good fittings, crisp linens on excellent beds and great taste. And you are bang in the middle of Bandon with a superb garden.

Price	€475-€525, including heating, electricity & linen.
Rooms	3 apartments for 2.
Meals	Restaurants within walking distance.
Closed	November-March.
Directions	From Cork N71 to Bandon; right at Methodist church, left at Post Office. Right signed Macroom. 250 metres up hill on right, next to Chaplins.

| | Catherine FitzMaurice
Bandon, Co. Cork |
|---|---|
| Tel | +353 (0)23 884 4935 |
| Email | kilbrogan.house@gmail.com |
| Web | www.kilbrogan.com |

Entry 98   Map 7

Co. Cork   Hotel

Pier House

Behind a 200-year-old exterior lies a strong and purposeful design that constantly delights. The wide estuary light floods in to Pier House, right on the harbour; enter through iron gates into the garden and follow the path. You will get a lovely Irish welcome. Behind stripped old doors – witnesses to the dockside bustle of Kinsale's past – a contemporary marine theme plays: the hotel is decorated with driftwood sculptures, scatterings of seashells, stocks of reeds, paintings by an artist friend. Natural is the key word: wickerwork sofas, feather duvets and crisp white linen on polished sleigh beds, dark timber floors and white walls, taupe and olive textiles, slate-tiled bathrooms and nothing to shock or jolt. Pat, formerly a master carpenter, oversaw the building of the clever storage spaces for hiding clothes and television sets. Bedrooms are not big but beds are generous, there's a private, plant-graced balcony for almost every room, one vast bath with a telly… a sauna on the deck, a pretty garden, and cheerful and knowledgeable local hosts. A wonderful find right at the heart of lovely Kinsale.

Price	€100–€160. Singles €100–€120.
Rooms	10: 8 doubles, 2 twins.
Meals	Choice in town. Guests may barbecue, or picnic on the balcony.
Closed	Christmas & New Year.
Directions	From Cork into Kinsale; follow round to left by Supervalu; 1st left at Tourist Office. House on right, opposite car park on Pier Road.

Ann & Pat Hegarty
Pier Road, Kinsale, Co. Cork
Tel   +353 (0)21 477 4475
Fax   +353 (0)21 477 4475
Email   pierhouseaccom@eircom.net
Web   www.pierhousekinsale.com

Entry 99   Map 7

Self-catering Co. Cork

Boland Townhouse

Built in 2001 beside Tony and Colette's own house, Boland Townhouse is immaculate and designed for comfort, a place you can slip into without a second's anxiety over cobwebs or broken chairs. Indeed, beside the realistic gas-fired logs, the red leather reclining armchairs and matching sofa are brand new, the Irish art modern, the flowers fresh, the books and mags up to date. Your quarters are on the first and second floors with boot, rod, golf club and surfboard storage below. The pristine pine-and-tile kitchen has just about everything. In colour-coordinated bedrooms, you will find masses of storage as well as floor-length paisley curtains for cosy softness but… which to choose, the power shower or the jacuzzi? Tony and Colette, friendly and helpful, are hugely knowledgeable about and great ambassadors for the area. With all the resources of buzzing Kinsale just below, you can choose the privacy of the rooftop patio for meals out on warm days. Readers are full of praise. *Off-street parking. Not suitable for small children.*

Price	€450–€860 per week.
Rooms	Apartment for 4 (2 twin/doubles, 1 bath, 1 shower).
Meals	Restaurants in Kinsale.
Closed	Never.
Directions	From Cork N27 to Cork Airport, then R600 to Kinsale centre. House opposite tourist office, next to Methodist church.

Tony & Colette Boland
Emmet Place, Kinsale, Co. Cork
Tel +353 (0)21 477 7584
Email boland@iol.ie
Web www.bolandkinsale.com

Travel Club Offer. See page 266.

Co. Cork   B&B

Gort-Na-Nain Vegetarian Guest House & Organic Farm

Just ask a ruddy-cheeked old boy the way to Gort-Na-Nain – you're most likely within touching distance of its hill-proud seat. Mists rise to uncover the new house, a distant sea and a lovingly cultivated market garden of organic riches that supplies some of the best restaurants in Cork. Ultan and Lucy's ecological vision doesn't stop at mouthwatering vegetarian food (try the parsnip tortellini) but reaches to planting hedgerows and protecting indigenous woodland. The sun supplies hot water and wood-burners heat the house, stocky fireplaces spreading from its country kitchen heart – a gorgeous smelling hub where something is always bubbling above dark flagstones. Across the hallway is the shared sitting room, fresh decorated with light oak floors, comfy sofas, wooden chests and Lucy's handmade curtains; another pair, golden with rich red flowers, frames a bedroom window. There is uncluttered comfort throughout, either on king-size sleigh beds or on a clever zip-link twin/double covered in deepening shades of lavender. Peace comes dropping slow, to borrow Yeats; here it stays the night.

Price	€85-€95. Singles €60.
Rooms	3: 2 doubles, 1 twin/double.
Meals	Dinner, 3 courses with glass of wine, €30. Packed lunch €10. Pub & restaurant 1.5km.
Closed	Rarely.
Directions	From Cork on Kinsale road, R600. Left between two pubs at Belgooly; signs to Oysterhaven; at x-roads turn towards Nohoval; 1st left, 3rd house on right.

Travel Club Offer. See page 266.

Ethical Collection: Environment; Food. See page 270.

Lucy Stewart & Ultan Walsh
Ballyherkin, Nohoval, Kinsale, Co. Cork
Tel   +353 (0)21 477 0647
Email   lucy@gortnanain.com
Web   www.gortnanain.com

B&B Co. Cork

Maranatha Country House

The wonderful fantasy world of Maranatha awaits you, up on a hill surrounded by rhododendron, monkey-puzzle and giant redwood. This late Victorian mansion has some of the most imaginative bedrooms in Ireland. Lounge in shimmering palatial luxury dreaming of Persia and the Orient as each room follows its own sumptuous theme, even unto the bathrooms. Gleaming fabrics flow across four-posters, pour from coronets and frame views of landscaped garden and secluded woodland. Walks lead in all directions. Olwen inherited the old house from her Scottish father in 1982 and, with no previous experience of interior design, she transformed the place utterly. She has a natural eye for lush, opulent colours – deep burgundy, claret red, forest green – and a love of inlaid French furniture. Olwen and Douglas have huge affection for the house and their enthusiasms rubs off on those who stay; many return year after year. Breakfasts, served in the floral-draped conservatory, are memorably good. A wonderful silk-flower place with real heart, it is exceptional value.

Price	€70-€120. Singles €45-€75.
Rooms	6: 1 double, 2 four-posters, 3 family.
Meals	Choice in Blarney.
Closed	November-February.
Directions	From Cork N20 then R617 through Blarney 2.5km. House signposted just after Tower village sign; right up hill.

	Olwen & Douglas Venn Tower, Blarney, Co. Cork
Tel	+353 (0)21 438 5102
Fax	+353 (0)21 438 2978
Email	info@maranathacountryhouse.com
Web	www.maranathacountryhouse.com

Entry 102 Map 7

Co. Cork

B&B

Allcorn's Country Home

Helen's wooden house is bright, jovial and open-hearted in warm yellows, fresh flowers, big skylights, bigger rooms and well-stocked bookshelves. Generous bathrooms, too: once extracted from your Egyptian cotton sheets, you can comfortably mambo on the mosaic among the spoiling smellies. Enchanted by the patient sounds of the River Shournagh on its way from hillside to ocean and the seclusion of the wooded valley, the Allcorns built the house themselves 30 years ago. It is still just as enchanting. Helen's simple philosophy is do-as-you-would-be-done-by. She loves animals and people in equal measure, her many pets are often strays in need of a good home – Betsey the black lab is a happy newcomer – and the dogbed is a pretty nice sofa. There are super pieces of family furniture everywhere, each room has real personality. On sunny days, or even drizzly ones, you can wander through the three acres of peace and garden, carefully landscaped with willow, dogwood and wildflower meadows down to the water's edge – and wait for the leap of a passing salmon. Breakfast is also a treat which should not be hurried.

Price	€70-€80. Singles €45-€50.
Rooms	4: 2 twins/doubles, 1 double; 1 single with separate bath.
Meals	Restaurants in Blarney.
Closed	November-February.
Directions	From Blarney R617 for Killarney 1.5km; right at major turn by River Shournagh, sign to house; entrance 2nd on left.

Helen Allcorn
Shournagh Road, Blarney, Co. Cork
Tel   +353 (0)21 438 5577
Email   info@allcorns.com
Web   www.allcorns.com

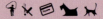

Entry 103   Map 7

Hotel   Co. Cork

Cafe Paradiso & Paradiso Rooms

Paradiso oatcakes with Knockalara sheep's cheese, tomatillo chutney and tomato and rocket salad... the breakfast menu alone is the most devilish temptation to push the door to paradise. Paradiso is the high-class vegetarian restaurant where Denis, who naturally belongs to Slow Food Ireland, has made an enduring name for himself. He is also the author of three stylish books in which he shares his passion for the ingredients he works with and the people and environment that produce them. The wines are chosen with similar zeal. So why not go the whole way and stay the night? On 'two floors over the shop' of this city-centre Victorian building are three sophisticated bedrooms – not afterthoughts to be ignored after a feast of feta, pistachio and couscous cake on citrus greens with sweet and hot pepper relish, but big and bold with superb modern bathrooms and a generous sofa each. Two of the rooms overlook the busy road and the River Lee, the other, with no view but masses of sky light, is quieter. Ask about the local arts and culture scene: your host knows it all.

Price	€160.
Rooms	3 doubles.
Meals	Lunch/dinner €15-€50. Wine from €22.
Closed	Sundays & Mondays.
Directions	From centre take Washington St & Western Rd towards University College Cork. Paradiso on right between Reidy's Wine Vault & The Thirsty (10-min. walk from city centre).

Travel Club Offer. See page 266.

Denis Cotter
16 Lancaster Quay, Cork, Co. Cork
Tel   +353 (0)21 427 7939
Email info@cafeparadiso.ie
Web   www.cafeparadiso.ie

Entry 104   Map 7

Co. Cork

B&B

Knockeven House

The impressive early Victorian house lifts its pillars to the admiring acres and has a regal interior to match. Red opulence in the main hall, smart golfing wallpaper at the back – a top designer has clearly worked here and you can guess that John is a golfing fanatic (the famous Fota Island golf course is nearby). Pam is a real people person whose warm hospitality will go to your heart: guests send her flowers from home. Having owned and run a successful supermarket, these two have a genuine talent for serving others. Big deluxe bedrooms are richly flounced and draped in florals or toile de Jouy. One has dramatically beautiful long silk curtains and matching throws, another has a superb old half-tester bed, all have fine antiques and the smartest white bathrooms with luscious goodies. Downstairs, white lilies, old timber and modern windows warm the smart sitting room, mahogany glows beneath your linen table mat and silver cutlery, the breakfast spread is sumptuous. But remember the famine-driven thousands who sailed from Queenstown (Cobh) to America in the 1840s; and the Titanic in 1912. Real value.

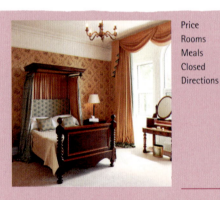

Price	€120-€140. Singles €75-€80.
Rooms	4 twins/doubles.
Meals	Restaurants in Cobh.
Closed	Rarely.
Directions	From Cork N25 for Rosslare; 3rd exit R624 to Cobh; pass gates, cross bridge, right to Great Island Motors, left here, first drive on right.

Pam & John Mulhaire
Rushbrooke, Cobh, Co. Cork

Tel	+353 (0)21 481 1778
Fax	+353 (0)21 481 1719
Email	info@knockevenhouse.com
Web	www.knockevenhouse.com

B&B   Co. Cork

Ballymaloe House   *well known!*

The iconic Irish country house run by unfailingly caring people, Ballymaloe is a brilliant place to stay – and eat. Superb grounds with memorable trees, modern rugs beneath classic plasterwork, a fine collection of the best 20th-century Irish painters and sculptors, multifarious dining spaces – formal Georgian, relaxed modern, little velvet corner – bringing intimacy to each part of the 100-seat restaurant. The food, much of it home-grown, is unforgettably good and rightly famous throughout Ireland. Some architectural details are amazing: an 18th-century house knitted into medieval walls; a 14th-century keep, reached through an innocuous cupboard behind the bar – like popping into Narnia – and blessed with fine views from the rampart; the ancient gatehouse now a sweet little apartment with a tiny staircase and arrow-slit windows. Bedrooms are all different, unfussy and eminently comfortable with up-to-date bathrooms: in the old house they breathe country-house history, in the extension they are larger, some have private little gardens.
Cookery & organic gardening courses on site.

Price	€240-€340. Singles from €150.
Rooms	33: 15 doubles, 15 twins, 3 singles.
Meals	Lunch €40. Dinner €75. Wine from €24.
Closed	Christmas; two weeks in January.
Directions	From Cork N25 for Waterford 30km; right R630 then R631 through Cloyne for Ballycotton. House 3km after Cloyne.

The Allen Family
Shanagarry, Midleton, Co. Cork
Tel   +353 (0)21 465 2531
Fax   +353 (0)21 465 2021
Email res@ballymaloe.ie
Web   www.ballymaloe.ie

Co. Cork   B&B

Sunville House

In all simplicity, Anna pampers her house and guests with fresh flowers, home-baked fruit cake, an enchanting giggle and loving kindness. Pat tends the garden (otherwise those Nicholas Mosse vases go empty), the goldfish pond, the hens for wonderful breakfast eggs and the blooming conservatory. They are a delight, these generous rural Cork folk who love having people to stay. Theirs is a place of contrasts: behind the uplifted modern bungalow (they raised the roof to add a floor) stands the historic granite ruin of William Penn's old house, he who founded Pennsylvania. A favourite colour inside is rusty orange with mellow cream carpets and pretty duvet covers to soften. Laid with Stephen Pearce pottery (do visit the workshop), fresh fruit and jars of nuts permanently on display, oranges squeezed to order, the all-pine breakfast room looks out to spectacular views over the garden (unusual ornaments include a red drill plough and ceramic ducks and hens) to ruins and fields. Bedrooms are pine furnished and thoroughly comfortable with soft carpets and space. Great value, genuine hospitality.

Price	€70-€80. Singles €50.
Rooms	6: 3 doubles, 1 twin, 2 family.
Meals	Choice in Ballycotton, 5-minute drive.
Closed	Rarely.
Directions	From Cork airport N25 for Rosslare to Midleton; R629 to Shanagarry; right for Ballycotton; over x-roads, right at T-junction; house 2km on right.

Anna & Patrick Casey
Ballycotton, Midleton, Co. Cork

Tel	+353 (0)21 464 6271
Fax	+353 (0)21 464 6271
Email	sunvillehouse@eircom.net
Web	www.sunville.net

B&B   Co. Cork

Ballyvolane House *Often stayed here in the 1950s*

Set in an idyllic private estate, Ballyvolane is one of Ireland's great old houses with owners to match: Anglo-Irish aplomb, great enthusiasm, charm incarnate, from generation to generation. The house was built in 1728 then remodelled in the Italianate style. The pillared hall with its fine ceilings, crackling fire and wonderful furniture has a Blüthner baby grand you are welcome to play. Fresh flowers, candles, shining all-wood floors run throughout; Egyptian lucifers stand attendant as guests dine at the baronial table for wonderful feasts. They even forage for wild foods here, and Justin's father tends seasonal rarities in the gardens and plans to reinstate the orchards. Bedrooms lie off a long narrow corridor, all different with huge beds – turned down before bedtime – antique furniture, armchairs, soft carpets, maybe an early 19th-century bath and tall windows onto the gardens. Wander through woodland, introduce the children to the treehouse, fish for salmon on their stretch of the Blackwater: just ask for rods and waders. The Greens deserve their reputation, they do it all brilliantly.

Price	€200-€270. Singles €135-€175.
Rooms	6 twins/doubles.
Meals	Dinner, 4 courses, €60. Wine from €17.50. Packed lunch for fisherfolk €17.50.
Closed	Christmas & New Year.
Directions	From Cork N8 for Fermoy about 24km. At River Bride right R628, before Rathcormac, for Tallow & follow signs.

Justin & Jenny Green
Castlelyons, Co. Cork
Tel   +353 (0)25 36349
Fax   +353 (0)25 36781
Email   info@ballyvolanehouse.ie
Web   www.ballyvolanehouse.ie

Entry 108   Map 7

Co. Cork

B&B & Self-catering

Glenlohane

A proper old Irish house where country pursuits have been actively pursued by the generations. Desmond's ancestor built Glenlohane in 1741, now Desmond and his American wife Melanie have turned the place into the most comfortable of country houses. 'Bird Sanctuary' at the gate simply means no shooting; there's nothing more exotic here than some guinea fowl, yet Desmond "lived for hunting" and still keeps several horses as well as myriad sheep on his 250 acres of parkland, paddocks and fields. Melanie, whose great interest is carriage-driving, takes in retired greyhounds – who are so grateful. Relax in the warm elegance of rooms filled with antiques, hunting ephemera and delightful family memorabilia (dolls house, rocking horse, old photographs and oils). Large, fresh bedrooms are done with consummate, easy taste, lots of windows and proper bathrooms. The best of the old and new worlds meet in harmony and humour with this wonderful couple, Desmond's entertaining tales, Melanie's intelligent humanity. One could spend a lot of time with them. Traditional comfort and great fun. *Children over 12 welcome.*

Price	€200. Singles €100. Cottage €750 per week. Whole house available.
Rooms	4 + 1: 1 double, 2 twins, 1 single. Cottage for 6.
Meals	Restaurants within 2 miles.
Closed	Rarely.
Directions	From Kanturk R576 for Mallow; bear left R580 for Buttevant; 1st right for Ballyclough; entrance on left after about 3km, signposted 'Glenlohane Bird Sanctuary'.

Desmond & Melanie Sharp Bolster
Kanturk, Co. Cork

Tel	+353 (0)29 50014
Email	info@glenlohane.com
Web	www.glenlohane.com

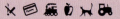

Entry 109   Map 7

Allo's Townhouse

Allo's is where the action is, in pretty Listowel. A little market town above the river Feale, it's home to Writers' Week, Ireland's top literary event. Thanks to Helen's loyalty to local artists, Allo's has an artistic streak too: the restaurant is bright with big paintings and photos. It also happens to serve outstanding food. The quality and creativity of Armel and Helen's menu comes as a fabulous surprise, as young staff ferry generous portions to tables laid with crisp linen, heaped with fresh flowers; join in the hubbub or retreat to an intimate corner. For romancers, and smokers, there's al fresco dining under the corrugated roof. Armel is justly proud of his collection of Irish whiskeys – one vintage malt commands €60 a shot – but he's prouder of his staff and his seasonal sourcing. Bedrooms are on three floors, reached via a winding narrow stair – all stylish, charming, even opulent (baroque mirrors, Irish linen, an antique four-poster). Gorgeous big bathrooms have roll top tubs and Connemara marble. No breakfast here but many coffee shops outside the door. A grand little place!

Price	€90–€100. Singles €55. Breakfast not served.
Rooms	3: 2 doubles, 1 twin.
Meals	Lunch €10.95–€18.50. Dinner, 2 courses, €35.
Closed	Sundays & Mondays. Christmas Day, New Year's Day, Good Friday.
Directions	From Limerick N69 to Tarbert then to Listowel. On left in High St, with bay trees outside. Ask about parking.

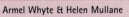

Armel Whyte & Helen Mullane
41 Church Street, Listowel, Co. Kerry

Tel	+353 (0)68 22880
Fax	+353 (0)68 22803
Email	allosbar@eircom.net

Co. Kerry   B&B

Mount Rivers

Mount Rivers has been in the family since 1869 and Liz keeps it the warmly welcoming home it has always been, with tea and delicious cakes on arrival, and communal breakfasts (the full Irish extravaganza) in the quirky red dining room, a lovely old-fashioned affair… there are dogs outside, cats in, a piano in the corner and books to read by the ever-smouldering fire. Bedrooms come in different shapes and sizes, the same laid-back décor covering all. One has wooden Bavarian beds (grandmother's dowry), with floral duvets and flowers from the garden; the big refurbished suite has matching headboard and curtains and a super big shower making it ideal for families. The other shower rooms are smaller. The big garden runs down the the Feale and screens you from the road beyond, so follow the river into town and pass the Garden of Europe and the castle on the way. Generous, charming Liz, fount of knowledge for all things Listowel, will point you in the right direction; Ballybunion is up the road (golfing stars have slept in these very rooms). Hunker down with one of those books, or stroll ten minutes into town.

Price	€60–€90.
Rooms	3: 1 double; 1 family suite for 4; 1 twin with separate bath.
Meals	Choice in Listowel 1.5km.
Closed	November to mid-April.
Directions	From Listowel, south over bridge & straight on (not right for Tralee); right after 100 yds; house imm. right.

Robbie Robitzki & Liz O'Reilly
Listowel, Co. Kerry

Tel	+353 (0)68 21494
Fax	+353 (0)68 23366
Email	robbie@iol.ie
Web	www.mountriverslistowel.com

Self-catering   Co. Kerry

An Tigh Beag

The long, low house is delightful, with its thick hemp-lined walls and benign buddha guarding over you. The drive here is stunning, up an ever-narrowing road with the mountains looming and the hedgerows filled with wild flowers. Outside is a waterfall; above is a dark lake set into a natural amphitheatre where you may cast your line in perfect tranquillity. John is a Kerry man with a love for hill walking and that is how he came across the almost derelict farmhouse, now surrounded by 17 acres of native woodland and with its own mountain river. He has done a sympathetic job on the restoration; there are geothermally heated tiled floors, a salvaged polished pine ceiling, a black leather sofa and a red leather chair, and a wood-burner for cosy nights in. Bedrooms lie off and beyond and are surprisingly large, there are books and DVDs (no reception for TV), a simple shower, a kitchen with all mod cons. There are enough walks from the front door to satisfy the most adventurous, so arrive with plenty of food and settle in. Go to the nearest pub and you will have a serious uphill stride home through forest park.

Price	€300-€550 per week
Rooms	Cottage for 4-6.
Meals	Pub 4km.
Closed	Rarely.
Directions	N86 from Tralee for 10 miles veering right at fork at Camp. On to Aughacasla; left for Glanteenassig Wood; 3km, then pass entrance to forest park & cross small bridge. At end of narrow road.

John & Patricia O'Connor
Glanteenassig, Castlegregory,
Tralee, Co. Kerry

Tel   +353 (0)87 779 3126
Email   info@tighbeag.com
Web   www.tighbeag.com

Co. Kerry   B&B

Gorman's Clifftop House & Restaurant

Vincent and Sile (Sheila in Gaelic) have done amazing things here, turning their modest café and B&B into a luxurious restaurant with rooms. Their philosophy is simple and reassuring, they provide everything you need: a genuine welcome, good food, homegrown organic veg, an excellent bed. You find wooden furniture crafted in Tralee, Louis Mulcahy pottery, arty sea-shell prints in rooms with warm colours where you feel you're almost walking into an Atlantic sunset ("a happy coincidence", says Sile) and organic fair-trade coffee at breakfast. The restaurant looks across Smerwick Harbour to the Three Sisters and the giant ocean beyond – stunning at all times. Vincent's robust and flavoursome Irish cooking uses local and organic ingredients where possible: Dingle Bay prawns, Irish Hereford beef, farmhouse cheeses. The Gorman family has lived on the land since the 1700s and this is one of the few areas left in Ireland where Gaelic is the first language. Hire bikes, explore the many archæological sites, or just curl up next to the turf fire. This is place of high standards, lots of space, great people.

Price	€120–€190. Singles €85–€125.
Rooms	9: 6 doubles, 3 triples.
Meals	Dinner €37.50. House wine €19.95.
Closed	Christmas; 5 January–12 February.
Directions	From Dingle take R559 with harbour on left to r'bout; straight on for An Fheothanach 6.5km; fork left. House 6.5km on left beside round house.

Travel Club Offer. See page 266.

Ethical Collection: Food.
See page 270.

Sile & Vincent Gorman
An Ghlaise Bheag, Co. Kerry
Tel   +353 (0)66 915 5162
Fax   +353 (0)66 915 5003
Email reservations@gormans-clifftophouse.com
Web   www.gormans-clifftophouse.com

Entry 113   Map 6

B&B   Co. Kerry

Greenmount House

Who would believe bread and butter pudding could taste so beautiful at breakfast time? Greenmount's breakfasts are the best in the world. Dramatically overlooking Dingle Bay, this may not be the prettiest house on the outside but it is resplendent within, a place of immense style, of wall-to-wall carpeting, slow-burning fires, easy living. There are two pretty sitting rooms (one with a massage chair) and a conservatory dining room drenched with light and views. Fabulous suites, some with balconies, have warm colours and toasty floors, deep carpets, even deeper baths, plump towels and charming toiletries, WiFi, satellite TV… at night, as beds are turned down, two exquisite chocolates appear on plump pillows, accompanied by sweet Irish prayers. John and Mary are the charming key-holders to all this pleasure, nothing is too much trouble and their knowledge of the area is immense. A short walk downhill and you're in Dingle itself; from here, fabulous walking across dramatic cliff, hill and sea, and scenery studded with prehistory. Out of season may be the best time of all.

Price	€100–€170. Singles from €70.
Rooms	14: 2 doubles, 12 suites.
Meals	Restaurants 4-minute walk in town.
Closed	Christmas.
Directions	N86 into Dingle, right at r'bout; right at next junction; up hill; house on left.

Travel Club Offer. See page 266.

Mary & John Curran
Gortonora, Dingle, Co. Kerry
Tel   +353 (0)66 915 1414
Fax   +353 (0)66 915 1974
Email info@greenmounthouse.ie
Web   www.greenmounthouse.ie

Entry 114   Map 6

Co. Kerry

B&B

Number Fifty Five

Wonderful art, well-designed bedrooms, rolling Dingle views – and Stella Doyle, star of this place. No. 55 was built as a staff house for Doyle's, her restaurant; now she has opened up the first floor so it is bathed in light. Take a peep at the open-plan living room, simple and stylish, with gleaming floors and white walls, fresh flowers and classy art. A characterful sofa faces the wood-burner, the dining table overlooks a wall of sliding glass. Bedrooms, on the ground floor, are restful and peaceful, a treat to come back to after an active day out. The smaller room at the front of the house is light and bright with an antique brass bed, an embroidered bed cover from Honduras and super linen. The larger back room also has a brass bed, and bright gingham curtains opening out into the small but very colourful courtyard garden; bathrooms are spotless and white. Over fruit smoothies, potato cakes and sizzling sausage, bacon and eggs Stella – ever a twinkle in her eye – will tell you where to surf, cycle, walk and sail. A charming, popular retreat which is just far enough out of the town centre to ensure a good night's sleep.

Price	€75-€80. Singles €55-€60.
Rooms	2 doubles.
Meals	Restaurants within walking distance.
Closed	October-April.
Directions	Main road Dingle/Tralee; right at r'bout. Right into John Street; house at top of road, on left.

Stella Doyle
55 John Street, Dingle, Co. Kerry

Tel	+353 (0)66 915 2378
Email	stelladoyledingle@gmail.com
Web	www.stelladoyle.com

B&B & Self-catering   Co. Kerry

Emlagh Country House

Big old country houses are an extinct breed in Dingle so the next best thing is Emlagh House, designed in 2000 as if it were an extension to an old Georgian house. The results are pretty awesome, the views are gorgeous and a few seasons' growth in the landscaped garden has softened the surroundings. There are ten bedrooms; each themed and painted in the colours of native Kerry flowers. All have wide beds, springy carpets, creative lighting, CD players, heated mirrors, creaky antique cupboards, and chocolates on the turned-down beds. Bathrooms sparkle. There's a John Bronsmead piano in the drawing room, Irish art all over the house, history books and internet in the library and views across Dingle Bay from the breakfast conservatory. Down by the waterside Gráinne has just constructed four apartments beautifully and stylishly with solid wood, Italian marble, gorgeous kitchens, comfortable sitting rooms overlooking the sea, and bedrooms you won't want to leave. Perfect for those who prefer a bit more independence but want to remain in the comfort zone.

Price	€190-€290. Singles €135-€185. Apartments €260 per week.
Rooms	10 + 4: 8 doubles, 2 twins. Waters Edge House: 4 apartments for 6.
Meals	Restaurants in Dingle.
Closed	November-mid-March. Self-catering open 12 months.
Directions	Entering Dingle on N86, 1st left after Shell garage; house on corner.

Gráinne & Marion Kavanagh
Dingle, Co. Kerry

Tel	+353 (0)66 915 2345
Fax	+353 (0)66 915 2369
Email	info@emlaghhouse.com
Web	www.emlaghhouse.com

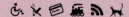

Entry 116   Map 6

Co. Kerry   B&B & Self-catering

The Phoenix

Bohemian meets gypsy meets Arabian nights and they all decided to dance because… why wouldn't you? Somewhere in this exotic whirl is a two-foot high statue of St Theresa: it's a celebration of colour, wood, exposed stonework and rare plants. Lorna and Billy bought the house some years ago and now run this relaxed place for open-minded devotees of organic vegetarian cooking: fresh breakfasts, tantalising lunches and seriously good dinners are served in the restaurant with its colourful art on the walls. Lorna also sells whole food, gluten-free house products and organic wine, and in the winter runs cookery classes, organises salsa and Egyptian belly dancing classes, and encourages live music. There's also a room for workshops and therapeutic groups. This place positively fizzes with colour, life and energy: bedrooms are large, comfortable and vibrant, with spangled bedcovers and spotless bathrooms. The garden is gorgeous, with wild areas for children to roam, treehouses, gypsy caravans (you can stay in them) and a very productive vegetable patch. You're bang on the Inch beach road, so surfers will delight.

Price	€76. Gypsy caravan €35. Chalet €450 per week.
Rooms	3 + 1: 1 double, 1 family, 1 single. Chalet for 2-3. Also gypsy caravans for 2+2.
Meals	Lunch €7. Dinner €25. Packed lunch from €6.
Closed	November-March.
Directions	From Castlemaine, R561 west for Dingle and Boolteens for 6km. House on right by road.

Ethical Collection: Environment; Community; Food.
See page 270.

Lorna & Billy Tyther
Shanahill East, Castlemaine, Co. Kerry
Tel   +353 (0)66 976 6284
Email phoenixtyther@hotmail.com
Web   www.thephoenixorganic.com

Self-catering   Co. Kerry

Fleur & Kizzie Cottages

These sweet hideaway cottages are ineffably romantic, the site is stunning, the views over to the Macgillycuddy Reeks, Ireland's highest mountains, will swallow your heart at any time of day. Set in a fine mature garden, the minute Kizzie for two and the larger Fleur for a family have been renovated, decorated and furnished with flair, loving care, well-chosen furniture on warm wooden floors, and delightful fabrics. The style is perfectly cottagey without ever being twee and the nostalgic aroma of an open turf fire is the best thing ever when you come in from a long day's fishing, walking or history-hunting. The two sofas in Fleur, the one in Kizzie just ask to be relaxed into. Their kitchens have the old-fashioned patina of slate floors and weathered pine – and all the modern bits you expect. Bedrooms rejoice in tempting quilted bedding on new old-style beds and good storage space. In Kizzie, you can lie in bed and gaze at those magic mountains. In Fleur, the sunroom draws them in. Each has its own patio or garden spot with barbecue and furniture. And pretty Killorglin is within walking distance.

Price	€315–€830. Prices per week.
Rooms	2 cottages: 1 for 5; 1 for 2-3.
Meals	Restaurants within walking distance.
Closed	Rarely.
Directions	From Killarney to Killorglin. Cross bridge, through town square, down narrow one-way ahead, over small r'bout; cont. 3km, cottages on left.

Joanne McNicholl
Sunhill, Killorglin, Co. Kerry
Tel   +44 (0)7919 982305
Email info@kerry-country-cottages.com
Web   www.kerry-country-cottages.com

Entry 118   Map 6

Co. Kerry   Hotel

Carrig Country House

At the end of a long wooded drive, this mid 19th-century country house looks onto the beauty and mystery of Caragh Lake, a supreme spot, discovered by Frank and Mary many years ago. They run their stylish house with a good-natured professional touch, he full of likeable charm and disarming patter, she ministering with sincere warmth and a big smile; she is also the interior designer. Breakfasts are memorable, dinners are divine; some say this is the finest restaurant in Kerry. Ponder the menu with an aperitif by the fire in one of six drawing rooms, then slip into the intimate dining room with its magical lake view. Superb bedrooms mix embossed wallpapers, sumptuous fabrics and fine antiques with more views; one stunningly exotic suite harks back to the Raj; each room has its own grace and charm. As for the grounds… four acres of secret pathways leading down to the lough, 1,000 species of flowers, shrubs and trees, a boathouse and summerhouse hidden amongst the glades. All you hear is the distant clunk of the croquet ball, the rustle of leaves and the trilling of birds. Bliss. *Children over eight welcome.*

Price	€150-€370. Singles €99-€140. Extra bed €40.
Rooms	17: 11 doubles, 3 twins, 1 single, 2 suites.
Meals	Dinner, 4 courses, €55. Wine €28.50-€61.50.
Closed	December-February.
Directions	From Killorglin N70 for Glenbeigh 5km; left for Caragh Lake 2.5km; right at village shop, entrance on left.

Frank & Mary Slattery
Caragh Lake, Killorglin, Co. Kerry
Tel   +353 (0)66 976 9100
Fax   +353 (0)66 976 9166
Email info@carrighouse.com
Web   www.carrighouse.com

Hotel   Co. Kerry

Ard Na Sidhe Country House

Great gardens are a hallmark of western Ireland and Ard Na Sidhe ('fairy hill') has a garden to rival most. Beside the lake you find 40 exhilarating acres of mature woodland, tiered beds, stone-flagged paths and trim lawns – a tranquil Irish Eden. Paths lead to the water and you can row across to Robert's Island for absolute stillness. The house, a sporting lodge built in 1913 by the Gordons, as in gin, looks much older than it is, while the mullioned windows that you find all over the house **are** old – 1713 to be precise, swiped from an Edinburgh mansion. In good weather you can breakfast on the terrace or take afternoon tea in the garden but two fires in the huge sitting room guard against the odd spot of rain and there's a grand piano on which to practise your Shostakovich. Inside, all is thick-carpet hush and gliding smiling staff in white shirts and black waistcoats. Bedrooms, five with lake views, the best in the main house, are country-house floral; expect repro beds and dressing tables, draped crowns and fluffy bath towels. Killorglin's eateries are a 15-minute drive.

Price	€170-€300. Singles from €150.	
Rooms	18 twins/doubles.	
Meals	Dinner à la carte from €55. Wine from €30. Restaurants 15-minute drive.	
Closed	October-April.	
Directions	From Killorglin N70 for Cahersiveen; 1st left for Caragh Lake; straight over x-roads for 1.6km; sign on right.	

	Caragh Lake, Killorglin, Co. Kerry
Tel	+353 (0)64 667 1370
Fax	+353 (0)64 663 2118
Email	reservations@ardnasidhe.com
Web	www.ardnasidhe.com

Entry 120   Map 6

Co. Kerry   Hotel

Arbutus Hotel

A star in today's hotel firmament, the Arbutus sings of an Ireland past. Solid, quietly prosperous, it was the stalking ground of wealthy farmers who gathered here on market days to chew the Killarney cud. Now Sean, Carol and their attentive, caring, extended family – some of whom have been working here for 40 years – pour love and devotion into keeping it all shine. The feel is crackling fires, polished floors, William Morris wallpapers, a chandelier in the ladies loo. Original woodwork has Celtic motifs carved into it and the hotel emblem is the *Arbutus unede* – the only tree native to Ireland. Bedrooms are havens, each with its own gem of Irish furniture, and brilliant value: plush fabrics, big old beds, crisp sheets, and blankets woven down the road; the quietest are at the back. There's Guinness and Gaelic music in the wood-panelled, fire-fuelled bar, rich Killarney rugs in the drawing room, superb breakfasts and fine dinners in the dining room – aglow with silver cutlery, jugs and tureens. In the heart of town, the perfect starting point for those setting off on the Kerry Tour. Glorious.

Travel Club Offer. See page 266.

Price	€130–€210. Singles €75–€135. Family rooms €140–€210.
Rooms	36: 27 twins/doubles, 3 family rooms, 2 four-posters en suite; 4 twins/doubles each with separate bath/shower.
Meals	Dinner, 3 courses, €35; also à la carte. Wine €20. Lunch €8–€16. Restaurant closed two evenings a week.
Closed	Mid-December to mid-January.
Directions	N22 to Killarney from north: left at r'bout for Cork 500m; 1st right to T-junc.; hotel directly opposite.

Sean & Carol
College Street, Killarney, Co. Kerry
Tel   +353 (0)64 663 1037
Fax   +353 (0)64 663 4033
Email stay@arbutuskillarney.com
Web   www.arbutuskillarney.com

Entry 121   Map 6

Hotel Co. Kerry

Killarney Royal

In the heart of town, a luxury hotel that breathes an atmosphere of friendly splendour. No self-righteous snobbery, just genuine attention, from staff who have been here a decade or more. The Scallys are justly proud of this great team spirit. The pair were nurses before Margaret inherited the Royal; her family has a long pedigree in hotel management. So she scoured Europe for new ideas and then became her own interior designer with remarkable, occasionally stunning, results. Luxurious rooms, some large, some smaller, are all different, doffing their cap to the restrained elegance of French and Italian styles. All are regularly redecorated, bathrooms flourish white robes and thick towels, comfort and gizmos go hand in hand. In the sitting room and mirrored bar a turf fire smoulders throughout the winter, vases burst with flowers, newspapers are dotted about. Breakfast is served on dazzling white cloths beneath glistening chandeliers, muffins keep warm in silver tureens, background muzak plays. The Royal is a cut above the rest of the hotel troop. Plus broadband, massage, receptions... *Amex cards accepted.*

Price	€140–€320. Singles €120–€205.
Rooms	29: 10 twins, 14 twins/doubles, 5 suites.
Meals	Dinner, 4 courses, €39. Wine from €25.
Closed	Christmas.
Directions	College Street is in Killarney town centre. Hotel opposite Arbutus Hotel.

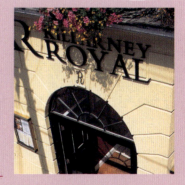

	Joe & Margaret Scally
	College Street, Killarney, Co. Kerry
Tel	+353 (0)64 663 1853
Fax	+353 (0)64 663 4001
Email	info@killarneyroyal.ie
Web	www.killarneyroyal.ie

Entry 122   Map 6

Co. Kerry

Hotel

The Cahernane House Hotel

Once a small stately home, Cahernane combines comfortable luxury with old Irish history. The neo-gothic house, built in 1877 by the Earls of Pembroke, rejoices in fine marble fireplaces and warm polished floors, huge creaking doors and wooden mullion windows, an extraordinary carved ceiling, an all-pervading calm. Cows chew the cud in the fields, deer wander the water meadows, acres of lawns drift down to the National Park. In the grand dining room fine dinner is served with typical Cahernane graciousness; simpler food is served in the bar in the cellar. Stags heads and family portraits peer down on you as you gaze on the mountains, or nod off in front of a roaring fire. Sunshine casts a glow over wood-encased walls, a grand piano stands majestically in a corner, a card table is set for bridge. The bedrooms in the main house are stunning: richly covered sofas, delicately papered walls, hidden nooks and crannies. In the fine new wing rooms are larger, furniture is repro, bathrooms have jacuzzis. All this a ten-minute walk from Killarney; listen out for the cathedral bells across the fields.

Price	€190–€320. Suites €320–€400. Singles €130–€210.
Rooms	38: 12 twins/doubles; 26 twins/doubles with separate bath/shower.
Meals	Dinner, 4 courses with coffee, €55; à la carte from €30. Lunch from €20.
Closed	Christmas & New Year.
Directions	From Killarney N71 for Kenmare, through traffic lights, over bridge, right at sign into long leafy drive.

Sarah Brown
Muckross Road, Killarney, Co. Kerry
Tel   +353 (0)64 663 1895
Fax   +353 (0)64 663 4340
Email   info@cahernane.com
Web   www.cahernane.com

B&B & Self-catering   Co. Kerry

Iskeroon

This is the place where the road runs out... in every direction are views of a blue sparkling sea. David knew Iskeroon as a child: his grandfather lived nearby and he'd sneak up for a glimpse. He and Geraldine, an utterly charming couple, have renovated marvellously, not just the main house, cradled by ridge and rock, but the apartment and the coach house in which the lovely new suites lie. All is colour and light, natural wood floors, skylights in the ceiling, bathrooms with azure blue tiling, super kitchenettes and first-floor balconies for the views (one of the sea, one of the hills). Back in the main house, spellbound by the view, you can breakfast (deliciously) while watching the locals pass by: seals, seagulls, the odd boat. And there's more magic outside: semi-tropical gardens full of rare Kerry lilies that lead to a cove and bracing swims in Derrynane harbour. Follow the path to the pub (20 minutes) or take the boat to the Skellig Islands, for immense vistas and walks in the wilderness. Little folk may play on pure beaches with white shells; secret paths meander down to the sea. Heaven. *Min. two nights.*

Price	€175. Apartment €500–€550 per week.
Rooms	2 + 1: 2 suites for 2, each with kitchen. Apartment for 2.
Meals	Pub 20-minute walk.
Closed	October–April. Please check website.
Directions	Between Caherdaniel & Waterville on N70. At Scarriff Inn take road for the harbour; at pier, left on unpaved private road along beach & through white gateposts.

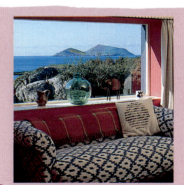

David & Geraldine Hare
Bunavalla, Caherdaniel, Co. Kerry
Tel   +353 (0)66 947 5119
Email res@iskeroon.com
Web   www.iskeroon.com

Co. Kerry

B&B

Picín

The loveliest hideaway for two where you may both decide to live in the bathroom, more opulent and original than most drawing rooms. A cast-iron roll-top bath stands on herring-bone boards, a wood-burning stove creates heart-warming cosiness, a velvet antique sofa embraces the non-bathing conversationalist and a Tudor wardrobe just looks benign. Amelia and Nick – young, artistic, warm and so happy to have brought their two children from London to grow up in Kerry – have stroked every little stone alcove back to life. You arrive via your own garden and terrace into a big light space rich in oriental rugs, a bold red sofa, a wall of books and an antique rocking horse. Through that amazing bathroom, steep stairs bring you to the softly muted bedroom in greys, blues and creams where touches of pure luxury finish the seduction: Egyptian cotton bedlinen, a silk bedspread, a painted chest, stone walls hung with a fascinating choice of paintings. All done with such loving care, this is no run-of-the-mill B&B and exceptional value. Their first guests kept saying "it's like the Waldorf Astoria."

Price	€100–€120. Singles €80.
Rooms	1 double.
Meals	Restaurants/pubs in Caherdaniel, 4km.
Closed	Rarely.
Directions	From Kenmare N70 for Waterville 45km; through Castlecove, continue 4km; sign on right.

Nick & Amelia Etherton
Brackaragh, Caherdaniel, Co. Kerry
Tel   +353 (0)66 947 5894
Email   netherton@eircom.net
Web   www.picincottage.com

Self-catering   Co. Kerry

Westcove Farmhouse

From the little reading corner to the sea pebble-floored bathroom to the magical views from every window, this is a special place to stay. You're up here above the harbour, among some of the most stunning scenery in Ireland – a delight in all weathers. Jane runs a small bakery so pop down for freshly baked sodabread, scones and speciality cakes. The charming and very private seaview apartment is on the first floor of a whitewashed wing, with its own small enclosed courtyard full of flowers and herbs for picking. Steps lead to the front door and the little pot-hung kitchen/dining room, well-equipped for those who love cooking. In the bathroom: a corner bath and a luxurious shower. In the bedroom: a padded window seat for that glorious ocean. Perfect simplicity and peacefulness – beams, creamy whites, a sofa, an old Mexican chest of drawers. The second bedroom downstairs, with its own access, is just as charming. It's five minutes to the pier, the seals and the grey herons nesting high in the pine trees. Go deep-sea fishing, walk the Kerry Way. Jane's love for this place is infectious and guests find it hard to leave.

Price	€330-€500 per week. 3-night break from €220 (not July/Aug). 2nd room (same group only) €150 p.w.
Rooms	Flat for 2-3. Additional double close by.
Meals	Restaurants in Caherdaniel & Castlecove, 3km.
Closed	Rarely.
Directions	From Kenmare N70 for Waterville 25km. House signposted on left 3km beyond Castlecove.

Jane Urquhart
Castlecove, Co. Kerry
Tel   +353 (0)66 947 5479
Email westcovefarmhouse@oceanfree.net
Web   www.westcove.net

Travel Club Offer. See page 266.

Entry 126   Map 6

Co. Kerry   Self-catering

Westcove House, The Stables and Garden Cottage

The history of beautiful Westcove House is as full of movement, human quirks and fine things as the house, which has looked proudly across Kenmare Estuary for 350 years. From the imposing hall, dominated by an ancestral portrait, move into the soft informality and open fires of the sunken sitting room and the bar – wonderfully relaxing. The views from the more ceremonious dining room will grab your eyes and the kitchen is superb: suffice to say it has two dishwashers. Katherine, the charming housekeeper, knows Westcove inside out and, for a total holiday, will cook some or all of your meals – deliciously, even organically. Bedrooms are full of personality too, there's a reading gallery, a sauna, a terrific games room in the Stables, shared by all, where local musicians may come to dance Irish reels with you. The charmingly furnished Stables are warm and comfortable, with pretty, soft bedrooms ('nanny's' room is a bit smaller) and loads of storage. Now the farmworkers' cottage has been revived, and its spacious living room opens to a stone suntrap terrace with a magnificent estuary view.

Price	House €2,500–€3,400. Stables €1,200–€1,600. Cottage €400–€600. Prices per week.
Rooms	House for 8-10. Stables for 9-11. Cottage for 5.
Meals	Cook at extra charge. Full breakfast €10. Dinner, 3 courses, €25-€32. Daily cleaning included.
Closed	Rarely.
Directions	Directions given on booking.

Mike & Susannah Adlington
Castlecove, Co. Kerry

Tel	+44 (0)1420 23113
Fax	+44 (0)1420 22063
Email	info@westcovelettings.co.uk
Web	www.westcovelettings.com

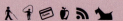

Hotel   Co. Kerry

Tahilla Cove Country House

If Tahilla Cove's 14 landscaped, wooded acres by the secluded cove sings of the south seas it's because there is a whiff of paradise in this part of 'Ireland's Riviera': lawns resplendent with palm trees run down to the sea and a private mooring. James now runs it all with son Charles and wife Deirdre, the local GP – two houses, built in the Forties by James's father, touched by an unusual melange of Art Deco and Greek villa. Sink into boldly floral sofa and chairs and gaze on palm trees and sea, put your feet up by the wood-burning fire and be charmed by the every-changing light; it is restful and delightful. Big unpretentious bedrooms are lifted by art on the walls and good strong colours; most have a private balcony or terrace and views of the legendary peninsula. Walk through oak groves to idyllic viewpoints where seals can be seen basking on rocks, swim off the private pier, mess about in a rowing boat before coming back for tea in the sun or drinks by the bar. The best possible therapy for speeded-up urbanites, to stay three nights (at least!) with these very welcoming people.

Price	€120-€150. Singles €100.
Rooms	9: 2 doubles, 1 twin, 6 twins/doubles.
Meals	Restaurant in Sneem, 10-min drive.
Closed	Mid-October to Easter.
Directions	From Kenmare N70 for Sneem 16km; house left down drive at sign.

	James, Deirdre & Charles Waterhouse
	Tahilla Cove, Tahilla, Sneem, Co. Kerry
Tel	+353 (0)64 664 5204
Fax	+353 (0)64 664 5104
Email	tahillacove@eircom.net
Web	www.tahillacove.com

Travel Club Offer. See page 266.

Entry 128   Map 6

Co. Kerry

Self-catering

Seal Rock Cottage

You are hardly aware of it but you are on an island and out there is the Atlantic with the mountains of Kerry forming part of the view; if you are not inspired by this landscape then you have no soul. The new cottage is stone built and sturdy, with a large gravelled area at the front... a plain enough exterior, but step inside to find a place of polished wooden floors and all the bleached beauty of the beach. In the large sitting room there are stones, driftwood mirrors and lamps, heavy wooden table tops, sheepskins and shaggy pile rugs, and an open fireplace with a pyramid of logs. Next is a sun room with wraparound windows and remote control blinds, which you operate from the comfort of two enormous sofas in tasteful grey. The state-of-the-art kitchen has a super table and black upright chairs. Upstairs: more spotless wooden floors, big beds, clean white walls, stylised pieces of furniture and bathrooms that are beautifully tiled. A terrace to the rear has small lights set into wooden sleepers and leads to a stone platform with a grey slate table and benches... have your meals watching the sea and the sky.

Travel Club Offer. See page 266.

Price	€1,200–€1,800 per week.
Rooms	Cottage for 4.
Meals	Restaurants in Sneem.
Closed	Never.
Directions	From Kenmare N70 for Sneem. Past Blackwater Bridge. Left signed 'Rossmore'. Cross stone bridge, pass house on right, thro' farm gate on right at top of hill; follow track to end.

Jane Madigan
Rossmore Island, Tahilla, Sneem,
Co. Kerry

Tel	+44 (0)7949 784016
Email	janemadigan@fsmail.net
Web	www.kenmareirishcottages.com

Entry 129 Map 6

B&B Co. Kerry

Shelburne Lodge

People in Kenmare say Maura has the Midas touch, excelling at everything she does. Her colourful personality is stamped all over the house, and the house glows: lemon yellow bedrooms with huge mirrors, beautiful limewashed furniture, antiques galore, modern art, thick rugs on polished boards – it all shows a keen eye for elegant, unstuffy interior design. The rooms are divided between the 1740s lodge and the secluded coach house which overlooks the ample grounds and grass tennis court. All are gorgeously different, full of flowers and bright art and modern country-house style. The house vibrates: tiny Maura creates the buzz. She or a daughter will settle you in with other guests by the ever-burning log fire for a cup of tea that appears to arrive by magic; at breakfast you swoon over porridge with whiskey cream in a room with canary walls. Tom's knowledge of the area is remarkable: a gentle, solicitous man, he'll inspire you to explore at length. You are just on the outskirts of delightful Kenmare; steep country lanes lead to sweeping views of the river and surrounding hills. Outstanding.

Price	€120–€190. Singles from €80.
Rooms	9: 6 doubles, 2 twins, 1 family.
Meals	Restaurants within walking distance.
Closed	December-February.
Directions	From Killarney N22 for 15km; right R569 to Kilgarven; continue for Kenmare. House signposted on right just before town.

Maura & Tom O'Connell-Foley
Cork Road, Kenmare, Co. Kerry
Tel +353 (0)64 664 1013
Fax +353 (0)64 664 2135
Email shelburnekenmare@eircom.net
Web www.shelburnelodge.com

Entry 130 Map 6

Co. Kerry   B&B

Seanua

A kindly, casual family atmosphere envelops you at Seanua with small children joyfully playing here and there. It is a new house where the old sense of hospitality is fully alive: *seanua* means 'old and new' in Irish. You are just a minute's drive from the attractive town of Kenmare with its bustling shops, restaurants and lively night life, but all is quiet here and there are lovely strolls from the house, one along the river where you may fish. The sitting room has stripped and polished wood floors, a textured plaster finish to the creamy yellow walls and a contrasting deep red on the chimney breast. Colourful prints dot the walls and the open fire belts out the heat; breakfast is taken here, and there are places to flop with a book. All four bedrooms have fresh flowers, there are lacy flounces in the yellow room and rich red tasselled cushions in another, where an open fire can be lit for romantic nights; bathrooms are bright and clean. You'll eat well: breakfast includes Clonakilty black pudding with potato cakes and free-range eggs, dinner is a family affair round one big table. Marvellous.

Price	€85–€125. Singles €45–€55.
Rooms	4: 3 doubles, 1 twin.
Meals	Dinner €30. Wine €12.
Closed	Rarely.
Directions	Take R569 for Kilgarvan/Killarney. 1.5km, right at crossroads. Seanua is second house on right.

Travel Club Offer. See page 266.

Alison & Andy Whelton
Gortagass, Crossroads, Kenmare,
Co. Kerry
Tel   +353 (0)64 664 2505
Email   info@seanua.com
Web   www.seanua.com

Entry 131   Map 6

B&B   Co. Kerry

Virginia's Guesthouse

They are a winning combination: Neil, who was born in Room 23 and has wonderful tales to tell, and Noreen, his 'young bride', an intelligent, energetic and inventive woman. Marvellously unposh, Virginia's is a great find – friendly, relaxing, full of its own good ideas. The marathon breakfast, much of it Noreen's own work, brings homemade breads and muesli, fresh orange juice, banana pancakes, blue cheese pears, the full Irish works, and champagne on New Year's Day. The sitting room has books and games, a kettle, loads of different teas and coffees: help yourself. Bright colours abound in bedrooms whose varnished wood beds are topped by teddies; shower rooms have lashings of water and fluffy towels. Those at the front look onto Henry Street, those at the back are less light but quieter, of course; all are spotless. Kenmare is one of the prettiest small towns in Ireland, a real treat. You can tour its streets in ten minutes, choose your restaurant, stop in a pub, chat with the locals. Great hospitality, great people, great fun – and much praise from readers for the restaurant below.

Price	€80–€120. Singles €55–€80.
Rooms	8: 5 doubles, 1 twin, 1 single, 1 triple.
Meals	Mulcahy's Restaurant below.
Closed	Rarely.
Directions	Kenmare has 3 main streets, all one-way. From post office on Henry Street, house 50 metres down hill (above Mulcahy's Restaurant).

Travel Club Offer. See page 266.

Noreen Harrington
Henry Street, Kenmare, Co. Kerry
Tel   +353 (0)64 664 1021
Email virginias@eircom.net
Web   www.virginias-kenmare.com

Co. Kerry   B&B

Sallyport House

An enterprising grandfather who exported railway sleepers to England is to be thanked for the antiques here: rather than use conventional ballast for the return boat journey, he brought back mahogany furniture. The Arthurs, a warm and attentive family, are justifiably proud of his collection and put it to full use in every room – even the bedroom tea cups are antique. This extraordinary man also bought the local workhouse, knocked it down and used the stone to build Sallyport in 1932 – you can see the worn stepping stone in the hall. Good Irish art enlivens the walls, and books, chess and dominoes the sitting room. Bedrooms are off a wide central landing and have silk bedspreads, thick carpets, big baths, lots of light… not a hair out of place. Views stretch over the orchard to Muxnaw and the Caha mountains, the gardens run down to the river and golfers are happy; the golf course is a short walk. Breakfast menus include smoked salmon, staff are delightful and Kenmare is a pretty town with lots of life. This is also a good base from which to explore the Ring of Kerry and, better still, Beara.

Price	€140-€170. Singles from €90.
Rooms	5: 2 doubles, 1 twin/double, 1 four-poster, 1 family.
Meals	Restaurants within walking distance.
Closed	November-March.
Directions	From Killarney N71 to Kenmare. Follow Bantry signs through town. On left before suspension bridge.

The Arthur Family
Kenmare, Co. Kerry

Tel	+353 (0)64 664 2066
Fax	+353 (0)64 664 2067
Email	port@iol.ie
Web	www.sallyporthouse.com

Self-catering   Co. Kerry

Somerton

Yes, a new house on the shores of Kenmare Bay with those devastatingly beautiful views. No, not another beastly bung but a superb architect-designed house set against the hillside, living sensitively in the landscape. Every room has vast sky-filled windows, the Mackintosh-style dining area opens onto a sheltered terrace, the outside rushes in to grab you: walk straight out into the Kerry wilderness. With matching sensitivity, the owners have furnished their well-loved house in natural materials, subdued tones and quiet opulence. You will love the sleek fitted kitchen – a cook's dream of steel and maple with all the gadgets – and revel in the rainy-day delights of the little library, the eye-catching art, the DVDs and the wraparound music system before the ultra-modern gas fire – and now there's broadband! Bathrobes and a welcome basketful of organic goodies add to the comforts that real people have chosen for themselves and there is a sense of family here – personal photographs here and there, soft fabrics on hand-crafted beds. Somerton is a wow, worlds away from the anonymity of a standard rental.

Price	€1,950–€2,900 per week.
Rooms	House for 8.
Meals	Restaurants 2km.
Closed	Rarely.
Directions	From Kenmare post office turn away from town; cross bridge; right for Beara 1.5km; house on left. More details on booking.

Colette Hamel
Killaha East, Kenmare, Co. Kerry
Tel   +353 (0)21 487 0820
Email   info@somertonkenmare.com
Web   www.somertonkenmare.com

Entry 134   Map 6

Co. Kerry

Inn

The Lake House

Mary is the warmest, most gracious south-Kerry soul, deeply committed to proper hospitality and the local community, working her apron off from dawn to dusk to cook the superb pub food that the Lake House is renowned for. The setting is gorgeous, peace wafts up from the surface of the lake and the silent hills around. Indoors, the atmosphere is alive with wild fishermen's tales of battling brownies and rare grilses. Bring your rods, hire a boat and by the evening you too can tell a tale over delicious food and drink. Two of the bedrooms are now completely refurbished with new carpets, curtains, comfortable beds and lovely views of the lake and mountains. The others will follow: Mary is doing all she can to keep her family place up and running. Her grandfather opened the pub in 1926 and also built the dance hall here which she turns over to the community for exhibitions and… the annual dance. She is thinking of setting up a cookery school there, quite rightly. Come for the food, come for the fishing, come for the marvellous *craic* and the Wednesday night traditional music session.

Price	€70.
Rooms	5: 2 doubles; 2 doubles, 1 twin sharing 2 bathrooms.
Meals	Lunch €4–€10. Dinner €15–€25.
Closed	Rarely.
Directions	From Kenmare N71 for Glengariff over bridge; right R571 for Castletownbere. Inn on this road; signposted. (15km from Kenmare.)

Mary O'Shea
Cloonee Lakes, Tousist, Kenmare,
Co. Kerry

Tel	+353 (0)64 668 4205
Fax	+353 (0)64 668 4205
Email	mary@clooneelakehouse.com
Web	www.clooneelakehouse.com

B&B Co. Limerick

Flemingstown House

Soft towels and sweet-clove apple tart: "Imelda is a lovely lovely lady," says one reader, and a fine cook who grows her own fruit. The square old farmhouse has been in the family for generations; lush lawns at the front, the family's herd at the back. Inside, pristine walls are hung with antique paintings and family photographs, and ancient family furniture soaks up the space. Upstairs, solid old rosewood beds are swathed in embroidered bed linen, then topped with fabulously comfy duvets and heaped with goose down pillows. Windows overlook fields and lush orchard, en suite showers are generous. (And there's a bath for all to use – a beautiful claw-footed tub.) There are also lots of peaceful walks around the farm and more in the surrounding golden vale and the Ballyhoura mountains. But what really sets this place apart is your enchanting hostess and her wonderful cooking, served at one big dining table in a conservatory sparkling with Waterford crystal. Imelda runs the house with the help of her daughter and daughter-in-law and breakfasts, laid before an open turf fire, are fit for kings and queens.

Price	€120-€140. Singles €70.
Rooms	5: 4 doubles, 1 family. Extra bath.
Meals	Dinner €45. BYO wine. Packed lunch on request.
Closed	November-February.
Directions	House 3km from Kilmallock on Fermoy road R512. Set on long avenue.

Imelda Sheedy-King
Kilmallock, Co. Limerick
Tel +353 (0)63 98093
Fax +353 (0)63 98546
Email info@flemingstown.com
Web www.flemingstown.com

Entry 136 Map 7

Co. Limerick   B&B

Ash Hill Stud

Come here for the experience. The house is ancient and rather magnificent, set in handsome parkland and with views to the hills. It is on the edge of town, but you'd not know it. Slightly daunted by the scale of it all, you meet Simon and the daunting stops. He is very English in style and so relaxed that it is hard to imagine him disapproving of anything; you have the run of the place. You enter off the splendid three-sided courtyard flanked with stables. The hall is small, carpeted as British pubs once were. There is a dark, cosy sitting-room for tea, reading and chats to Simon, then more carpet, past the splendid dining-room and up modest stairs to a long corridor and one enormous and handsome, 4-poster bedroom. It has PVC windows down to the floor and over the parkland. It is not without its oddities – so no 'luxury', though the mattress is superb. But handsome it is, and you can wander to a vast and half-furnished sitting room. The small twin room is for children and the big twin, gorgeous at heart (witness that ceiling), awaits decorators. With a sense of history and humour you can have a grand time here.

Price	€100–€120.
Rooms	3: 2 twins, 1 four-poster.
Meals	Restaurants within 1.6km.
Closed	Rarely.
Directions	From Limerick, south ring road at Tipperary r'bout; at next r'bout, R512 to Kilmallock 32km; right in town centre onto R515; 1st gates on right after 1km.

Simon Johnson
Ash Hill, Kilmallock, Co. Limerick
Tel   +353 (0)63 98035
Email   ashhill@iol.ie
Web   www.ashhill.com

Entry 137   Map 7

Hotel　　　　　　　　　　　　　　　　　　　　　　　Co. Limerick

The Mustard Seed at Echo Lodge

The Mustard Seed (a biblical quote) gets top marks on all counts. Dan's cheerful energy has made the place sparkle. Step over the sleeping cat into a sumptuous world of understated excess, a shrine to colour and hospitality. Many backpacking journeys have fathered all this far-flung exotica: hangings, silk prints, maps and other worldly goods to delight the senses. Luxury and lovely views (lawns, church, trees) wash over you: deep sofas and carved marble fireplaces, elephants and a few thrones, crackling fires and bedrooms full of lovelinesses – big armoires, lacquered screens, more exotic wall hangings, rugs on warm wooden floors. There are ten rooms in the main house and six in the old schoolhouse where immaculate ground-floor suites have windows onto terraces. There's even a Thai masseur at your disposal. Then there's the restaurant with its superb atmosphere of candles and opulent flowers on every table, traceable ingredients beautifully cooked, veg from the immaculate patch, eggs from the hens. We haven't even scratched the surface, so come and dig deeper yourself. *Pets by arrangement.*

Price	€190-€330. Singles from €130.
Rooms	16: 6 doubles, 2 twins, 1 family, 3 singles, 1 four-poster, 3 suites.
Meals	Dinner, 2-4 courses, €43-€65. Wine from €26. Light lunch for residents. Restaurant closed on Mondays November to spring.
Closed	Rarely.
Directions	From Limerick N21 to Rathkeale; left R518 to Ballingarry; through to bottom of village; follow signs.

Travel Club Offer. See page 266.

Daniel Mullane
Ballingarry, Co. Limerick
Tel　　+353 (0)69 68508
Fax　　+353 (0)69 68511
Email　mustard@indigo.ie
Web　　www.mustardseed.ie

Co. Limerick

B&B

Fitzgerald's Farmhouse & Riding Centre

Riding centre, animal sanctuary and B&B (self-catering coming soon), this place has a cheerful, youthful, happening atmosphere. There are poultry, rabbits and, of course, horses and ponies galore. Tim, former athlete and gentle giant, has built special pens so children can wander safely. A two-mile walk leads past the stream to a gazebo with lovely views, then to an exhibition of antique farm machinery. Comfortable, jolly bedrooms have bright yellow walls and wooden floors. The ever-bubbly Kathleen serves meals in the dining room, among the family snaps but you're always welcome in the kitchen or the guest sitting room with its open fire and the family's riding and athletics trophies. They own 30 horses and specialise in riding and riding holidays: anything from a couple of days to children's summer camps or riding-and-English for young foreigners. Tackle the cross-country course, trek through stunning countryside, gallop on Beale beach... Non-riders can go golfing, fishing or walking in the Stack Mountains, knowing the young are in safe hands. Fun and welcoming for parents and children alike.

Price	€70–€105. Singles €50.
Rooms	6: 1 double, 3 twins, 2 family rooms.
Meals	Dinner from €30.
Closed	Rarely.
Directions	From Limerick N21 for Tralee 64km to Abbeyfeale; left in square, between O'Rourke's Bar & Cellar Bar. House up hill on left 1.5km, signposted.

Kathleen & Tim Fitzgerald
Mount Marian, Abbeyfeale Hill,
Abbeyfeale, Co. Limerick

Tel	+353 (0)68 31217
Fax	+353 (0)68 31558
Email	fitzfarmhouse@eircom.net
Web	www.fitzgeraldsfarmhouse.com

Hotel   Co. Limerick

Glin Castle

Dripping with history, stuffed with exuberant, exotic, ancient art, Glin is one of Ireland's treasures. Desmond FitzGerald, its 29th Knight (the family have lived here since 1200) is a passionate collector. Drive through cow-grazed parkland to find the sublime river Shannon flowing 400 yards from the front door. Enter to fanfares of aristocratic splendour: Corinthian columns, swords fanned on the walls, staggeringly beautiful ceilings, pictures of George III, an Arbusson tapestry made for Marie Antoinette. Open fires leap in the deep-blue library, the sinful red smoking room, the fine drawing room that floods with river light. Not a hotel, something grander, rarer: a castle home. As you proceed up the unique flying staircase the rooms become smaller but the grandeur remains: majestic bedspreads and embossed drapes, armchairs waiting by claw-footed baths. Tumble back down and a huge window frames the formal garden... beyond: fruits and vegetables for the kitchens and 400 acres of woodland walks. There are other things to do locally but you'll probably spurn them for Glin. *Children over ten welcome.*

Price	€310–€495. Whole property (max. 30 people) €5,900 per day.
Rooms	15: 4 doubles, 10 twins/doubles, 1 four-poster.
Meals	Dinner, 4 courses, €60. Wine from €26.
Closed	December–February. Off season by arrangement.
Directions	From Limerick N69 west 51km to Glin; left up main street; right at top of square; entrance straight ahead. Tabert car ferry 6.5km.

Desmond & Olda FitzGerald
Glin, Co. Limerick

Tel	+353 (0)68 34173
Fax	+353 (0)68 34364
Email	knight@iol.ie
Web	www.glincastle.com

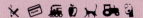

Entry 140   Map 6

Co. Limerick   Hotel

No. 1 Pery Square

A quiet oasis looking over the park, but within walking distance of the city centre, good shops, vibrant bars and restaurants; old Limerick bricks and mortar are here combined with contemporary Irish style. The bones of this 1830s building are beautiful: wooden shutters, lofty sash windows, haughty stone and marble fireplaces, high ceilings. Patricia is busily creating four bedrooms upstairs in the main house, all with views, heritage colours, grand beds, thick carpeting, fabulous bathrooms with roll tops, double sinks and pummelling showers. There's a huge, elegant drawing room on this floor too, with leafy views through enormous windows. Meals are taken in the brasserie style restaurant – from a pre-theatre snack or full à la carte there is a commitment to Irish food; try Limerick cheeses or seaweed sausages from County Mayo. Along a corridor from here find 15 'club' bedrooms, smaller but with everything you need, a more modern feel and a penthouse suite on the top floor. There's a small garden and terrace for outdoor dining to the rear of the building, and the famous People's Park is across the road.

Price	€145–€185. Suite €185–€210.
Rooms	20: 19 doubles, 1 suite.
Meals	Dinner from €20. Wine €22. Lunch from €13.50.
Closed	24–29 December.
Directions	From Shannon Airport, N19 to Limerick City. Further directions on booking.

Travel Club Offer. See page 266.

Ms Patricia Roberts
Pery Square, Limerick, Co. Limerick
Tel   +353 (0)61 402402
Email info@oneperysquare.com
Web   www.oneperysquare.com

Self-catering Co. Tipperary

Tir na Fiúise Cottages

In utter peace on an organic farm whose very air vibrates with all things natural. Lovingly restored by the Heenan family and painted with non-toxic paints, these three stone cottages are ideally placed for learning rural Ireland hands-on, touring the west (bikes come free) and discovering great Lough Derg. Lime Kiln even has an enclosed patio that makes it safe for young children. The strong red paintwork follows you inside for a bright cheerful splashing against clean whitewashed walls and original stones. Each cottage has a welcoming wood-burning stove, books to flick through, simple country furnishings, candles for atmosphere, comfy chairs. The neat tiled kitchens have all the equipment you could wish for on a holiday while the shared laundry is at the end of the block. Living rooms and bedrooms are warmly floored in wood, the odd rug, furniture is clean-limbed pine-clothed with light natural fabrics. Up the road in Terryglass is Paddy's pub, and the Derg Restaurant for excellent food. Guests are encouraged to go to stock up at the farmers' market but they usually end up at the local supermarket!

Price	Granary €280–€400. Stables €350–€530. Lime Kiln €400–€580. Prices per week; electricity & heating extra.
Rooms	Granary for 2 (1 double, 1 bathroom). Stables for 4 (1 double, 1 twin, 1 bathroom). Lime Kiln for 6 (1 twin, 1 family, 2 bathrooms).
Meals	Pub & restaurant 2km.
Closed	Never.
Directions	Directions given on booking.

Niall & Inez Heenan
Terryglass, Borrisokane, Co. Tipperary
Tel +353 (0)67 22041
Fax +353 (0)67 22041
Email info@countrycottages.ie
Web www.countrycottages.ie

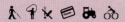

Entry 142 Map 4

Co. Tipperary   B&B

Kylenoe House

Coming to Kylenoe, set in this beautiful wooded spot near Lough Derg, is like coming to visit a favourite aunt: Virginia spoils you rotten with tea, sympathy and garden roses. And moreover, she draws your curtains and turns down your bed in the evening, those little attentions that are going out of fashion. You are immediately made to feel part of the family in her cosy old farmhouse. Pets are very welcome, too – they've won an award for being the most pet-friendly B&B in Ireland – though Virginia's special love is the thoroughbreds she has been breeding professionally for years. You will see the mares from the window of your cosy, lacey-covered (but un-twee) bedroom. The other has a balcony onto the woods; all you hear are the house martins and swallows. Sitting and dining rooms wear the same family-worn antique-comfortable air – relaxing and easy. Virginia's other great strength is cooking: readers have told us about her delicious country dinners. Kylenoe also has its own pier on the lake where you can swim or take a boat out, and the pretty harbour village of Terryglass is a short drive.

Price	€110–€140. Singles €60.
Rooms	3: 2 doubles; 1 double with separate bath.
Meals	Dinner, 4 courses, €42.
Closed	Rarely.
Directions	From Nenagh N52 to Borrisokane 17.5km; left for Ballinderry 8km; pass village store on left, continue 3.5km, entrance on right: house in trees up drive.

Virginia Moeran
Ballinderry, Nenagh, Co. Tipperary
Tel   +353 (0)67 22015
Fax   +353 (0)67 22275
Email ginia@eircom.net

Entry 143   Map 4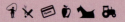

B&B   Co. Tipperary

Ashley Park House

Refreshingly Irish and old-fashioned, Ashley Park bathes in its 18th-century time warp by the trout-filled waters of Lough Ourna, blissfully detached from modern madness. A giant trout greets you in the hall; the sweet smell of endless turf fires wafts over quiet, ornate rooms, dark polished floors and deeply carved 17th-century furniture. The circular reading room with its exquisite Chinese art is lighter. Big bedrooms rejoice in heavy curtains, old-style linen on fine old beds, armchairs for quiet gazing over vast swathes; fadedly Victorian bathrooms have chequered floors and original fittings. Take tea on the crumbling colonial veranda, ponder the ruins of the island castle or listen to Sean's inexhaustible repertory of stories: he is a true character, an ever-present force here while daughter Margaret applies all her drive and imagination to reviving house and garden. Children love the cobbled farmyard with its peacocks, guinea fowl and doves; there's a walled garden, a nature reserve where ancient woodland protects red squirrels, dreams to dream. An authentic, unsmart delight – the kind of place we love.

Price	€110–€150. Singles €60–€75.
Rooms	5: 3 doubles, 2 family.
Meals	Dinner €40–€45. Wine from €22.
Closed	Never.
Directions	From Nenagh N52 for Borrisokane 5.5km; entrance on left after big lake.

The Mounsey Family
Nenagh, Co. Tipperary

Tel	+353 (0)67 38223
Fax	+353 (0)67 38013
Email	margaret@ashleypark.com
Web	www.ashleypark.com

Entry 144   Map 4

Co. Tipperary   B&B

Bayly Farm

These terrifically kind and welcoming people whose sons have grown and flown (one of them was the 2001 world champion Mirror-dinghy sailor), are still hard at work on their 130-acre farm and love entertaining guests in the comfortable family atmosphere of their Georgian farmhouse, owned by Baylys for 200 years. Enjoy breakfast at the fine mahogany table, once used to store harnesses, lounge by the crackling drawing-room fire, sleep in huge, handsome bedrooms with good beds, a few antiques, family pictures, wonderful views. Bathrooms are another pleasing mix of old and new, smart modern fittings, black-and-white floors, underfloor heating. The house stands among beautiful trees and well-tended shrubs, the south-facing patio is a real sun trap on a fine day, beyond lie the dramatic Silvermines Mountains. It is a tranquil, lovely spot. A stay in this caring, intelligent house would cheer and comfort any weary traveller – or indeed enthusiastic sailor, fisherman, golfer, hill-walker, castle-gazer: all will find grist to their mills within half an hour's drive. *Dogs welcome to sleep in the boot room.*

Price	€80–€90. Singles €50–€55.
Rooms	3: 1 double, 1 twin; 1 twin with separate bathroom.
Meals	Dinner €35. By arrangement.
Closed	Rarely.
Directions	From Nenagh R498 for Thurles; over railway 600m; over river, immed. right for Ballinaclough 2km; lane on right (sign); house 800m along.

Jacqueline & Desmond Bayly
Ballinaclough, Nenagh, Co. Tipperary

Tel	+353 (0)67 31499
Email	bayly@eircom.net
Web	www.baylyfarm.ie

Entry 145   Map 4

B&B   Co. Tipperary

Saratoga Lodge *family friend*

Valerie is hospitable, funny, full of chat and extremely talented: one of Ireland's great characters, she does the heart good. She lives on the stud farm where she restores ceramics, bronzes and stoneware, organises hunting, shooting and fishing parties (there are some magnificent bogs here), and great cookery courses when required. An accomplished cook, she uses fresh things from her garden, eggs from her hens, honey from her bees, meat and game from local farms whenever possible: meals are a treat. In its fine big garden, she designed this practical Georgian-style house herself. Books, racing and hunting memorabilia, soft sofas, antiques and log fires make it relaxed and homely; bedrooms are simple and inviting with deeply sleep-inducing beds. Beneath the the Devil's Bit mountain, Saratoga lies on 120 acres of rolling pastureland in the lovely Golden Vale where mares and foals and cattle graze in peace. There's sailing on Lough Derg; walks and hunts start from the door. Bring your own horse and ride or walk out to explore the castle-strewn, legend-laden heart of Ireland. *Pets by arrangement.*

Price	€90–€100. Singles €45–€50.
Rooms	3: 2 doubles, 1 twin.
Meals	Dinner €30. Wine €15 or BYO wine. Packed lunch €7.
Closed	23 December–3 January.
Directions	From Templemore R501 for Borrisoleigh 3km; 2nd right 1.5km; left at T-junc.; entrance with white gate 300m on left.

Valerie Beamish
Barnane, Templemore, Co. Tipperary
Tel   +353 (0)504 31886
Fax   +353 (0)504 31886
Email saratogalodge@eircom.net
Web   www.saratoga-lodge.com

Entry 146   Map 7

Co. Tipperary   B&B

Rusheen House

Rusheen is a horse-lovers' paradise, a place to ride them, pat them, and sit on them all day. The whole place breathes a love of horses and Clare spreads the love, taking in folk for horse holidays and riding courses. But there is more to Clare, for she still teaches a bit of criminology at the university and has wide-ranging interests – with a sitting room full of books to quicken your own. There is a Bechstein, which she plays (you can too), books all down one side, a wooden floor, fine furniture and rugs, an old pine table to dine at and a comfortable sofa. You'll probably have it to yourselves. The 'yellow' bedroom is engagingly old-fashioned, the little double with pale blue walls is very little but attractive and there is a twin room too. One giant and colourful bathroom, with jacuzzi, serves all the rooms. Clare is a vegetarian so don't expect bacon for breakfast, but few mind the smoked salmon and scrambled eggs. Delicious dinners are vegetarian and pescetarian. You can stay around all day, but do sally forth into the countryside, for it is lovely and there are views across hills and dales.

Price	€70-€90. Singles €50-€75.
Rooms	3: 1 double, 1 twin, 1 family, all sharing bathroom.
Meals	Lunch €15. Dinner, 5 courses with wine, €30. Restaurant 3 miles.
Closed	Never.
Directions	R498 or R501 to Borrisoleigh. There, take road beside church. 1 mile on, follow Kilcommom Rd through junction. 1 mile, keep right at fork, signed left after 0.5 miles, house at end of road.

Travel Club Offer. See page 266.

Clare Rattray
Borrisoleigh, Thurles, Co. Tipperary
Tel   +353 (0)50 451055
Email rusheenhouse@eircom.net
Web   www.timotrec.com/rusheen.html

B&B Co. Tipperary

Inch House

Recline in a Prince Albert bed or beneath an antique lace canopy, then soak in a wood-panelled bathroom before an exquisite breakfast (just try the homemade bread) or dinner served on silver in the hushed but celebrated restaurant: the food is special. The approach, past beech woods and waving fields of wheat, is stately; the house exudes comfort and hospitality. The Egans have created a generous temple of ease and good taste – country living in the grand style. In the chapel, recently finished, you may find a family relation saying Mass. John and Nora work well together, she the neat and practical nurse, he the farmer bursting with grand plans; the rest of the family lend unflagging support. Certain features stand out: the fine relief of the serpent ceiling rose, the 44-foot pitch-pine floorboards in the blue, white and gilt drawing room, the wide double oak staircase, the rich stained glass of the Ryan family with its motto, 'Death before Dishonour'. Mysteriously, the Ryans survived where fellow Catholics were dispossessed by Cromwell's penal law. Today, Inch House is blissfully free of intrigue.

Price	€130. Singles €75.
Rooms	5: 1 four-poster, 2 doubles, 2 twins.
Meals	Dinner, 5 courses, €60. House wine €25. Restaurant closed Sunday & Monday.
Closed	Christmas & Easter.
Directions	From Dublin N7 to Port Laoise; N8 for Cork 50km; N75 to Thurles; through town square, R498 for Nenagh 6.5km. Stone entrance just past 'The Ragg' crossroads.

John, Nora & Máirín Egan
Thurles, Co. Tipperary

Tel	+353 (0)504 51348
Fax	+353 (0)504 51754
Email	mairin@inchhouse.ie
Web	www.inchhouse.ie

Entry 148 Map 7

Co. Tipperary   B&B

Dualla House

A poem hangs in the hall: "Go placidly amid the noise and haste and remember what peace there may be in silence." Mairéad knows it by heart – and lives it. She and Martin love welcoming guests to their splendid, well-lived-in Georgian house, its marvellous views across pastures to the mountains, its romantic ruined coach house. Farmers come from afar to learn about pedigree sheep breeding: there are over 1,000 ewes here and you can watch the lambing and shearing in season; it's instructive fun for children, too. Irish racehorses are another passion: Tipperary is the cradle of Ireland's thoroughbred industry and the 1926 Irish Grand National winner Amberwave lived here. Well-proportioned rooms are furnished in a traditional farmhouse style, with some antiques, original polished floorboards in the breakfast room, fresh flowers, paintings brought back from Korea by Mairéad's sister, who is a nun. Big, comfortable bedrooms have good mattresses and clean, modern bathrooms. Come to walk, visit The Rock of Cashel, enjoy the country peace, not to see perfect Georgian architecture.

Price	€90-€110. Singles €60-€70. Discount for children.
Rooms	3: 1 double, 1 twin/double, 1 family.
Meals	Restaurants in Cashel, 5km.
Closed	December-February.
Directions	From Dublin N8 into Cashel. Take R688 300m, pass church on left, left R691 for Dualla 5km. Entrance on left as road dips.

Travel Club Offer. See page 266.

Mairéad Power
Cashel, Co. Tipperary

Tel	+353 (0)62 61487
Fax	+353 (0)62 61487
Email	duallahse@eircom.net
Web	www.duallahouse.com

Entry 149   Map 7

Self-catering | Co. Tipperary

The Cottage

Bowl along a quiet country road, drive through an iron farm gate and be dazzled by a strumpet of a red front door. The little stone cottage began life as an animal shelter but is now a fetching hideaway for two, independent of the main farmhouse and with its own pretty garden. Inside: an open-plan sitting room, a high beamed ceiling, exposed stone walls, wooden floors, fresh flowers in jugs on deep window sills – all rather light, bright and alpine in feel; here you can loll on the sofa with a book or plot outings. Your galley kitchen with gleaming checked tiles has all that's needed to rustle up a meal, though the buzzing bars and restaurants in Kilkenny might be a headier pull. Beyond the kitchen is the bathroom – not swish, but spotless and generously towelled up. Climb wooden spiral stairs to a loft-style mezzanine where you sleep in a comfortable bed with a jolly patchwork quilt. Lovers or lazy lumps may want to stay put, but the adventurous can walk, watch birds, play golf, visit castles, have picnics by rivers, go fishing or riding and have oodles of fun. A super place to stay.

Price	€335-€385 per week.
Rooms	Cottage for 2-4.
Meals	Restaurants 6.5km.
Closed	Never.
Directions	From Kilkenny, N78 towards Callan/Clonmel. At Callan, right for Kilkenny Crystal Factory Shop. On for 3.5 miles; cottage on right.

Chris & Grainne Perkins
Modeshill, Mullinahone, Co. Tipperary

Tel	+353 (0)86 336 7366
Fax	+353 (0)86 336 7366
Email	stay@thecottage.ie
Web	www.thecottage.ie

Entry 150   Map 8

Co. Tipperary

B&B & Self-catering

Kilmaneen Farmhouse

A magic spot. Look out onto a landscape untouched for centuries: not a pylon in sight, wonderful lush hedgerows, fine trees. Its totally unspoilt beauty makes Kilmaneen very special, in large part thanks to the O'Donnells' loving care of their land, their animals and their rivers. The Tar and the Suir flowing through the farm to meet at one corner of the property have inspired them to develop model environmental practices (superb trout fishing: book a ghillie). You are welcomed with gentle grace to their compact and crisply modernised farmhouse where discreet mod cons hide behind country antiques, pretty wallpapers match the unintrusive floral fabrics and lovely watercolours by a local artist give you reason to pause on the landing. The peace outside is reflected in the house and cottage and Bernadette's attention to detail shines out; her succulent breakfasts have won awards. These are open, genuine, warm people. All set against the breathtaking backdrop of the Knockmealdown Mountains and their great hill walks (book a guide).

Price	€80–€85. Singles €45–€50. Cottage €250–€500 p.w.
Rooms	3 + 1: 1 double, 1 twin/double, 1 twin. Cottage for 2-5 (1 double, 1 family).
Meals	Dinner €30. BYO wine. Picnic on request.
Closed	November-February.
Directions	From Cahir R670 or from Clonmel R665 to Ardfinnan; through village to 'Hill Bar'; left up hill; Kilmaneen Farm signposted.

Kevin & Bernadette O'Donnell
Ardfinnan, Newcastle, Clonmel,
Co. Tipperary

Tel	+353 (0)52 613 6231
Fax	+353 (0)52 613 6231
Email	info@kilmaneen.com
Web	www.kilmaneen.com

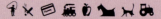

B&B   Co. Waterford

Ardsallagh Lodge

In this wonderful watery world, the rooms at Ardsallagh Lodge look out either to the sea or to the River Blackwater – as private as you could wish yet only a few miles from lively, arty Youghal and the gentle spirit of East Cork. Inside the house find neutral carpets, gilt mirrors, glass-fronted cabinets containing best crystal, tapestried chairs, lace-edged cushions and a huge Italian marble carved fireplace. You eat breakfast at one table in the grand dining room with a crystal chandelier and displays of fresh flowers: try proper porridge, then kedgeree, or a feast of Irish cheeses and meats. Two bedrooms upstairs are large and pristine with good furniture, orthopaedic mattresses, flowing curtains and floral bedcovers. One downstairs is equally charming with colourful floral prints in thick curtains, all will suit traditionalists and it is supremely comfortable; traffic noise during the day will not disturb at night. Elizabeth wants people to come to a home environment where they will feel involved and Tim is dying to take you on a tour down to the river in his old Model T Ford. Fun!

Price	€100-€160. Singles €80.
Rooms	3: 2 doubles, 1 twin.
Meals	Pub/restaurant 1.5 miles.
Closed	20 December-15 January.
Directions	From Cork N25 to Waterford by-passing Youghal; continue on N25 across Blackwater River bridge. 1st left (as you come off bridge). House 1st on right.

Travel Club Offer. See page 266.

	Elizabeth Kee
	Youghal, Co. Waterford
Tel	+353 (0)24 93496
Email	ardsallaghlodge@eircom.net
Web	www.waterfordhouseireland.com

Entry 152   Map 7

Co. Waterford   B&B

Newtown House

The wind blows gently across the Blackwater estuary, over the strip of beach and straight across the lawn to the house: at low tide you can almost walk the mile to Youghal (birdlife is rich and ever-present). It is a place of deep beauty and the Penruddocks are lucky people. But they deserve it, for they have also transformed a small, if elegant, country farmhouse into something far bigger by adding a long, low, very open and attractive kitchen-dining room behind it. The bedrooms are wonderful, the big double looking out over the estuary and filled with river light. There is a large sitting room with a log fire where idle hours can be spent, and enough space everywhere for people not to tread on each other. Georgie was once the Honey Queen of Ireland and still has four hives. So you will breakfast well, talk a lot with Georgie and Michael, wander out to enjoy local folk music, hire a boat on this beautiful river, explore some great gardens, or do nothing. You may well sit out as the sun sets over the water, with a fishing rod in one hand, a drink in the other, and wonder why on earth you had planned to move on.

Travel Club Offer. See page 266.

Price	€90–€130. Singles €80–€100.
Rooms	2: 1 double, 1 twin.
Meals	Dinner by arrangement only. Packed lunch €15. Restaurants Ardmore 6km.
Closed	1st weekend in November to last weekend in April.
Directions	From Youghal N25 for Dungarvan. Left on R671 for Clonmel; double back under flyover thro' Pilltown. Right at x-roads towards Ferry Point; on right after 1km.

Georgie Penruddock
Ferry Point Road, Kinsalebeg, Youghal,
Co. Waterford
Tel   +353 (0)58 54424
Email georgie@lismoretown.com
Web   www.stayatnewtown.com

Entry 153   Map 7

B&B   Co. Waterford

Little House on the Hill

There is no fisherman in sight, but the river is not far away and you can bring a rod. This is a surprising and delightful experience; the cottage, although authentic and rare for modern Ireland, is modest – you may wonder how you will fit in – but Ken and Cathleen have worked magic on this small house. The two bedrooms are beautifully decorated and colourful (doors may be green, wooden windows painted bright red), each with its own impressive and attractive bathroom. Find excellent mattresses on wrought-iron beds, roll-top baths, coir carpets and curtains of thick, handsome fabric. Above all there is art on the walls, a painted wooden carving, and books everywhere… for books, perhaps, are the clue to being here. There will be reading, good Irish conversation, wonderful food if Ken does some cooking (he was once a Rick Stein local food hero in his previous incarnation running the Glencairn Inn), and a wry sense of what it takes to be well together with other people. Don't come for grandeur and space, but to be surprised at what has been achieved and to enjoy some great company.

Price	€70-€100. Singles from €50.
Rooms	2 doubles.
Meals	Restaurants within 2 miles.
Closed	November-January.
Directions	From Lismore, right at Hornibrooks signposted Ballyduff. Straight over crossroads, then first right. Lismore to house 8km.

	Ken & Cathleen Buggy
	Lyons Cross, Ballyduff Upper,
	Co. Waterford
Tel	+353 (0)58 60895
Email	info@lismore.com
Web	www.lismore.com

Entry 154   Map 7

Co. Waterford
Inn

Glencairn Inn & Pastis Bistro

Glencairn Inn exudes that incomparable mixture of old wood, delicious food and warm friendly chat, all gathered in the small pub, restaurant and B&B that Fiona and Stéphane have taken over from the renowned Buggys. Fiona has come home to her native Ireland to apply her outgoing nature and organisation skills to this marvellous place; her quietly chatty French husband is absolutely the right man in the kitchen. Perch on a stool in the snug old heavy-beamed pub, joyfully eavesdropping on the local gossip while waiting for dinner. The even cosier restaurant has more stone floors, old pictures – including Stéphane's ancestral farmhouse – and a definite French *auberge* flavour. As has the really good food: no jumped-up fussiness, just excellent ingredients, most of them local and fresh, treated with care and inspiration. After coffee, amble back to the bar for a nightcap and more chat. Upstairs, an eclectic mix of non-precious antiques wonderfully put together makes for utterly charming bedrooms: patchwork quilts on super beds, lots of pictures and books. Early sleepers may need their earplugs.

Price	From €95. Singles from €60.
Rooms	4: 3 doubles, 1 twin.
Meals	Dinner from €35.
Closed	Christmas & January.
Directions	From Lismore N72 for Tallow 1km; right at Horneybrooks car showroom for Glencairn. House 3km on right in village, opp. T-junc.

Stéphane & Fiona Tricot
Glencairn, Co. Waterford
Tel +353 (0)58 56232
Fax +353 (0)58 55840
Email info@glencairninn.com
Web www.glencairninn.com

Entry 155 Map 7

Self-catering   Co. Waterford

Dromana House *Known by my family*

High above the River Blackwater, Dromana House seems to carry much of Ireland's history in its stones – and in the stones that it has lost. In 1966 the magnificent Georgian front with its bow-fronted ballroom was pulled down as it was too expensive to maintain. What is astonishing is how the remainder of the house can be so impressive, shorn of its 'façade'. It has the elegance of a modest French château and looks entirely at ease with itself. There are 30 acres of grounds, beautiful enough to attract the public during the summer months, and those renting the apartments can use the grounds as their own. The river is one of Ireland's prettiest, as much of the riparian is ancient and protective of the banks. One can potter up the river in a boat and see nothing but woods, fields and some fine old houses. The apartments are generous, with sitting rooms, a log fire in the main flat, space everywhere and everything you could need. The atmosphere is traditional and comfortable, with enough modern touches – spanking smart kitchens, roll-top baths and coir carpeting – to please the most demanding guests.

Price	€305–€780 per week.
Rooms	East Wing for 7 (1 double, 2 twins, 1 single; 2 bathrooms). River Duplex for 4 (1 double, 1 twin; 2 bathrooms).
Meals	Restaurants 4km, pub 2km.
Closed	Never.
Directions	On east bank of Blackwater River, 3 miles south of Cappoquin. Further directions on booking.

	Barbara Grubb
	Cappoquin, Co. Waterford
Tel	+353 (0)24 96144
Fax	+353 (0)24 96144
Email	bgrubb@eircom.net
Web	www.vee.ie

Entry 156   Map 7

Co. Waterford B&B

Richmond House

A charming Georgian house, with a tranquil, understated comfort and smiling Irish staff. Paul, relaxed, professional and Swiss-trained, has put huge energy into the kitchen and has been showered with praise; guests and locals eagerly pour over their menu by the drawing room fire. The appealingly traditional linen-clad dining room overlooking the gardens hosts high-quality local produce: fresh scallops from Helvic, lamb from the fields of Waterford, game in season, home-grown chicken and vegetables – all cooked to simple perfection in a gloriously light version of country cuisine. A separate, imaginative vegetarian menu shines. Harmonious ground-floor rooms, welcoming hall and wide staircase testify to the generous architecture of 1704 when the house was built by the local Lismore estate. Up those stairs are comfortable bedrooms. The prize goes to the huge master room but all are nicely maintained in relaxed country style with a feminine touch and longing views of the Knockmealdown Mountains. The loyal return – for the warm family welcome, the wonderful cooking, and the fishing and walking of the area.

Price	€75-€240. Singles €85-€100.
Rooms	9: 2 twins/doubles, 5 doubles, 1 twin, 1 single.
Meals	Dinner, 4 courses, €55. Wine €24. Early Bird menu 6.30pm, €40 (Tues-Thurs).
Closed	Two weeks Christmas & New Year.
Directions	From Cappoquin N72 for Dungarvan 1km; house signposted.

Paul & Claire Deevy
Cappoquin, Co. Waterford

Tel	+353 (0)58 54278
Fax	+353 (0)58 54988
Email	info@richmondhouse.net
Web	www.richmondhouse.net

Entry 157   Map 7

B&B   Co. Waterford

Powersfield House

The glowing highlight here is Eunice's cooking: she's a national hero, a Slow Food adept, runs courses at Powersfield, appears on television and, of course, cooks succulent organic dinners. And breakfasts. Which may include goats-cheese and bell-pepper croustade, if you please. All that plus looking after three young children and busy farmer Edmund – how does she do it? An inextinguishable ball of fire, she says "this is a night house" and the atmosphere in the evening is supremely relaxed among the flickering candles. The dining room is a gem, intimate, modern, with polished floors and Eunice's art collection on the walls – Barry Fitzpatrick's head is always a talking point and dinner is a revelation. For someone who didn't know the difference between a tagine and a daube until a few years ago, she brings food to life: piadina with goat's cheese, crispy roast duck, maybe sticky pear and ginger cake. Nothing seems beyond her ken. The deeply comfortable bedrooms are pretty funky, too, with Eunice's plates a constant theme – she just loves plates. Come for lots of fun and fabulous eating.

Price	€110-€120. Singles €65-€75.
Rooms	4: 3 doubles, 1 twin.
Meals	Dinner, 3 courses, €27-€37. 24 hours' notice required.
Closed	Rarely.
Directions	From Dungarvan centre R672 for Killarney; over Kilrush roundabout; 2nd left; 1st house on right.

Eunice & Edmund Power
Ballinamuck West, Dungarvan,
Co. Waterford
Tel   +353 (0)58 45594
Email   eunice@powersfield.com
Web   www.powersfield.com

Entry 158   Map 7

Co. Waterford   B&B

The Castle Country House

National Farmhouse of the Year, no less! These are the kindest country people who give you tea and scones when you arrive; Emmett runs the large dairy farm and is passionate about his undulating garden watered by the pretty Finisk, Joan grows her own berries and vegetables, both ooze warmth and friendship. But why the name? Because it is just that: an 18th-century house built onto the remains of the McGrath clan's 16th-century round stone tower house. The grand gilded gates are original, you will see one old arch in the long thin dining room, thick walls and high ceilings in Lady Mary's room, part of the old tower on the way to the McGrath room; the rest has the gentle proportions of a later age. Joan and Emmett have been caring for guests for 20 years, brilliantly, and have passed the gift to daughter and daughter-in-law, now part of the team that produces imaginative breakfasts and delicious local dinners. There's a fine new sitting room and soft-coloured bedrooms with a sitting space each, snow-white linen and candles. Time-warp Millstreet is a must-see.

Price	€100–€120. Singles €50–€60.
Rooms	4: 3 doubles, 1 twin.
Meals	Dinner, 3 courses, €35. Wine €17–€19. Packed lunch on request.
Closed	November to mid-March.
Directions	From Dungarvan R672 then N72 for Lismore 15km; second right R671 for Millstreet; first right in village, first house on right.

Emmet & Joan Nugent
Millstreet, Cappagh, Dungarvan,
Co. Waterford

Tel	+353 (0)58 68049
Fax	+353 (0)58 68099
Email	castle@castlecountryhouse.com
Web	www.castlecountryhouse.com

Entry 159   Map 7

B&B   Co. Waterford

Sliabh gCua Farmhouse

Irish high tea by the log fire – heaven! Sliabh gCua is an authentic place with views to die for but come above all for Breeda and Jim. Jim, a beef farmer, is soft-spoken and humorous while Breeda, warm and full of energy, could talk about anything until the oxen came home; they could not be kinder. She makes her own bread, scones, muesli and jams, keeps her well-loved farmhouse clean and fresh, the roaring fire in the drawing room is gorgeous, the beautifully laid-out dining room looks over Jim's fine lawn and outhouses ("the neatest farm we've seen in Ireland", a visitor said). Breeda has cleverly fitted little shower rooms into the bedrooms without compromising their good proportions. They all have lovely furniture, tall windows, impeccable bedding and a heart-warmingly nostalgic atmosphere. You are welcome to play the piano, son Jamie may be persuaded to play the accordion, Irish-dancing guests have been known to tread the boards. This is a house of light and laughter where the shyest child will join in; there's even a treehouse in the much-pampered garden – and not a leaf out of place.

Price	€90. Singles €50.
Rooms	4: 2 doubles, 2 twins/doubles.
Meals	Pub 5km. Restaurants in Dungarvan, 16km.
Closed	November-March.
Directions	From Dungarvan R672 for Clonmel, 16km. Take first sign left for Touraneena, after petrol station. First house on left (signed) before village.

	Breeda & Jim Cullinan
	Touraneena, Ballinamult, Dungarvan,
	Co. Waterford
Tel	+353 (0)58 47120
Email	breedacullinan@sliabhgcua.com
Web	www.sliabhgcua.com

Entry 160   Map 7

Co. Waterford

B&B

Glasha

Kindness itself, Olive is formidably houseproud, her hall slathered in framed awards testifying that she gives herself 110% to her guests. Breakfast is the greatest demonstration of her mastery: just try homemade rhubarb and strawberry compote with home-baked courgette and walnut bread for a taster – there's masses more in the basket. It's a feast served on the renowned Stephen Pearce crockery. Her colour mixes are joyous and bright – regal red, cranberry cream, blue, mustard, burgundy and buttercup – and her fanciful spirit is personified in the quirky statues and water features that decorate the garden: it gurgles and bubbles at every turn. Olive's standards shine forth inside, too: the sitting room is so luxurious in its cream sofas and gold candelabras that you feel bound to be on your best behaviour. No dust from the log fires: they're electric! The all-seasons conservatory is a lovely room, more appealing for that breakfast experience than the rather dark dining room. Colourful welcoming bedrooms, comfortable bathrooms and superb walks into those beckoning mountains.

Price	€100–€120. Singles €50–€60.
Rooms	8: 2 doubles, 4 twins, 2 triples.
Meals	Dinner €45. Wine €20–€35. Packed lunch on request.
Closed	1-28 December.
Directions	From Clonmel R671 for Dungarvan 13km; right at sign for Glasha Accommodation 1.5km.

Travel Club Offer. See page 266.

Olive & Paddy O'Gorman
Ballymacarbry, Clonmel, Co. Waterford

Tel	+353 (0)52 36108
Fax	+353 (0)52 36108
Email	glasha@eircom.net
Web	www.glashafarmhouse.com

Entry 161   Map 7

Hotel　　　　　　　　　　　　　　　　　　　　　　　　　　Co. Waterford

Hanora's Cottage

The cottage is still in there. Around it, the Walls designed and decorated a refuge of luxury on the banks of a crystal-clear brook deep in the beautiful Nire valley where the road stops and nature takes over, rising into the Comeragh Mountains and up to majestic Knockanaffrin. The ever-singing brook is floodlit at night, to delightful effect. Rooms, many facing the river, have all the discerning guest could ask for: thick carpets, voluptuous beds, swish jacuzzis, baskets of exotic fruits… and lashings of hot water for grateful walkers. Mary thinks of everything, the place runs like clockwork and the food is outstanding. Sadly, Seamus died, but his legacy lives on in his bread recipes and special bakes. Son Eoin performs culinary magic with his wife Judith and dinner here after a day in the mountains is a long, lingering, candlelit delight. Next morning, the breakfast table deserves a photograph: every variety of fruit, muesli and bread; creamy porridge, scones, cheeses, smoked salmon… not to mention scrambled eggs, sweet bacon and coffee. Total indulgence – just for grown-ups.

Price	€170-€250. Singles from €95.
Rooms	7: 1 double, 5 twins/doubles, 1 triple.
Meals	Dinner about €50. No dinner Sundays. Wine from €20. Free picnic for walkers.
Closed	Christmas (open for the New Year); 1 week in spring; 1 week in autumn.
Directions	From Clonmel south bank, south on R671 for Dungarvan. At Ballymacarbry turn off at the Pubs. House 5.5km up twisty road signed Nire Church. House by church.

Mary & Eoin Wall
Nire Valley, Ballymacarbry,
Co. Waterford

Tel	+353 (0)52 613 6134
Fax	+353 (0)52 613 6540
Email	hanorascottage@eircom.net
Web	www.hanorascottage.com

Entry 162　Map 7

Co. Waterford

B&B

The Coach House

Only ten minutes from coast and mountains here: catch a ferry to Co. Wexford, walk the stunning countryside, discover fabulous beaches. This 18th-century house is cosy and comfortable to return to and Des, a local lad, is an affable, charming host – ask him about the history. Grab a book and flop in the comfortable sitting room with its patterned carpet, open fire, gilt-framed pictures and mirrors, leather club chairs and squashy sofas; no need to stand on ceremony here. Bedrooms have American-size beds, mainly stripped wood furniture, flounces on canopies in blushing pinks or soft greens and a folding ironing board and iron so you can get rid of those creases! The overall feel is comfortingly old-fashioned, and bathrooms are neatly tiled. Fill up on a full Irish, or delicious pancakes, then go to explore: there's masses to do, starting with four acres of garden around the house (which includes the ruins of a tower and earlier house). Lovely to wander through the mature trees and ancient walls to find a secret walled garden, filled with flowering plants and with a little patio area for guests.

Price	€110–€125. Singles €70–€85.
Rooms	7: 5 doubles, 2 twins.
Meals	Pub/restaurant 2.7km.
Closed	November-March.
Directions	From Waterford, N25 to Cork. Pass Waterford Crystal factory; straight on through the Butlerstown r'bout & continue for 1.6km. Turn left at signpost; house 0.8km on right.

Des O'Keeffe
Butlerstown Castle, Butlerstown,
Co. Waterford

Tel	+353 (0)51 384656
Fax	+353 (0)51 384751
Email	coachhse@iol.ie
Web	www.butlerstowncastle.com

B&B Co. Waterford

Sion Hill House & Gardens

George and Antoinette are a gentle couple – until it comes to Sion Hill, when they wax passionately about their historic house and garden. It's easy to see why. In 12 years they have recreated this wonderful garden from jungle using old plans discovered in Waterford Library. The result is a living encylopædia of botany with over 1,000 species of rhododendron, azalea, rose, hydrangea and rare trees. Pathways lead to fragrant groves, a walled garden, a glorious fountain amongst ancient tree ferns and an 11th-century Coptic monk lodged in an old wall. Such a flower fiesta without must mean a colour and pattern fiesta within: the house is alive with embossed wallpapers, bright paintings, gleaming mahogany, Venetian chandeliers, Victorian memorabilia – nothing is without a story and everything 'fits'. Calm-inducing bedrooms lead off the spacious armchair'd landing overlooking the river, some with French beds quilted and flounced, all with fresh white cotton and busy views of the river – or garden palms. Loquacious George, chair of the Waterford National Trust, gives you the best garden tour this side of Kew.

Price	€80-€116. Singles from €65.
Rooms	4: 1 four-poster, 3 family.
Meals	Restaurants within 15-minute walk.
Closed	Christmas & New Year.
Directions	From Waterford city centre, N25 over main bridge for Wexford & Rosslare; on left entrance signed, sharp left up drive (100m after Ardree Hotel, before Texaco garage).

George & Antoinette Kavanagh
Ferrybank, Waterford City, Co. Waterford

Tel	+353 (0)51 851558
Fax	+353 (0)51 851678
Email	sionhill@eircom.net
Web	www.sionhillhouse.com

Travel Club Offer. See page 266.

Entry 164 Map 8

Co. Waterford   B&B

Foxmount Country House

One of Ireland's best-kept secrets. Porridge comes with cream and honey, water (delicious) from their spring, scones warm from Margaret's oven. David and their son work the 200-acre farm while welcoming Margaret, whom some call a domestic goddess, greets you with a confidence that comes of years of practice – 34 to be exact. She is justly proud of her home, its smart family-comfortable feel and lush gardens. A house-party atmosphere often develops as guests mingle – after a day's hard gaze at Waterford's renowned sparkling crystal and an exploration of the town's many and various eating places – for a beautifully served cup of tea or coffee in the big drawing room, warmed by the grand marble fireplace. The lovely fresh, thick-carpeted bedrooms are the highlight, with split levels, nooks and crannies, cosy bathrooms and creeper-clad windows overlooking a valley on one side, the farmyard on the other. Feather duvets, Foxford blankets, posies on the dressing table – the treats are many. The area is stuffed with ruins and history and Foxmount is three miles from dunes and sea. No wonder people return.

Price	€130. Singles €85.
Rooms	4: 2 doubles, 2 twins.
Meals	Restaurants 4km.
Closed	November-February.
Directions	From Waterford R684 for Dunmore East 5km; left for Passage East & follow signs to house.

Travel Club Offer. See page 266.

Margaret & David Kent
Passage East Road, Waterford,
Co. Waterford

Tel	+353 (0)51 874308
Fax	+353 (0)51 854906
Email	info@foxmountcountryhouse.com
Web	www.foxmountcountryhouse.com

Entry 165   Map 8

B&B   Co. Waterford

Gaultier Lodge

The other side of this 18th-century hunting lodge almost tips you onto a clean, sandy beach and the estuary that separates Waterford from Wexford – a fabulous spot. On sunny days, walk for a mile with the sand between your toes; on bracing days, let the wind and surf inspire you. Built on rock, surrounded by impregnable walls breached by one stone entrance under the gnarled boughs of an evergreen oak (there's an entrance for cars beyond), the house is intriguingly 'upside down' with exceptionally horse-loaded décor. Bill is American, a keen carriage driver and has bred Arabs; Sheila is Irish, energetic and loves country pursuits. They are a strong-minded and interesting couple. The square, whimsical hall with its antique table, books, games and other busy things to look at opens onto two very fine bedrooms, both with sweeping sea views, and the rich, dark and luxurious four-poster room with painted floorboards, tall windows and an astounding great wardrobe. In the guests' sitting room you'll find a log fire, more big views and a bountiful brunch. Sheila also runs painting courses. *Children over eight welcome.*

Price	€130-€180. Singles €95.
Rooms	3: 1 double, 1 twin, 1 four-poster.
Meals	Restaurants in Dunmore East & Passage East, within 7km.
Closed	October-May.
Directions	From Waterford R684 for Dunmore East 9.5km; left for Woodstown; as far as beach, right at T-junc. Lodge 0.5km on left behind high wall, drive through gates at end.

	Sheila Molloy
	Woodstown, Co. Waterford
Tel	+353 (0)51 382549
Fax	+353 (0)51 382549
Email	gaultierlodge@yahoo.ie
Web	www.gaultier-lodge.com

Entry 166   Map 8

Leinster

Photo: istockphoto.com

Co. Carlow   B&B

Lorum Old Rectory

Step through the door and feel instantly at home. Bobbie is cosy and warm, her three daughters, all professionals in their own fields, live across the yard, the family atmosphere is tangible. Bobbie will usher you into the drawing room to a soft sofa by the lovely fireplace for the compulsory tea and chat; the piano is there for all to talk to. Up the creaky stairs are bedrooms full of character with a carved four-poster, interesting antiques and peaceful views of the Blackstairs Mountains. The best treat of all is dinner at the big old dining table. Bobbie, an award-winning – yet modest – cook and an exponent of Slow Food, uses locally sourced meat and organic produce to stunning effect; her Irish cheeseboard must be one of the most comprehensive in the country. She also turns her hand to stained glass in her workshop in a converted outbuilding. There's a heart-soothing walk by the nearby Barrow river, or you can hire bicycles and explore the sunny south-east where it's said the climate is as gentle as the hills. Even cycle to another lovely house, with your luggage taken on ahead. Readers adore this place.

Price	€150–€160. Singles €90.
Rooms	4: 2 doubles, 1 twin/double, 1 four-poster. Extra bathroom available.
Meals	Dinner, 6 courses, €48. Wine €18–€35.
Closed	December–March.
Directions	From Bagenalstown R705 for Borris 6.5km; house signposted on left.

Bobbie Smith
Kilgreaney, Bagenalstown, Co. Carlow
Tel   +353 (0)59 977 5282
Fax   +353 (0)59 977 5455
Email info@lorum.com
Web   www.lorum.com

Entry 167   Map 8

B&B   Co. Carlow

Mulvarra House

On one of the most sensational spots in Carlow, this angular building stands above the River Barrow, facing the tree-clad mountains that fold in over the river as it meanders below and protects the ancient marvel that is St Mullins with its famous abbey, graveyard and aura of spirituality. With determination and amazing open-heartedness – extended to all guests plus four rescue dogs and three pet goats – the owners have transformed a fading B&B into an unpretentious, deliciously Irish haven. Nothing is too much trouble for Noreen: you can be collected from the station in Bagenalstown, go chad fishing for a day, join her in preparing a huge barbecue for that special evening. Each pretty, freshly-painted room has a little balcony onto the river, flower-embroidered duvets and a crisp clean shower room. The food is genuine home-cooking, organic where possible: do book dinner. On dimmer days when cultural Kilkenny, great hill walks, sport fishing or river swimming (for the brave) cannot tempt you, indulge in Noreen's brand new treatment centre. Remarkable value and such lovely people.

Price	€84. Singles €60.
Rooms	5: 2 doubles, 2 twins, 1 family. Extra bathrooms.
Meals	Dinner, 5 courses, €35.
Closed	Rarely.
Directions	From Carlow N9 for Kilkenny 16km; left R724 for Bagenalstown 1km; right R705 thro' Borris; R729 for New Ross; in Glynn right at Post Office for St Mullins; left, left again, follow signs.

	Noreen Ardill
	St Mullins, Co. Carlow
Tel	+353 (0)51 424936
Fax	+353 (0)51 424969
Email	info@mulvarra.com
Web	www.mulvarra.com

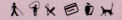

Entry 168   Map 8

Co. Dublin — Hotel

Number 31

The discreet entrance promises something special. Radically revamped, visibly and invisibly, into a chic little city-centre hotel, Number 31 holds fast to its essential family-run Irish personality: Noel employs upbeat and intelligent young staff knowing that, especially in a city, the personal touch matters. In the mews to the rear (where the coach house was) the sitting area is sunken and funky — whitewashed stone, squishy black leather, open turf fire. Cross the charmingly pebbled and box-hedged courtyard, shaded by an old acacia tree, to the more demure Georgian townhouse on Fitzwilliam Place — for lofty bedrooms and astounding cornicing (and a couple of rooms at basement level). But your favourite may be the diminutive coach house den with its own secluded patio. Breakfast is in the dining room upstairs: a joy. Whitewashed brick, simple white china, fresh fruits, perfect kippers. Just a ten-minute walk from Grafton Street, this is a peaceful and personable haven in the heart of Dublin Town. Brilliantly designed, too. *Children over 10 welcome. Secure parking. Noel also owns The Crooked Cottage, in Mayo.*

Price	€140–€300.
Rooms	21: 8 doubles, 12 twins, 1 family.
Meals	Restaurants close by.
Closed	Never.
Directions	From St Stephen's Green past Shelbourne Hotel, up Merrion Row, right Pembroke St to end, left Leeson St; Leeson Close, 1st left. Entrance on right through arched wooden gate in high wall.

Noel Comer
31 Leeson Close, Dublin 2,
Co. Dublin

Tel	+353 (0)1 676 5011
Fax	+353 (0)1 676 2929
Email	info@number31.ie
Web	www.number31.ie

Entry 169   Map 5

Self-catering   Co. Dublin

The Merrion Mews & Stables

One of the city's finest addresses, discreet, quiet and perfectly placed for the sights you're in clover here. Stepping into the Georgian coach house of a fine townhouse in Merrion Square is like slipping back in time. Through the high gate you enter 'working' courtyards, still used to refresh the police horses (fun to watch), then it's up wooden steps and into your first-floor quarters – pine floors, tongue-and-groove panelling, crewel-curtained windows. Furniture is comfortable and traditional, giving the place a homely fresh feel. The three simple double bedrooms are country-cottage snug with colourful panelling, shelves of books, pretty rugs and Shaker pegs. One has a four-poster bed, another a double shower, and there's a fine Victorian roll top in the main bathroom. The charming 'parlour', with its rosebud wallpaper, has a wood-burning stove, but you'll most likely spend family time around the pine table in the big charming kitchen. No TV, just sweet simplicity. Leinster House, the National Gallery, museums, canal walks, restaurants and bars are a stroll. Modestly special. *Minimum two nights.*

Price	€300 per night.
Rooms	House for 6.
Meals	Restaurants at end of street.
Closed	Never.
Directions	From Baggot St left into Lower Fitzwilliam St. Immediately left under arch into Fitzwilliam Lane. Big green gateway on right.

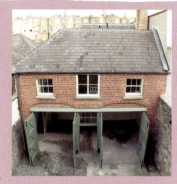

The Irish Landmark Trust
63 Fitzwilliam Lane, Dublin 2, Co. Dublin

Tel   +353 (0)1 670 4733
Fax   +353 (0)1 670 4887
Email bookings@irishlandmark.com
Web   www.irishlandmark.com

Travel Club Offer. See page 266.

Entry 170   Map 5

Co. Dublin   Hotel

Waterloo House

On a peaceful Georgian terraced street close to St Stephen's Green and Trinity College this hotel is in fact two large 1830s townhouses melded into one, whose shiny twin doors say 'come right in'. Evelyn spent years in the hospitality 'industry' before striking out on her own, but what sets this apart from many similarly priced places in Dublin is the friendly welcome, a relief from busy urban anonymity: staff go out of their way to make sure you're treated as an individual. The conversion has preserved the lofty ceilings and elegant big windows, while bedrooms, all similar in layout, are neat and clean, with thick carpets, retro furniture and decent bathrooms. Beds have white duvets and crisp pillowcases, bedside lights could be brighter. On the street side, you will find useful noise-reducing shutters and heavy curtains; the back bedrooms overlook the garden where two resident dogs play. Croissants, waffles and full Irish are served in the conservatory, the reception area doubles as a comfortable sitting space, and the bus to the centre runs right outside. *Parking for eight cars at front.*

Price	€99–€199. Singles €76–€130.
Rooms	17: 12 doubles, 5 twins.
Meals	Restaurants within walking distance.
Closed	23-28 December.
Directions	From Merrion Row, near St Stephen's Green, to Baggott St into Upper Baggott St. 1st right after bridge into Waterloo Rd; house on left. 15 minutes walk from city centre.

Evelyn Corcoran
8-10 Waterloo Road, Ballsbridge,
Dublin 4, Co. Dublin

Tel	+353 (0)1 660 1888
Fax	+353 (0)1 667 1955
Email	waterloohouse@eircom.net
Web	www.waterloohouse.ie

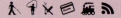

Hotel   Co. Dublin

Aberdeen Lodge

Pat fought hard to start his super little hotel amid the Regency mansions and embassies of leafy Ballsbridge. He won the neighbours over by promising to protect their peace and quiet and Aberdeen Lodge is indeed a refuge from the hullabaloo of Dublin city, yet the metro is close enough to catapult you back into the fray within minutes. Pat is a friendly hotelier, with a quiet deferential manner and his logo on the bathrobes, for whom nothing is too much trouble. His Irish staff have helpful charm, too. This modest Victorian villa has been cleverly converted into a variety of contemporary rooms with all mod cons and Egyptian cotton sheets. Candy-striped curtains remind you that the seafront is only 200 yards away and Biedermeier-style furniture adds a touch of luxury. Rooms at the back look over the good big garden onto a cricket pitch, an unusual sight in a country devoted to Gaelic football. Everything seems to run effortlessly and Pat's partner Ann's award-winning breakfast to piped classical music is deeply revitalising. Ideal for those wanting the best of both worlds in this fair city.

Price	€120–€160. Singles €99–€119. Suites €199–€249.
Rooms	17: 11 twins/doubles, 2 family, 2 triples, 2 suites.
Meals	Room service menu €15–€30. Wine €25.
Closed	Never.
Directions	From city centre by DART railway. From Merrion Square, Northumberland Rd to Merrion Rd; left into Ailesbury Rd, cross Sydney Parade DART Station, 1st left into Park Avenue; on left.

Pat Halpin
53 Park Avenue, Ballsbridge, Dublin 4, Co. Dublin
Tel   +353 (0)1 283 8155
Fax   +353 (0)1 283 7877
Email marketing@halpinsprivatehotels.com
Web   www.aberdeen-lodge.com

Travel Club Offer. See page 266.

Entry 172   Map 5

Co. Dublin   B&B

Druid Lodge

Is this magnificent house on the cliff a parody? a museum? a crazy concoction? A Titian-copy cardinal glares down upon innumerable pieces of art and artefacts, Irish, African and Italian, that hang, lie, squat in his shadow. Ken is an unstoppable collector of the unusual, the arcane, the merely beautiful. He was a sociologist in Africa (hence the Macondi carvings) and now paints – he has the temperament. Cynthia, a maths teacher who brought up six children here once they had put a roof on the crumbling mansion, welcomes guests with her gently efficient manner into the grand Georgian rooms upstairs (book early for their high views to the almighty ocean and the purifying east wind) or the smaller inward-looking basement retreats with more African interest to admire and barred windows to the roots of the tangled garden and the 'Spite' Tower that stands there. All are pleasingly personal in their quiet fabrics, family antiques, good beds and bathrooms. In winter, the warm dark drawing room is superbly atmospheric, in summer the conservatory elf enlivens the green space, and breakfast is a feast all year round.

Price	€80-€100. Singles €60-€70. Children under 7, €20.
Rooms	4: 2 doubles, 2 twins/doubles.
Meals	Restaurants in Dalkey, 2km.
Closed	24-28 December.
Directions	From M50 southbound exit 16 for Dun Laoghaire onto dual carriageway; right at top of hill, immed. left into Killiney Avenue; at T-junc. right; next T-junc. left; next gate on left opp. white stones.

Ken & Cynthia McClenaghan
Killiney Hill Road, Killiney, Co. Dublin

Tel	+353 (0)1 285 1632
Fax	+353 (0)1 284 8504
Email	dlodge@indigo.ie
Web	www.druidlodge.com

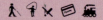

Self-catering   Co. Dublin

The Cottage

This perfect little cottage for combining fabulous hill walking (the Wicklow Way is two miles away), golf (12 courses within 5 miles: 'golf heaven') and Dublin's buzzy culture and night life (the station is five minutes' drive) was built in the 1800s – and looks brand new. It has all the finish and fittings of modern life yet is bright, cheerful and comfortable, just as a cottage should be, with incredible views of the sea from its five acres. Hilary, a warm, caring person, provides the basic foodstuffs any kitchen needs and all possible guidance to make your stay a complete success. Inside, the rooms are surprisingly light: the low windows are bigger than in most Irish cottages, the light bounces off the fresh flowers that always greet new arrivals from the solid-pine kitchen table, the open-plan living space has a pleasing rustic-pine simplicity. You could happily read all day here in dimmer weather. Bedrooms are equally easy and comfortable, with excellent new bedding, and there's a little private garden for balmy days. Don't miss the original Saturday-morning Irish country market in Kilternan. *Minimum stay three nights.*

Price	€735 per week.
Rooms	Cottage for 3.
Meals	Pub/restaurant within 5km.
Closed	Rarely.
Directions	Directions given on booking.

Hilary Knott
Ballybetagh Hill, Kilternan, Co. Dublin
Tel   +353 (0)86 846 2450
Email   ballybetaghhill@eircom.net

Entry 174   Map 5

Co. Dublin   Hotel

Redbank House & Restaurant

Terry McCoy, a true Irish original with an infectious sense of humour and a love of cooking, has built an excellent reputation for food and service. His guest house in charming Skerries, converted from an old bank, is just as unpretentiously good. Hotel-style rooms with old-look furniture, classic colour schemes and all the mod cons are split between the Old Bank House, next to the restaurant, and an extension. There's a small lounge with a fire but it is the restaurant that is the mainstay of this place. (The old safe complete with original vault door is now a well-stocked wine cellar, its bright walls making up for the lack of natural light.) Terry sources fresh fish from the harbour, Dublin Bay prawns and, more unusually, razorfish, whose long fluted shells are collected from local beaches. Be seduced by velvety soups, sizzling mushrooms, hearty breads; the long Sunday lunches are legendary. Leave the car at home – you really don't need it. Take a train to Dublin for the day, play some great golf, or come for one last fabulous meal before leaving.
Dublin airport is a 20-minute drive.

Price	€120–€140. Singles €60–€80.
Rooms	18: 12 doubles, 4 twins, 2 family.
Meals	Dinner from €50, 6.30pm. Wine from €24. Sunday lunch €33.
Closed	Never.
Directions	From Dublin N1. Follow signs for Skerries; under bridge, 1st left, continue. Church St on right opp. AIB. No. 6 has its own bell.

Terry McCoy
6 & 7 Church Street, Skerries, Fingal, Co. Dublin

Tel	+353 (0)1 849 1005
Fax	+353 (0)1 849 1598
Email	info@redbank.ie
Web	www.redbank.ie

Entry 175   Map 5

B&B   Co. Kildare

Martinstown House *been to lunch here!*

Worth any number of missed turns! A neo-gothic flight of fancy unlike any other, a *cottage orné*, no less, sitting grandly on an immaculate green sward, reigned over by tall trees. Roisin's dinners are proper country-house style at one big table with silver cutlery and cut glass; fruit, vegetables and flowers are mainly from the walled garden. At dinner you'll meet Edward, a lover of good food and wine, who adores entertaining and is a fountain of knowledge about the history of the house. The pastorals and pillars mural in the hall is riveting; the drawing room, twice as high as the rest of the ground floor, garlands galore, good furniture, is staggering – a room fit for a king; the Blue Room bathroom blows you away: it's covered in clouds. The beautiful bedrooms are country-house and peacefully TV-free, the style and elegance remain comfortably informal, the fires are lit, the garden provokes the same admiration. A perfect mix of old-fashioned hospitality, modern comfort, and a working farm nearby. *Horse racing locally. Unsuitable for young children.*

Price	€180–€240. Singles €115–€140.
Rooms	4: 1 double, 1 twin/double; 1 double, 1 twin, both with separate bathroom.
Meals	Dinner €55. Wine from €30. By arrangement. Restaurants 4km–5km.
Closed	Christmas.
Directions	From Dublin N7 south onto M7/M9; 1st exit for Athy onto N78 1.5km; right for Martinstown 2.5km; left at sign 1km; entrance on left.

Edward & Roisin Booth
The Curragh, Kildare, Co. Kildare

Tel	+353 (0)45 441269
Fax	+353 (0)45 441208
Email	info@martinstownhouse.com
Web	www.martinstownhouse.com

Entry 176   Map 5

Co. Kildare

B&B

Griesemount

Carolyn and her handsome Georgian house mirror each other: adventurous and entertaining. There is nothing trendy or super-stylish here, she is not afraid to mix Robert's beautiful Irish antiques with her African prints and furniture, prizes from an earlier life in Zimbabwe. The draped and canopied four-poster bed is striking, with echoes of the Princess and the Pea: guests ask to take it home, once they've dragged themselves out of the book-stocked bathroom. The Topiary Room is named after its topiaried wallpapers in soft green and yellow and the bathroom is concealed behind double doors; the twin has a touch of China. Also, a well-lived-in drawing room with furniture crowded round the fireplace and views perfectly framed by tall windows: paddocks or old rooftops, the walled garden or the River Griese and its ruined mill. This is a treasure trove of stuff redolent of 'Out of Africa' or a Somerset Maughan story, grandly faded and interesting; Carolyn has created a cacophony of memorabilia that is, overall, charming. She and Robert are entertaining company and you breakfast on freshly squeezed orange juice and the tastiest local produce.

Price	€80-€140. Singles from €50.
Rooms	3: 1 double, 1 four-poster; 1 twin with separate bathroom.
Meals	Dinner €25-€30, on request.
Closed	Rarely.
Directions	From Dublin N7 off M50 for Naas 32km; N9 for Carlow 19km. After Texaco garage right for Ballitore; left in village 1.5km past mill, over bridge; 3-storey yellow house, no sign at gate.

Robert & Carolyn Ashe
Ballitore, Co. Kildare

Tel	+353 (0)59 862 3158
Fax	+353 (0)59 914 0687
Email	griesemount@eircom.net

Entry 177 Map 5

B&B   Co. Kildare

Coursetown House

You could talk natural history and plants for hours with both Iris and Jim: she's a plantsman whose passion is gardening, he's an agricultural scientist – lovely, real, eco-friendly people. Their early Victorian farmhouse stands in one of the best-tended gardens in Ireland, full of colour, texture and, most important of all, scent; just smell those old-fashioned roses. Jim has a library of natural history books and grows crops on 270 acres, working closely with agri-researchers from University College Dublin. From the front bedrooms the woodland garden bursts into life in the spring. Well-sprung mattresses, electric blankets, crisp linen and luxurious pillows ensure the soundest sleep; soft towels and classy smellies lie in wait in all the bathrooms. From the yellow-washed breakfast room you look over groomed lawn and teeming border; from the fully wheelchair-friendly ground-floor bedroom, too. Over a slice of delicious homemade cake, you can ask about the sea bean or the huge whale bones in the yard. Engaging company and a great example of Irish hospitality. *Children over eight welcome.*

Price	€130. Singles €80.
Rooms	4: 2 doubles, 2 twins/doubles. Extra bath.
Meals	Restaurants in Athy, 3km.
Closed	Mid-November to mid-March.
Directions	From N78 at Athy, or N80 at Stradbally onto R428. 3km from Athy & 9.5km from Stradbally, signposted.

| | Jim & Iris Fox
Stradbally Road, Athy, Co. Kildare |
|---|---|
| Tel | +353 (0)59 863 1101 |
| Fax | +353 (0)59 863 2740 |
| Web | www.coursetown.com |

Entry 178   Map 4

Co. Kilkenny

B&B

Butler House

A high-class Russian-doll experience: through a rather unexciting façade you enter what looks like a grand country house built on the estate of a medieval castle. Next morning, you walk through superb formal gardens to the estate's refurbished stables for breakfast – then step out into the heart of an historic city. Those stables now house the Kilkenny Design Centre which masterminded the 1970s renovation of Butler House. Originally home to the Earls of Ormonde, it is now owned by the Kilkenny Civic Trust. Grandeur is all about you: those fluted columns, high ceilings, fabulous plasterwork and floods of light that the Georgians loved so much, none of it spoilt by frills or curlicues. Furniture in the big high bedrooms (the four best overlook the gardens) is sleekly, discreetly modern, fabrics are understatedly stylish, muted colours are enhanced by the occasional deep-hued cushion or good-looking rug. A plushness that will make you feel distinguished and exclusive. Gabrielle Hickey is a most attentive host and her staff are both friendly and efficient. *They also do seminars & company events.*

Price	€120-€220. Singles €80-€155.
Rooms	13: 12 twins/doubles, 1 suite.
Meals	Restaurants within walking distance.
Closed	Christmas week.
Directions	From Dublin N10 into Kilkenny; cross river, over High Street & Parade crossroads, hotel on left.

Gabrielle Hickey
16 Patrick Street, Kilkenny,
Co. Kilkenny
Tel   +353 (0)56 772 2828
Fax   +353 (0)56 776 5626
Email   res@butler.ie
Web   www.butler.ie

Entry 179   Map 8

B&B & Self-catering Co. Kilkenny

Blanchville House

Monica and Tim found trees growing inside this big Georgian farmhouse in 1970 but kept the wallpapers in the drawing room, the intricate plasterwork, the golden pelmets – all superb. They are practical people, Tim a shy and busy farmer, Monica a perfect host who generates an atmosphere of relaxed sophistication that you won't forget. Big traditional bedrooms with thick carpets and wonderful leap-onto half-testers are less grand, bathrooms are old-fashioned, mattresses are deeply comfortable, the enamelled taps warrant a photograph and the pastoral views belong in an oil painting. There are two apartments in the magnificent stone stables, sharing the carriage yard set up with tables and barbecue. And you can always wander over to the main house for a slap-up Irish – served beautifully off white linen – if you're tired of your own boiled egg. Monica cannot bear the thought that guests might feel neglected: she looks after you with natural, unfussy ease, her food is delicious, and she runs a holistic centre here, too. Blanchville is a place you'll remember, and there's masses to do in sweet Kilkenny.

Price	€120-€130. Singles €75-€85. Houses €350-€650 per week.
Rooms	4 + 3: 3 doubles, 1 twin. Cottage for 3-4; 2 Coach House apts for 5-6.
Meals	Dinner €45. By arrangement only.
Closed	November-February.
Directions	From Kilkenny N10 for Carlow/Dublin; 1st right, 1km after Pike Inn. Follow signs for Dunbell 4km. Left at x-roads. 1.5km, first large stone entrance on left.

Monica & Tim Phelan
Dunbell, Maddoxtown, Co. Kilkenny

Tel	+353 (0)56 772 7197
Fax	+353 (0)56 772 7636
Email	mail@blanchville.ie
Web	www.blanchville.ie

Entry 180 Map 8

Co. Kilkenny   B&B

Lawcus Farm Guesthouse

Leave the lane, drop down to the end of the track and find the King's River pottering along at the bottom. Woodlands rise on the far bank, as do some modern houses, but fields encircle you, chickens and ducks meander. A smooth arc of stone on the river bed creates a small weir and a heron fishes here most mornings. So can you – Mark bought Lawcus for its exceptional fishing – or follow the river, looking out for otters, badgers, foxes, leaping salmon, kingfishers, swans and ducks – but no tourists. Mark has found his slice of heaven, Dutchman Robin and Anne-Marie add to the generous, boho feel, pack you off on local adventures (working potters and watermills, the Augustinian monastery at Kells), even cook your wild trout for breakfast if you've been lucky. Mark renovated this 200-year-old cottage single-handedly, adding a wing, a conservatory/kitchen, a water garden. Rough hewn stone walls and vast open fire make a rustic foil for red velour, fancy shades and the odd prancing gilt horse. Sit out on the planked terrace with a beer, picnic by the river, have a barbecue – or dine in charming Kilkenny.

Price	€100. €80 singles.
Rooms	5: 3 doubles, 2 family.
Meals	Pub 1km.
Closed	Rarely.
Directions	From Kilkenny N10 south to Stonyford. Enter village & immed. right for Kells; house signposted right down lane at top of hill.

Mark Fisher
Kells, Stonyford, Co. Kilkenny

Tel	+353 (0)56 772 8949
Email	info@lawcusfarmguesthouse.com
Web	www.lawcusfarmguesthouse.com

B&B Co. Kilkenny

Ballaghtobin

Happy Americans follow their nose to Ballaghtobin, and no wonder: it's a beacon of contented hospitality amid the lush pastures of County Kilkenny. Catherine, warm and efficient, and Mickey, relaxed and funny, are renowned for their entertaining: be it friends, colleagues or guests, everyone is treated with the same easy-going generosity. Mickey farms 450 acres, growing cereals and the Noble Fir commercially. In his spare time, he competes in classic car rallies: ask to meet the prized automobiles. Catherine is also a doer, full of energy and ideas, the kind of person who puts you in a good mood. Inside the elegant Georgian house garnished with creeper are stylish colours and lots of sofas, period furniture and china they've been collecting since they got married. Gorgeous bedrooms are all done with taste and luxurious country-house style: fabrics chosen for subtle matching, beautiful beds, the best linen and spoiling extras. Walk on immaculate lawns surrounded by trees full of song; play tennis, wander off down the lane. It's all authentic, totally relaxed and brilliant value.

Price	€100. Singles €55. (5% extra if paying by credit card.)	
Rooms	3: 1 double, 1 twin/double, 1 family.	
Meals	Pub 6 miles.	
Closed	November-February.	
Directions	From main x-roads in Callan, take road signed Mill Street; cont. for 5km, passing Callan Golf Club on left. At end of straight road, sharp bend to left. 0.5km Y-junction, bear left. 0.5km on left, grand stone gates.	

Catherine & Mickey Gabbett
Callan, Co. Kilkenny

Tel	+353 (0)56 772 5227
Fax	+353 (0)56 772 5712
Email	catherine@ballaghtobin.com
Web	www.ballaghtobin.com

Travel Club Offer. See page 266.

Entry 182 Map 8

Co. Kilkenny

Self-catering

Croan Cottages

Discover beautiful Kilkenny from your own holiday cottage on this ten-acre estate; you are surrounded by stunning walking trails, ancient monasteries, lush forests. The little clutch of whitewashed cottages all face inwards in a mature garden and you find all you need inside. Downstairs is open plan in pine and in country-cottage style, there are comfy chairs and wood-burners in the sitting rooms, good beds, floral curtains and straightforward pine furniture in the bedrooms – no surprises on the design front but all is squeaky clean and the views from each window are tranquil and green. Kitchens have tiled flooring, all mod cons and plenty of space for rustling up meals, bathrooms have a mix of baths and showers. Each cottage has its own patio area and all are cleverly built so that one overlooks nothing but cherry trees. Families will love it here, with the neat farm to stroll through and pigs to pat, chickens, goats and spring lambs to admire. There's great fishing and golf on the doorstep, and a shed to store your gear, so no excuse to be bored. Home-cooked meals can be delivered to the door.

Travel Club Offer. See page 266.

Price	€395-€725 per week.
Rooms	5 cottages: 2 for 4, 3 for 6.
Meals	Dinner, 2 courses, €66-€120 (min. 4). Wine €10.
Closed	Never.
Directions	Cottages are signed off the R699 between Dunamaggan & Knocktopher in South Kilkenny.

Mr Francis Nesbitt
Dunamaggan, Co. Kilkenny

Tel	+353 (0)56 776 6868
Fax	+353 (0)56 776 6868
Email	info@croancottages.com
Web	www.croancottages.com

Entry 183   Map 8

B&B & Self-catering   Co. Kilkenny

Ballyduff House

Wander the bank, feed the swans or cast a rod for leaping trout and salmon: Ballyduff is B&B heaven. The gentle curved drive, the graceful, spaceful Georgian architecture fringed with wisteria, the big lawn surrounded by noble trees. Ring the bell: Brede will come and wrap you in lively smiles. This human dynamo runs the show single-handedly, plus two children, several hens, 240 acres of farmland, and a pony club. She has genuine warmth, possibly the product of ten years in the restaurant business in America, while the house is the epitome of Anglo-Irish refinement with legions of Solyfloods in view, Regency furniture, Venetian glass, the odd Napoleonic teddy. The library is a sort of aristocratic rumpus room with ancient tomes in the four corners and comfy lived-in sofas – "just the place to kick back in," she says. Lovely bedrooms are all generously big and different with beautiful antiques, two are prettily cottagey (one with a little vaulted bathroom), two are grander with views of the river Nore flowing widely at the bottom of the garden. A rare, relaxed, very happy place. *Whole house available.*

Price	€100. Singles €50.
Rooms	4: 1 double, 1 twin; 1 double, 1 twin both with separate bath.
Meals	Restaurants in Thomastown 6km.
Closed	November-February.
Directions	From Thomastown R700 for New Ross 5km. After crossing Brownsbarn Bridge take hard right. After 2km take right on x-road. Entrance on right after 200m: white gates, no sign.

	Brede Thomas
	Thomastown, Co. Kilkenny
Tel	+353 (0)56 775 8488
Email	ballydhouse@eircom.net
Web	www.ballyduffhouse.com

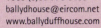

Entry 184 Map 8

Co. Kilkenny

B&B

Ballyogan House

Robert and Fran live beside the beautiful stretch of the River Barrow that cast its spell on them many years ago. They waited 25 years to live there but they're making up for it now and want you to enjoy their good fortune, too. Hidden down a narrow lane just outside the tongue-twisting town of Graiguenamanagh ('demesne of the monks'), Ballyogan looks over the river to the Blackstairs Mountains. Built by the Joyce family around 1830, it was 'the Joyce house' until the last in the line, a local vet, died in 1998. Redecorated throughout with conservative good taste, the whole place feels at ease. Bedrooms are comfortable, Lilac the prettiest. The thick tick-tock of the grandfather clock sets a genteel pace. Walk past the well-used croquet lawn down a wooded path, with cats and hens in tow, to where their boat, *La Brouette* ('wheelbarrow'), is moored. Robert may take you on a gentle picnic cruise, just as he and Fran first did in 1973. Fran serves hearty home-cooked food, the large garden delivering lots of produce, even melons, and Robert knows a properly authentic Irish pub for afters.

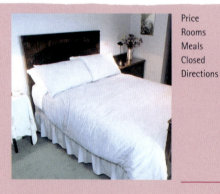

Price	€96–€110. Singles €58–€65.
Rooms	4: 1 double, 2 twins, 1 family.
Meals	Dinner €35–€45. By arrangement.
Closed	November–March.
Directions	From Graiguenamanagh R705 for New Ross 4km; sharp left down lane, signposted.

Robert & Fran Durie
New Ross Road, Graiguenamanagh,
Co. Kilkenny
Tel   +353 (0)59 972 5969
Email   info@ballyoganhouse.com
Web   www.ballyoganhouse.com

Hotel & Self-catering   Co. Laois

Roundwood House

Frank has a dry chuckle that makes you feel he knows all the jokes Ireland has ever told. He and Rosemarie are thoughtful, lovely people, as relaxed as the dogs that doze outside, and have endless time for visitors. Which doesn't mean they neglect the cooking: Roundwood's reputation for good food and wine is reliable and deserved. That supreme doll's house Palladian façade, built by Quakers in 1680, hides a charming, unpretentious family house which the Kennans have loved and lived in for 25 years. There are griddle scones for breakfast and books abound... botanical, philosophical, musical (Rosemary plays the harp). Elegance salutes you in the building's fabric, old family portraits in the hall, old oils in the drawing room – so what matter a few cracks or some worn upholstery? The beauiful rooms in the main house are big, bright and leap with colour, the four in the scented herb-garden courtyard, one a four-poster, are newly dressed in rush matting and all-white bedcovers. Dine with your amusing, well-informed hosts by the fire in the cosy dining room. You won't regret or forget a single human moment.

Price	€160-€180. Singles €105-€115. Cottages €280-€500 per week.
Rooms	10 + 3: 5 doubles, 2 twins, 3 family rooms. 3 cottages for 2-7.
Meals	Supper €35 (Sun/Mon). Dinner, 5 courses, €50 (Tues-Sat). Wine from €16.50.
Closed	Christmas.
Directions	From Dublin M7/N7 to Mountrath; right R440 for Birr & Slieve Bloom Mountains 5km; signpost & gate on left.

Frank & Rosemarie Kennan
Mountrath, Co. Laois
Tel +353 (0)57 873 2120
Fax +353 (0)57 873 2711
Email roundwood@eircom.net
Web www.roundwoodhouse.com

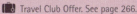 Travel Club Offer. See page 266.

Entry 186   Map 4

Co. Laois

B&B & Self-catering

Ballaghmore Manor House & Castle

Grace by name, graceful by nature, grand fun. An endlessly fascinating fount of Irish history, Grace will hold you spellbound with the story of Ballaghmore, and more. She has put a lifetime into this extraordinary house, bought as a ruin "last lived in by the King of Ossory", and the 15th-century tower castle in its back garden which you can rent for a medieval experience week. Grace relates the histories with a scholar's enthusiasm while making absolutely sure you are looked after. A gilder and gallery owner before moving here to restore the house and castle, she is one special, unusual lady, and her daughter Sorrel breeds Connemara ponies on the manor's 30 acres. Luxurious bed chambers are scattered in vast spaces – exposed stones and beams, heavy wooden doors, gothic arches; the four-poster room is glorious. Ballaghmore, off the main Dublin-Limerick road, is surrounded by golf courses, riding, fishing and boating, and there's swimming in the lake for the hardy. The dining hall is magnificent, with a great fireplace and seating for 35; the smoked salmon and scrambled egg breakfasts are peerless.

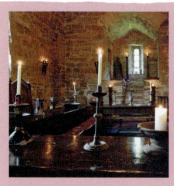

Price	From €120. Singles from €60. The Castle €2,000 per week.
Rooms	3 + 1: 1 twin, 1 four-poster; 1 family suite with separate bath. Castle for 10-20.
Meals	Restaurants 1.6km.
Closed	Rarely.
Directions	From Dublin N7 for Limerick between Borris-in-Ossory and Roscrea. House signed after 1km; entrance on right.

Travel Club Offer. See page 266.

Grace Pym
Borris-in-Ossory, Co. Laois
Tel   +353 (0)50 521453
Email gracepym@eircom.net
Web   www.castleballaghmore.com

Entry 187   Map 4

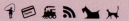

B&B Co. Longford

Viewmount House

Beryl and James have spent the past decade restoring this house, built in the 1750s. Now, unstoppable enthusiasts that they are, they are converting the old coach house into a small, refined restaurant. James gave up pedestrian accountancy to devote himself full-time to the house and grounds and he rejoices in realising his dream of running a restaurant (with a professional chef, of course). Young and eager to please, they have done the guest wing with flair and lots of colour. The bannistered staircase climbs past warm red walls to the fine green library and excellent bedrooms with a good mix of old furniture, big antique beds, wooden floors, woven rugs and garden views. Now there's a new wing of two-storey suites: solid mahogany beds downstairs, extra beds up – perfect for families. Breakfast is served in a stunning blue vaulted dining room. The Kearneys are a sincere, friendly couple who laugh easily and plan endlessly; James is working on an ambitious Japanese garden, too: try out his grand seated swing. An ideal staging post for Mayo and Donegal, and do stop by Ardagh village before you go.

Price	€110–€160.
Rooms	11: 3 doubles, 1 twin, 1 suite. Wing: 6 family suites for 3-4.
Meals	Dinner around €50. Wine from €20.
Closed	Rarely.
Directions	In Longford R393 for Ardagh 1km; right up sliproad following signs to house; entrance 200m on right.

Beryl & James Kearney
Dublin Road, Longford, Co. Longford

Tel	+353 (0)43 334 1919
Fax	+353 (0)43 334 2906
Email	viewmt@iol.ie
Web	www.viewmounthouse.com

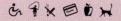

Co. Louth   Hotel

Ghan House

Enter the low, beamed hall with its blazing log fire – and know 18th-century Ghan House for the much-loved family inn that it is. Yet Joyce, who started her cookery courses here, and son Paul who is taking over (he's a honey), give more than just love: attention to detail is paramount. Food is important, too, so do book dinner. Enclosed within the ancient walls of Carlingford, probably the best-preserved medieval town in Ireland, the house looks over the pond, the road and Carlingford Lough to the distant Mourne Mountains. Some guests prefer a room in the creaky timeworn old house, others the peace and quiet of the new annexe. There are arched doorways, mouldings, old-style velvet with tassels, proper bathrooms – everything is impeccably done, everywhere you find thick wool carpets, family antiques, personal bits, a sense of deep comfort, plus books in the cosy little sitting room. The Carrolls know and enjoy what they are doing and are genuinely friendly with it. You won't be short of things to do, either. Restaurants, pubs, watersports, hill-walking or the simple pleasure of sitting by a turf fire.

Price	€190–€250. Singles from €85.
Rooms	12: 11 twins/doubles, 1 single.
Meals	Dinner €30; 5-course menu €55. Wine from €20. Book ahead. Restaurants within walking distance.
Closed	Christmas & New Year.
Directions	From Dublin N1 north 85km; junction 18 signed Carlingford. House 1st on left entering village, 10m after 50kmph sign.

Paul & Joyce Carroll
Carlingford, Co. Louth

Tel	+353 (0)42 937 3682
Fax	+353 (0)42 937 3772
Email	info@ghanhouse.com
Web	www.ghanhouse.com

Entry 189   Map 2 & 5

Self-catering   Co. Meath

The Cottages

Once through the 'village gate' you are secluded, safe in magical surroundings; the beautiful organic flower gardens wind through the thatched hamlet and you can walk along the spreading beach to pubs and restaurants. Liz's family has been letting cottages beside this safe seven-mile sandy beach since 1908 and her warm Irish welcome, with hot scones from the oven and homemade jam, proves she inherited the hospitality gene. She and Roger have impeccably refurbished the cottages, making them state-of-the-art practical, dressing them in oak and pine. With their quilted bedcovers on excellent beds, modern bathrooms with underfloor heating, double ended baths and power showers, CD and DVD players, local art and pottery, comfy sofas and fully-fitted kitchens, everything is just so: you will surely be content. All you can hear is the sea. There's even a thatched Wendy house for children, a barbecue, a gourmet farm shop at the gate, those head-clearing beach walks. The best antidote to city madness, 20 minutes from Dublin Airport. *Min. stay three nights.*

Price	€980–€2,900 per week. €70 pppn. 3-night break €420–€1,250.
Rooms	6 cottages: 2 for 2; 2 for 4; 1 for 5; 1 for 6.
Meals	Restaurants in Bettystown.
Closed	Rarely.
Directions	Directions given on booking. Full details on website. 20 minutes from Dublin airport.

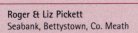
Travel Club Offer. See page 266.

Roger & Liz Pickett
Seabank, Bettystown, Co. Meath
Tel   +353 (0)41 982 8104
Fax   +353 (0)41 982 7955
Email info@cottages-ireland.com
Web   www.cottages-ireland.com

Entry 190   Map 5

Co. Meath

B&B

Annesbrook

Such a quiet, out of the way feel. Modernity has passed Annesbrook by, which is part of its appeal. A vast banqueting hall was added for George IV's visit in 1812; Voltaire and Shakespeare eye each other across the hall. This slightly eccentric, slightly faded Georgian house has fine proportions and masses of space: it would be a super place for small groups travelling together, or a big family. Kate is a great ambassador for the house, a thoughtful, calmly relaxed host who grows her own fruits and veg, keeps hens, makes bread. Flop in soft sofas round a carved marble fireplace beneath a lofty turquoise ceiling, lose yourself in one of the books, forget TV (there is none!). Works by contemporary Irish painters, including Kate's daughter, crowd the walls as you make your way down corridors and landings. Bedrooms are enormous, uncluttered, full of light, one with a terrific German Art Nouveau sleigh bed. Those at the front have the gorgeous view, the others look onto a courtyard with an old and rare meat safe. Ideal for the historic Boyne Valley – and the bus to Dublin passes the front gate.

Price	€112. Singles €66.
Rooms	5: 1 double, 2 twins, 2 family.
Meals	Restaurant in Duleek.
Closed	April-September. Groups by arrangement in winter.
Directions	From Dublin N2 for Derry. Right onto R152 for Drogheda & Duleek. Entrance 7km on left.

Kate Sweetman
Duleek, Co. Meath

Tel	+353 (0)41 982 3293
Email	sweetman@annesbrook.com
Web	www.annesbrook.com

Entry 191   Map 5

B&B & Self-catering   Co. Meath

Ballymagarvey Village

The 18th-century house has a round battlemented tower, no pomposity, oodles of charm and a flax-mill village behind, all in cut stone, all superbly, sensitively restored. With Vincent's energy and vision and the eye of a talented designer, the house has become an intimate, opulent country-house hotel whose rich warmth will wrap you in silks, velvets and brocades falling to ripe walnut-coloured floors or thick pale carpet in swathes of soft gold and orange, old rose and burgundy. The furniture is a stylish mix of old and new, Irish and continental, lampshades are feathered and beaded, there's nothing plain anywhere – and ten lovely, luxurious bedrooms. A fine conservatory growing Mediterranean fruits and vines opens onto the walled garden, and you can walk the 100-acre grounds and out into the forest. The mill buildings, coach houses and two-storey workers' houses round the tranquil 'village square' are now beautifully converted self-catering cottages but "tenants" can eat out… on the spot. Just the place for a small wedding or your special party.

Price	€80-€120.
	Cottages €60-€80 p.p. per night.
Rooms	10 + 8: 10 twins/doubles.
	8 cottages for 4-8.
Meals	Pub & restaurant on the premises
	(avail. April 2009). Dinner €20-€50.
	Lunch €5-€20.
Closed	Rarely.
Directions	M50 Exit 3 at Fingals for N2
	Ashbourne. Follow N2 to Marriot
	Hotel r'about. Continue towards Slane
	9 miles. Outside Balrath Cross, white
	gates to Ballymagarvey on left.

	Vincent Callan
	Ballymagarvey Village, Balrath, Navan,
	Co. Meath
Tel	+353 (0)41 982 1450
Fax	+353 (0)41 982 1410
Email	vincent@bmvillage.ie
Web	www.bmvillage.ie

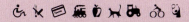

Entry 192   Map 5

Co. Meath   B&B & Self-catering

Ballinakill House

The big solid old house is surrounded by well-tended grounds – Mary is a keen gardener. She enjoys running B&B too and has redecorated top to toe (much appreciated by Ryder Cup fans) so all is fresh and squeaky clean. There's a yellow striped drawing room for guests in which a fire is lit every night, and two pretty bedrooms with painted brass bedheads and lovely country views. A very charming bathroom in which a white slipper bath takes centre stage lies at the end of the hall; the twin has an en suite shower. These were the daughters' rooms – now the daughters have flown and the cat and the dog remain. The cat is the boss and the dog fears the cat but any pets you may bring will be welcomed here; children too. With her background in tourism Mary is a font of all knowledge – on Trim Castle and neolithic chambers, on golf courses and where to fish, and grand 18th-century estates. And the bus gets you to Dublin in one hour. Breakfasts are lovely but if you seek independence there's a spic and span, one-storey cottage in its very own walled garden. *Minimum stay three nights.*

Travel Club Offer. See page 266.

Price	€100. Cottage €400-€500 per week.
Rooms	2 + 1: 1 twin; 1 double with separate bath. Cottage for 4.
Meals	Dinner €35, by arrangement. Pub/restaurant 5km.
Closed	December-March.
Directions	From Dublin N4 to Enfield. Straight over roundabout at end of town. 1st right up small road, signed Rathcore. 2.5 miles on left.

Mary O'Malley
Enfield, Co. Meath
Tel   +353 (0)46 954 1835
Email ballyk2@iolfree.ie
Web   www.ballinakillmews.com

Self-catering   Co. Meath

Clonleason Gate Lodge

Clonleason sets the standard for self-catering in Ireland. Sinead has converted the Georgian lodge into the dandiest cottage that indulges the senses and yet, despite the luxury and attention to detail, never feels overly perfect: roses meet honeysuckle, country-house elegance meets cosy cottage. It lies secluded among trees at the end of her drive with only the odd tractor to interrupt the peace. You enter by the kitchen: hand-printed wallpaper, a Welsh dresser storing patterned Portmeirion china, red deal cupboards distressed to create a limewash effect, oven, dishwasher, microwave and all the basics generously provided. Left is the sitting room: books, paintings and a comfy cream sofa in front of an open fire – so civilised. The sabre is purely for decoration. French doors open onto a terrace and a beautiful secret garden that leads to a small stream and the wild fields. The bedroom has lots of storage, fresh white linen on an excellent bed, coir matting and a pretty shower room. If you can drag yourself away, there are lovely river walks. Enchanting. *Linen, logs & turf included.*

Price	€300-€480 per week, plus electricity & heating.
Rooms	Lodge for 2 (1 double, 1 shower).
Meals	Restaurants in Fordstown.
Closed	Christmas.
Directions	From Athboy R154 for 3 miles. Turn right signed Fordstown. Second house on right.

Sinead Connelly
Fordstown, Co. Meath

Tel	+353 (0)46 943 4111
Fax	+353 (0)46 943 4111
Email	clonleason@eircom.net
Web	www.clonleason.com

Entry 194   Map 5

Co. Meath   Self-catering

Decoy Country Cottages

Less than two miles off the main Dublin/Navan road, but all is peaceful, quiet and with a suburban feel. Decoy House has a set of black iron gates and sits high overlooking the countryside. Sweep straight in to a stable yard and here are the converted cottages, all with stable doors, neat paths and pretty pots on the gravel. All eight cottages are decorated in the same way: Travertine marble tiles or light oak flooring, pale ginger walls, plenty of space, light and views. Beds are well dressed with pillows and cushions, kitchens boast black polished granite work tops, wood-burning stoves and geothermal underfloor heating will keep you toasty even on the chilliest of days. Perfect for families is the den, a general sitting/games room for use by all, with games, TV, books and magazines, billiards; out the back door find a playground with barbecue, sandpit and garden furniture – a safe place for children to play while you have a workout in the gym or a bit of beauty therapy. You are in the famous Meath Boyne Valley with many important historical sites; excellent golf and fishing are nearby.

Price	€480-€1,680 per week.
Rooms	8 cottages. 1 for 8, 2 for 6, 1 for 5, 2 for 4, 1 for 4 + 2, 1 for 2.
Meals	Restaurants 6.5km.
Closed	Never.
Directions	Dublin road out of Navan. 4 miles; left at Garlow Cross (Tara Na Ri pub on right). 1.5 miles, signed left for Decoy Cottages.

Travel Club Offer. See page 266.

Mrs Paula Irwin
Garlow Cross, Navan, Co. Meath
Tel   +353 (0)46 902 6960
Fax   +353 (0)46 902 6961
Email   info@decoycountrycottages.ie

Entry 195   Map 5

B&B & Self-catering   Co. Meath

Tankardstown House

The treat begins with the wonderful high stone wall; then, beyond the decorative gates, a scene of stately beech trees, bluebells, pheasants and fresh-cut parkland unfurls... culminating in the great Cedar of Lebanon and a house that is simply and beautifully Georgian (with a delightful Victorian bustle at the rear). Stone lions greet you at the door but Patricia's welcome is decidedly warmer as she leads you into traditional public rooms dressed in contemporary style with modern wallpapers and lavish curtains; only decorum stops Patricia from draping herself in the fabric. Painted a deep red, the library holds a fine collection of children's books, inspired by four young daughters who have given their names to fabulous bedrooms, each one individually decorated; 'Lara' has a trendy brown scheme and custom-made beds of regal proportions. For night owls, a wicked treat of hot chocolate and cake can be plundered on the landing. Everywhere there is Conroy enterprise on display, and that includes the seven sophisticated self-catering cottages that open off a courtyard. Worth the splurge! *Spa & beauty treatments.*

Price	From €200. Cottages from €400 per night.	
Rooms	6 + 7: 2 doubles; 4 doubles sharing 2 baths. 7 cottages: 5 for 4, 2 for 2.	
Meals	Breakfast €20. Lunch from €35. Dinner from €65. By arrangement. Pub/restaurant 8km.	
Closed	Never.	
Directions	From Slane, road to Kells. Right at Slane Castle main gates, signed Tankardstown. Pass Slane Farm Hostel, take left fork. House 4km on right. Please ring bell for gates to open.	

Patricia Conroy
Slane, Co. Meath

Tel	+353 (0)41 982 4621
Fax	+353 (0)41 982 4622
Email	info@tankardstown.ie
Web	www.tankardstown.ie

Entry 196 Map 5

Co. Meath   B&B & Self-catering

Loughcrew House

Inspired by peerless views and their fabulous historic gardens down by Oliver Plunkett's church, Emily and Charlie are an artistic couple, bursting with non-stop creative and organising energy, and excellent company. As well as the B&B, Emily runs a gilding school in the beautiful Grecian-style yard and a family castle in Wales; Charlie designs, prints, engineers (the chip-fat generator...) and writes. This was the orangery: the mansion burned down, the victim of a priest's curse, it is said; bits of its grand entrance stand in classical ruin nearby. The Napers took over the derelict, sheep-run remains of the old family home and, with ingenuity, artistry and patience, created a house that oozes style and things from Emily's showroom – French furniture, gilded pineapples, small masked faces peering from pelmets. The 17th-century gardens now have a water feature, fairies in the grotto and a wooden coffee pavilion. Do explore their megalithic tombs, too. An exceptional experience in a stunning history-steeped place. They do weddings, of course – up to 100 people – and their annual opera season is a music-lover's must.

Price	€150. Singles €75. Full house rental €3,500 per week.
Rooms	8 + 1: 3 doubles, 3 twins, 2 singles, each with bathroom nearby. House sleeps 12-14.
Meals	Restaurants 6.4km.
Closed	Christmas.
Directions	From Kells R163 into R154 for Oldcastle 17.5km; ignore turn to Oldcastle, 3km until blue railings on left. Signed opp. gatehouse.

Emily Naper
Oldcastle, Co. Meath
Tel   +353 (0)49 854 1356
Email   info@loughcrew.com
Web   www.loughcrew.com

B&B   Co. Meath

Knockbrack Grange

The views here are hard to beat for beauty: this is the lovely heart of County Meath, with its gardens and historical treasures. Having lived all over the world, Kitty and Richard are happy to be home. Her effervescent enthusiasm will pick you up at the door and carry you into her love for Ireland, her family furniture and portraits and her B&B summers. She's an inspired cook, too, while Richard knows all the history. They have repainted and recurtained this friendly late-Georgian rectory, furnishing it with good pieces that have old charm and no arrogance. The library's picture windows may be 'out of period' but they capture wonderful views over the megalithic tombs at Loughcrew to perfection, and the yellow and white bedroom has the hugest dressing/ bathroom. Upstairs, rooms are their proper original shapes – one with a red four-poster, the other done in beautiful blue fabric from America – and as Kitty refuses to spoil them by putting in bathrooms the yellow cast-iron bath and clean fresh shower are across the landing. Leave time for the amazing multiple beech tree.

Price	€140. Singles €95.
Rooms	3: 1 four-poster; 1 double, 1 four-poster, each with separate bath.
Meals	Dinner €35. Wine €15.
Closed	October-May except by arrangement.
Directions	From Kells R163 for Oldcastle; after Ballinlough ignore sign to Oldcastle; 800m after Loughcrew gardens, house on right (beech trees, stone wall).

Kitty Kinsella-Bevan
Oldcastle, Co. Meath
Tel   +353 (0)49 854 1771
Email   kittybevan@eircom.net

Entry 198   Map 4

Co. Offaly   B&B

Brendan House

Bohemian eccentricity in the centre of Birr — a place of joy for creative spirits. Brendan House is a listed building that spans history and culture in one generous human brushstroke — poets, artists, musicians flock. It's comfy and quirky and sometimes Rosalind warms weary travellers with pink sloe vodka. Nepalese prayer flags flutter outside, fabulous masks enchant the corridors, art and antiques jostle. French, Tudor, Victorian bedrooms have canopy beds, reclining cushions and no telly. Shutters and sash windows are original, as is the amazing (shared) 19th-century bath, the second to be fitted in Birr, with its gaudy looks and Rosalind's loving restoration. Catch the sun in the small courtyard garden or snuggle up to the roaring fire in the drawing room. Derek, mountaineer, poet and accomplished walking guide, has a bushy red beard and is a dapper dresser. Rosalind the stage-setter, and writer, gives art classes; her father gives castle tours. All are engaging, unusual company and are doing their best to protect the planet. Breakfast, fulsome, hearty, local or organic, is totally memorable.

Price	€80–€90. Singles from €55.
Rooms	3: 1 double, 2 singles, all sharing bathroom. (Studio available.)
Meals	Dinner €45. Supper €20. Wine €12–€20. By arrangement (min. 2). Cream tea €15.
Closed	Rarely.
Directions	Arriving in Birr from Dublin, left at central square, down main street, then left by Market House Tavern. On right.

Travel Club Offer. See page 266.

Rosalind & Derek Fanning
Brendan Street, Birr, Co. Offaly
Tel   +353 (0)57 912 1818
Email   tinjugstudio1@eircom.net
Web   www.tinjugstudio.com

Ardmore House

Pretty Kinnitty marks the crossroads of Ireland: this is the heart of it all. And soon your walking books will be parked under the bench in the hall, in eager anticipation of the Slieve Blooms hills. So lovely are the walks, up hill and down dale (on a clear day you can see the highest point of every province from the top) that a Walking Festival is hosted in the village the first week of May. Christina will happily lend you maps, podcast, poles, prepare you a picnic, organise a guide. The clear light of the Irish heartland washes into her handsome 1840s house, and her rooms illustrate her calm take on life: a well-worked quilt here, an amazing carved bedend or a fine oval-mirrored wardrobe there. In the same vein, the house sits sure and square in its large plot of well-tended trees, shrubs and borders: space to sit out in summer. On cooler days, turf brings a warm aroma to the living room where breakfast flourishes just-baked sodabread, homemade preserves and prize-winning cheese. You are right on the edge of the village with two churches and two pubs; join Christina as she plays the Irish fiddle.

Price	€80–€90. Singles from €60.
Rooms	5: 1 twin, 2 doubles, 2 family rooms.
Meals	Choice in village.
Closed	Rarely.
Directions	From Dublin N7 towards Cork. Exit 15 for Mountmellick. Take R422 for Kinnitty. On right entering village.

Travel Club Offer. See page 266.

Christina Byrne
The Walk, Kinnitty, Birr, Co. Offaly
Tel +353 (0)57 913 7009
Email info@kinnitty.com
Web www.kinnitty.com

Entry 200 Map 4

Co. Westmeath   B&B

The Bastion

Old Athlone, an historic staging post between Dublin and Galway on the banks of the Shannon, is now the trendy 'culinary capital of the Midlands'. On the Left Bank, around King John's 13th-century castle, the houses are ancient, the narrow streets full of good restaurants and swinging pubs. *Sean's* is so old it's mentioned in the 9th-century Clonmacnoise Annals. At the Bastion, brothers Vinny and Anthony have turned the house above the family shops into a very special B&B that meanders from level to landing. Their slightly bohemian style is gentle and definitely 'green': space to recline, happy plants, an eclectic collection of original art, globetrotters' mementoes. The snug bedrooms, where apprentice tailors once lived, have a clean spartan elegance, crisp white linen, floorboards, oak dressing tables, hangers on hooks, designer lamps, modern art – impeccable. A healthily natural buffet breakfast, a welcome change from Irish Fry, is served in the colourful communal room over the street. Great fun, delightful easy people. Ask about boat trips to prehistoric Clonmacnoise, bog walks and nearby Lough Ree.

Price	€75-€90. Singles €45-€50.
Rooms	6: 2 doubles, 2 family; 1 double with separate bath. Annexe: 1 double studio.
Meals	Restaurants within walking distance.
Closed	Rarely.
Directions	From Dublin N6 for Galway to Athlone; follow signs to town centre; cross bridge to Left Bank, left round castle, follow street round, house 100m on right.

Vinny & Anthony McCay
2 Bastion Street, Athlone,
Co. Westmeath

Tel	+353 (0)90 649 4954
Fax	+353 (0)90 649 3648
Email	info@thebastion.net
Web	www.thebastion.net

Hotel   Co. Westmeath

Wineport Lodge

Step down from the quiet little road, through a strip of flourishing garden and onto the deck of a glorified boating club. Low-slung, weather-boarded Wineport Lodge is designed to be utterly discreet against the spreading lake – and a glorious spot for birds. A watery peace washes the gorgeous rooms and their balconies (only a couple miss the lake view). The décor shares the philosophy: solid pieces of real timber, gleaming white cotton, simple classy furniture by Jane's designer brother, all natural, respectful and yet contemporary, furnishings and fabrics as genuine as the timber. It's a lesson in "sober needn't be boring". An easy-going, efficient couple, Ray and Jane have firm good taste and show their knowledge of modern art in the public spaces where ceiling heights can bring a touch of drama. The harmony of this organic building is palpable against the unparallelled, changing waterscape. Swim if you're tough enough, boating can be organised, Feargal O'Donnell's cooking is said to be divine, a complimentary drink is waiting in your room. *Dublin Airport under 90 minutes.*

Price	€195–€295. Singles €145. Suites €325–€590. Half-board available.
Rooms	29: 24 twins/doubles, 1 family, 4 suites.
Meals	Dinner €75 or à la carte. Wine from €25. Snack lunch available for residents.
Closed	Christmas.
Directions	From Athlone ring-road N55 for Longford & Cavan 4km; entering Glasson village, left at the Dog & Duck, 1.5km on left.

Ray Byrne & Jane English
Glasson, Athlone, Co. Westmeath

Tel	+353 (0)90 643 9010
Fax	+353 (0)90 643 9033
Email	lodge@wineport.ie
Web	www.wineport.ie

Entry 202   Map 4

Co. Westmeath

Self-catering

Greenhills

On the edge of the rural village of Killucan sits this very pretty 1854 house and its bubbly, youthful owner. The area is well known for its lakes and the popular waterway from Dublin – the Royal Canal; horse racing is at Navan and Kilbeggan. By the house in the tub- and flower-strewn yard find a bright red door and The Stables: a hall with a kitchen nook with creamy flooring and an eating counter, a simple sitting room with manger and hay rack still intact, comfy leather sofas, family furniture and pictures, and a wood-burning stove. From here are two double bedrooms – one reached through the other – with good new mattresses dressed in bright pink tartan blankets. Limewashed stone walls create a plain and simple feel. Off the sitting room with its fresh flower arrangements on deep sills is a simple shower room with creamy wood panelling. The two-storey Loft, spacious, lovely and full of light, is on the other side of the yard, with a garden terrace at the back. Sweet peas, fruit trees and donkey flourish in the grounds; Nanny Quinn's pub on the canal serves breakfast, lunch and dinner.

Price	€300-€500 per week.
Rooms	Stables for 2-4. Loft for 2-4.
Meals	Pub 2-minute walk. Pubs/restaurants in Mullingar 8 miles.
Closed	Never.
Directions	From Dublin M4 to Kinnegad. Through Kinnegad, first right signed Raharney. Continue for 8 miles to Killucan. First left after Ennis Pub. 500yds house on right after Ivy Court.

Travel Club Offer. See page 266.

	Nicola & Kieran O'Malley Killucan, Co. Westmeath
Tel	+353 (0)44 937 4170
Email	nicolaomalley@gmail.com

Entry 203 Map 4

B&B   Co. Westmeath

Lough Owel Lodge

So often in Ireland you only need to turn off a main road to find yourself in beautiful countryside. Lough Owel Lodge is just off a dual carriageway north of Mullingar, yet you are deep enough in the country to forget the road is there. Nothing spoils the view from this nature-surrounded 1940s house. The open-plan sitting/dining room has full-length, timber-framed windows that seem to draw the outside in; in winter you can see writer J P Donleavy's house through the trees. There is nothing to spoil this view for miles. The Lodge's land stretches past terraced garden and tennis court to the lake below. Unusually shaped bedrooms are scrupulously clean, have patterned carpeting and family furniture; two have fine old beds. Walkers will appreciate the library of books on the region known as the 'Land of Lake and Legend' – fishing fans will know the name already. Trout fishing can be arranged with ghillies and boats, racquets are to hand for tennis. Aideen and Martin – he busy with his farm, she a competent painter and mother of teenagers – run a good-natured, unpretentious family home.

Price	€80. Singles €45-€50.
Rooms	5: 1 double, 1 twin, 2 four-posters, 1 family suite.
Meals	Restaurants 3km.
Closed	November-April. Off season by arrangement.
Directions	From Dublin N4 for 80km. Just past Mullingar, as lake comes into view, left at sign; 1km, entrance on right.

	Martin & Aideen Ginnell
	Cullion, Mullingar, Co. Westmeath
Tel	+353 (0)44 934 8714
Fax	+353 (0)86 324 6427
Email	aideen.ginnell@ireland.com
Web	www.loughowellodge.com

Entry 204   Map 4

Co. Westmeath   B&B

Mornington House

Seclusion here is absolute, ancient, untouched. The house has a four-part history which the O'Haras, whose family settled here in 1858, relate with verve: they love their old-style family seat and wonderful garden. A fine Afgan rug cheers up the landing off which old-fashioned, mostly large, bedrooms lie, with bright colours and bathrooms of character; views include the mighty solitary oak on the front lawn. A path has been mown through the meadow to Lough Derravaragh with Knock Eyon beyond. Downstairs, carpets fade as they approach long ranks of park-facing windows, the gleaming gold drawing-room wallpaper was put up in the 1800s (Warwick has no intention of changing it), velvet cushions are sprinkled over a variety of antique sofas and chairs and a huge potted lime tree in the dining room catches the sunlight in the morning. Warwick and Anne are genuinely dedicated hosts and produce delicious meals for the big candlelit table, growing much of the produce in the fabulous walled garden. Roses scent the air, dogs doze, wood pigeons coo.

Travel Club Offer. See page 266.

Price	€150. Singles from €95.
Rooms	5: 4 twins/doubles; 1 single with separate bathroom.
Meals	Dinner, 4 courses, €45. Wine €18-€36.
Closed	November-March.
Directions	From N4/Mullingar bypass R394 for Castlepollard 8km; left at Wood Pub in Crookedwood 2km; right at 1st junc. House 1.5km on right, down long drive.

Anne & Warwick O'Hara
Multyfarnham, Mullingar,
Co. Westmeath

Tel   +353 (0)44 937 2191
Fax   +353 (0)44 937 2338
Email stay@mornington.ie
Web   www.mornington.ie

Entry 205   Map 4

B&B   Co. Westmeath

Lough Bishop House

A wonderful smell of freshly baked scones on arrival: Helen's vitality is infectious. She breeds rare Irish Draught horses and loves cooking (preserves galore). Christopher, with equal enthusiasm, deals with myriad sheep, tends the pretty young orchard, the honey bees and the Irish Moiled cattle. Lough Bishop is a slice of quintessential Irish country life, including a view of the lake and the hills rolling round. The typical 19th-century, white-painted, red-tipped Irish farmhouse has a delightful courtyard and a chequered hall floor. Cosy rooms come in warm pinks, greens and yellows without an ounce of twee and some lovely old furniture. Everything is well loved and cared for, done with natural fabrics and a mix of styles that carry the Kellys' story. They share their super sitting room with you, friendly with its family-worn leather sofa, open fire and many books. Guest rooms are bright and inviting, there are interesting pictures to intrigue, no clutter to annoy and lovely views over the stable yard or the countryside to draw you out into the peace. Lough Bishop refreshes the spirit and warms the heart.

Price	€110. Singles €55-€65.
Rooms	3: 1 double, 1 single, 1 family.
Meals	Dinner €30. Book before noon.
Closed	18 December-2 January.
Directions	From Mullingar or Castlepollard take R394. At Whitehall church & school take narrow lane opposite school for 3km. Sign on gate on right.

Helen & Christopher Kelly
Derrynagarra, Collinstown,
Co. Westmeath
Tel   +353 (0)44 966 1313
Fax   +353 (0)44 966 1313
Email chkelly@eircom.net
Web   www.derrynagarra.com

Travel Club Offer. See page 266.

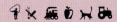

Entry 206   Map 4

Co. Wexford

B&B

Glendine Country House

Hide yourself away from the cares of the world. On a hill in 50 acres of private farmland, looking over the Barrow Estuary to the hills beyond, Glendine is a plush family home with a farm feel to it: scenic Jacob sheep, Highland cattle, Silka deer hang around for all to love. The 1830s house has grown and the four bedrooms in the extension are large with superb sea views. The King's Bay Suite has a fabulous bathroom, a Victorian repro bed and rich colours fit for… a king. Those warm colours, Victorian-style beds, glowing pitch-pine floors make all the rooms inviting. Relax in the drawing room where family photographs mix with antiques and comfy sofas await your collapse. Annie serves home-grown organic rhubarb, bread and scones, organic porridge and strawberries, and masses more – all part of her gourmet breakfast that will sustain you along the spectacular coastal walk to the Hook Peninsula. Award-winning restaurants and pubs abound – including the famous Dunbrody House Hotel – and you're near enough to Kilkenny, Wexford and Waterford for a day of exploring the wonderful south east.

Travel Club Offer. See page 266.

Price	€110–€140. Singles €70–€100.
Rooms	6: 2 doubles, 2 twins/doubles, 1 family, 1 suite.
Meals	Dinner from €40 Wed-Sat (min.10 people). Wine from €20. Hotel restaurant & pubs within walking distance.
Closed	Christmas.
Directions	From Rosslare N25 for Wexford 8km; left 1st r'bout; left 2nd r'bout R733 for Wellingtonbridge 32km. Entrance on right as road dips into Arthurstown.

Tom & Annie Crosbie
Arthurstown, Co. Wexford
Tel   +353 (0)51 389500
Fax   +353 (0)51 389677
Email   glendinehouse@eircom.net
Web   www.glendinehouse.com

Entry 207   Map 8

B&B & Self-catering   Co. Wexford

Kilmokea Country Manor & Gardens

With its incomparable heritage gardens and long history, Kilmokea is hard to fault. Mark and Emma could not be nicer: gracious, welcoming and so very helpful, they somehow find time to bring up three young children as well. Bedrooms, four in the main house, two in the converted courtyard suite, are in luxurious good taste: thick carpets, lovely beds, smart antiques, voluminous towels. In the evening guests meet over a drink and your hosts make sure everyone is introduced before sitting down in the formal Regency dining room. Cooked to order by the chef, whose speciality is seafood, many ingredients come from the organic walled kitchen garden, eggs from hens that graze the pretty apple orchard: integral parts of Kilmokea's chemical-free botanical treat. Breakfast is deliciously fresh and unusual, too. The gardens cover seven acres, peacocks strut by the Italian loggia, paths and bridges lead past a trout lake to a hide whence you can watch coastal birds swoop over the estuary. Plus the heated pool, gym, jacuzzi, sauna. Like staying in a five-star hotel owned by friends – quite remarkable. *David & Joan Price lived here.*

Price	€75-€300. Singles €75. Apts €750-€1,250 per week.
Rooms	6 + 2: 3 doubles, 1 four-poster, 1 family; 1 twin with separate shower. 2 apts: 1 for 2, 1 for 4-8.
Meals	Lunch €7-€25. Dinner €45-€55. Wine €20-€45.
Closed	Mid-November to January. (Self-catering open all year.)
Directions	From Waterford to Passage East; R733 north 2.5km; at sharp right bend, straight on for Great Island; left at T-junc. 2km to house.

Travel Club Offer. See page 266.

Mark & Emma Hewlett
Great Island, Campile, Co. Wexford

Tel   +353 (0)51 388109
Fax   +353 (0)51 388776
Email kilmokea@eircom.net
Web   www.kilmokea.com

Entry 208   Map 8

Co. Wexford

Self-catering

The Coach House

For years they had been looking for an old house to restore, with lovely big trees and a pasture for a herd. Dick and Susan found it here, high on the Hook Peninsula, where there's history in hatfuls and unpopulated beaches. The charming family with "a weakness for old ruins" live in the big house down the drive; the kettle is always on. Grounds and gardens (the flagged kitchen garden is being restored) flow into each other, song birds abound, a peacock hops onto the window sill when the TV is on… timelessness and tranquillity prevail. Enter the hall, off which the kitchen lies: be cheered by a fresh pine-and-gingham feel, a big family table, a dear little area for children's books and toys. The sitting room is solidly, old-fashionedly comfortable, with log fires for winter nights; the bedrooms, the best upstairs, are carpeted, sweetly furnished, airy and light. The bathrooms are spotless but 'no-frills' – bring your potions and lotions! This is a place for buckets and spades, wellies and rods (with a boiler room for drying them). Shop and pub are two miles, beaches not much further, monasteries abound.

Travel Club Offer. See page 266.

Price	€300-€550 per week.
Rooms	House for 6.
Meals	Pubs/restaurants 4km.
Closed	Never.
Directions	From New Ross, R733 south towards Campile; right for Great Island. 1st left then right, after 6th house.

Mrs Susan Devane
Fruit Hill, Campile, New Ross,
Co. Wexford
Tel   +353 (0)51 388694
Email   fruithill@gmail.com
Web   www.fruithillholidayhomes.com

Entry 209   Map 8

B&B   Co. Wexford

Healthfield Manor

As Irish and as eccentric as they come, Mayler and Loreto are warm, helpful, full of stories – and Healthfield is matchless. Built in 1820, it lies above the languid River Slaney. When Cromwell sacked Wexford in 1649 the people fled upriver to escape the plague and found an untainted well in a field: health field. You reach the house via a tunnel of overgrowth that winds uphill to a stunning view of the river and the towering house. Inside is an incredible mix of antique and kitsch; the ornately-framed oil painting of Princess Diana seems perfectly normal here, as do the dated floral wallpapers and fake flowers. Beds, breakfast and welcome are as huge as the old-fashioned rooms. Loreto is lovely, her style of B&B almost theatrical. Mayler, a bearded ex-shot-putter, farms the estate with ingenuity, selling eels to the Dutch, growing reed-beds for thatch – and creating a water garden in what was probably Ireland's first heated outdoor pool. The walled garden rambles past wild potting sheds, ancient vineries and a perfect fig tree. Utterly original and great fun. *Children over seven welcome.*

Price	€90. Singles €58.
Rooms	3: 1 family suite; 2 twins, each with separate bathroom.
Meals	Restaurants in Wexford, 3km.
Closed	Mid-November–Easter.
Directions	From north, N11 for Wexford; over River Slaney; right for Heritage Park; under r'way bridge, sharp right; follow river 3km. Entrance on right, signpost; up long drive.

Mayler & Loreto Colloton
Killurin, Co. Wexford

Tel	+353 (0)53 912 8253
Fax	+353 (0)53 912 8253
Web	www.healthfield.8k.com

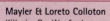 Travel Club Offer. See page 266.

Co. Wexford   B&B

Cuasnóg

Catríona has the warmest smile, the twinkliest eyes, an artistic temperament – and sings in two choirs. Musicians stay for the Opera Festival. Sociable and hugely caring of her guests, she cannot possibly let you leave for the early ferry without breakfast. Catríona's small 1930s house, inherited from her great-aunt, is a simple, comfortable, easy place to be. Breakfast is as organic as she can make it, the brown bread, scones and muffins (with home-grown raspberries) are her own, her herby vegetarian omelette is made with a friend's free-range eggs whose shells are then baked, crushed and returned whence they came – as hen food. She is a fanatical recycler. In the living room great-aunt's antique sideboard holds the packets of cereals, the Kachelofen wood-burning stove glows and there's a soft sofa, CD-player and books. Bedrooms are pine-simple, print-pretty, cottagey and intimate and have good new bathrooms with solar heated hot water. And you'll discover the fine modern kitchen – all stainless steel and fancy coffee maker! She is a lovely person. *Irish spoken.*

Price	€70-€100. Singles €40-€60.
Rooms	3: 2 doubles, 1 twin.
Meals	Restaurants within walking distance.
Closed	Rarely.
Directions	From Rosslare N25 to Wexford. House in town centre. Map provided on request.

Caitríona Ní Chatháin
St John's Road, Wexford, Co. Wexford
Tel   +353 (0)53 912 3637
Email   cuasnog@eircom.net
Web   www.cuasnog.com

B&B   Co. Wexford

Churchtown House

Although it looks like a small hotel, this is the Cody's family home and they create the mix exceptionally well. They have gradually added pieces onto the 300-year-old house, and introduced some plastic anodized windows, but the solidity of the old farmhouse remains. The giant cedar that rules the luxuriant lawns is pretty ancient too... benches are scattered throughout the grounds creating many delightful spots for tea, or a pre-dinner G&T. An atrium draws in the sunshine to reveal bright-coloured pristine rooms (not a speck of dust to be seen) while bedrooms vary greatly – bring a hottie in winter! Sherry before dinner is served in the airy garden room overlooking the courtyard. The Codys are relaxed, generous hosts, a delight to talk to: Austin and Patricia bring the whole place to life. Nothing is too much trouble: they will find a spot for your bike, your trailer, even your boat – just ask when booking. Ideal for the Rosslare ferry but do stay longer for an abundance of super walks on unspoilt beaches, birdwatching and historic sites as well as riding, sea fishing and the Wexford opera festival.

Price	€130-€190. Singles €85-€110.
Rooms	12: 6 doubles, 4 twins, 1 family, 1 single.
Meals	Dinner, 4 courses with sherry, €42 (Tuesday-Saturday). Wine €25-€35. Packed lunch €15. By arrangement.
Closed	Mid-November to early March. Off-season by arrangement.
Directions	From Rosslare ferryport N25 for Tagoat 5.5km; right on R736. House 1km on left.

	Austin & Patricia Cody
	Tagoat, Rosslare, Co. Wexford
Tel	+353 (0)53 913 2555
Fax	+353 (0)53 913 2577
Email	info@churchtownhouse.com
Web	www.churchtownhouse.com

Entry 212   Map 8

Co. Wexford   Hotel

Kelly's Resort Hotel & Spa

Yes, a vast 'resort' hotel – and it's wonderful! Family-grown by four generations of Kellys beside five miles of safe sandy beach, it is ideal for short breaks, has a priceless collection of modern art perfectly hung as if in a private home – and never more than 50 children present; all the latest in spa, aqua, gym and games things yet aiming to become carbon neutral. Not only is Bill the greenest man in Irish business today, he's a perfectionist whose life's work is to make and keep Kelly's superb. He runs the place with common sense, an excellent eye, the easiest manner – chatting to all and sundry, including little kids – and endless lovely staff. The décor is cool, funky, bright and bold, there are myriad sitting and eating rooms, a teenage hang-out room, no false pomp, nothing tacky, and breathtakingly high standards. So if you love a buzzy, happy-families atmosphere and everything to hand (library, hairdresser, snooker, more), disregard the ugly block of a face, step into the light and colour of the great hall and learn why some people talk of Kelly's with almost religious fervour.

Price	Full-board €325 p.p. + 10% service charge.
Rooms	118 doubles, twins/doubles, twins, singles & family rooms.
Meals	Full-board only. Lunch €25–€28. Dinner €48.
Closed	Early December to late February.
Directions	From Wexford N25 for Rosslare Strand 16km & follow signs.

Bill Kelly
Rosslare, Co. Wexford
Tel   +353 (0)53 913 2114
Fax   +353 (0)53 913 2222
Email info@kellys.ie
Web   www.kellys.ie

Entry 213   Map 8

B&B   Co. Wexford

Ballinkeele House

The columned portico sets the tone: this 1840 house has a sense of easy, lived-in grandeur. At the turn of the carpeted stair Mercury, a Grand Tour momento, lifts and delights on his winged heel. Ballinkeele, its spacious rooms beautifully proportioned, was designed for John's great-grandfather by Daniel Robertson, an Adam son-in-law, with space and light in mind. Original furnishings reflect the nobility of the main rooms. John and Margaret, very relaxed, very charming, love this house, where family pictures sit easily with vibrant contemporary art and generous bedrooms, overlooking the gardens, are seriously comfortable. John maintains the grounds – lawned, terraced and shrubbed – with their 'laundry' pond, once used for washing flax, and acres of trees. Margaret, something of a perfectionist, presides over succulent meals in the rose-striped, chandelier-hung dining room with just the right period feel. The housekeeping is immaculate, the bathrooms are excellent, the spring water is their own. Recover from the ferry journey, wander the grounds, cast a rod in the lake – or head for the Wexford Opera.

Price	€150-€170. Singles €95-€105.
Rooms	5: 2 doubles, 2 twins/doubles, 1 four-poster.
Meals	Dinner €45. Wine from €18. Book by 11am the same day.
Closed	December-January.
Directions	From Rosslare N25 to Wexford, then N11 to Oilgate. Right at lights in village for Ballinkeele 6.5km; left in Ballymurn, 1st black gates on left.

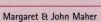

Margaret & John Maher
Ballymurn, Enniscorthy, Co. Wexford
Tel   +353 (0)53 913 8105
Fax   +353 (0)53 913 8468
Email john@ballinkeele.com
Web   www.ballinkeele.com

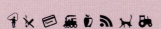

Co. Wexford   B&B

Woodbrook House

The long sweeping drive, the Georgian house protected by massive old hardwoods, tucked under the snowcapped mountain, the pillared entrance flanked by two marble lions… so far, so Anglo-Irish. The hall, lit by two-storey windows and with a Mediterranean-toned frieze, suggests a warmer clime. Giles and Alexandra are no strangers to the wider world; she is half-Italian, he capped a diplomatic career as British ambassador to Venezuela. They toured Italy and India before starting the restoration work on their intriguing, 1770s, somewhat ramshackle house which has Ireland's only 'flying staircase' – it quivers as you climb. Lions from Florence and painted furniture from Rajasthan came home with them; bedrooms are big, family-friendly, unposh; some have balconies for long parkland views. Giles, well-travelled and well-read, has strong convictions, a wry humour and is a leading Irish Green: Woodbrook is host to the annual Irish Green Gathering. Alexandra and their four children lend youth and vitality to this memorable family home. All take part in the local opera-à-la-carte circuit: picnics with Mozart.

Ethical Collection: Environment; Food. See page 270.

Price	€160–€180. Singles €100–€110.
Rooms	4: 2 doubles, 1 twin; 1 family with separate bathroom.
Meals	Dinner €45. Wine from €15.
Closed	November-April. Groups off season by arrangement.
Directions	From Enniscorthy R702 to Kiltealy. Through village towards Rathnure 2.5km; left down small lane with tall trees; entrance, not signed, 300m on left down drive.

Giles & Alexandra FitzHerbert
Killanne, Enniscorthy, Co. Wexford

Tel	+353 (0)53 925 5114
Fax	+353 (0)53 925 5114
Email	fitzherbert@eircom.net
Web	www.woodbrookhouse.ie

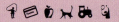

B&B   Co. Wexford

Woodlands Country House

Philomena is everyone's dream hostess, sweet, old-fashioned and cosy – and loves doing B&B after all these years. She'll do anything to help, even spending hours tracing family roots with visiting Americans. The Irish Georgian farmhouse and its pretty courtyard stand in the loveliest setting: two acres, a copse, a river and a little lake, all kept trim and inviting by John's hard work, when he's not out chairing something or other. Light peeps into the cosy farmhouse bedrooms to show off the fresh white sheets that hug the wooden beds. They have florals and crochet and proper old furniture and a good shower room each; three have balconies, the four-poster is the most striking but even the smaller ones are appealing and eminently sleep-worthy. If you prefer a bath, you may use the free-standing tub in the gorgeous main bathroom. The sitting room feels like the best old-world parlour with its velours and brass and fox-furs draped over the chaise-longue; Philomena's breakfast menu includes fresh fruit, her own brown bread, scones and jam on crochet cloths in a dining room shining with silver.

Price	€110-€130. Singles €70.
Rooms	6: 3 doubles, 1 twin, 1 single, 1 four-poster. Extra bath.
Meals	Pub in village, 1.5km; restaurants in Gorey, 8km.
Closed	October-March.
Directions	From Dublin Airport M50/M11. Take Arklow/Gorey bypass. Exit 22 for Gorey. Right at fruit farm and follow signs.

John & Philomena O'Sullivan
Killinierin, Gorey, Co. Wexford
Tel   +353 (0)402 37125
Fax   +353 (0)402 37133
Email info@woodlandscountryhouse.com
Web   www.woodlandscountryhouse.com

Entry 216   Map 8

Co. Wicklow   B&B

Barraderry House

True Irish family hospitality and grace, in a house with a solid proper farmhouse feel. Life hums along to a cheery tune in a peaceful, bucolic setting in the shadow of Lugnaquilla, Ireland's second highest mountain. The main house – early Georgian with Victorian additions – is approached along a drive that dips and curves through an avenue of trees. The setting is lovely, nicely set off by the Connemara ponies; at the back, an amazing grafted Siamese beech tree – make a wish as you walk through its trunk. After the last of six daughters left home, Olive decided to spruce it all up; she did a wonderful job. The large uncluttered hall, warmly coloured with a lively black and white floor, leads to a dining room where silver gleams and delicious breakfast is served at a huge table – and a drawing room with beautiful porcelain, a century-old rosewood grand piano and a bay window to the garden. Nice, well-furnished bedrooms have pretty fabrics, shuttered windows, the odd fireplace, fantastic beds, neatly squeezed-in showers. John and Olive are delightful.

Price	€100. Singles €55.
Rooms	4: 3 doubles, 1 twin.
Meals	Restaurant 7km.
Closed	Mid-December to mid-January.
Directions	From Dublin N81 through Blessington to Baltinglass (56km); left R747 for Kiltegan. Entrance on right 1km before edge of village.

Olive & John Hobson
Kiltegan, Co. Wicklow
Tel   +353 (0)59 647 3209
Fax   +353 (0)59 647 3209
Email jo.hobson@oceanfree.net
Web   www.barraderrycountryhouse.com

B&B Co. Wicklow

Ballyknocken House

Catherine is a joy, the young heart and soul of this traditional guest house, creating a cheerful atmosphere with her family and staff. Her cooking is wonderful; indeed, such is her pleasure and interest in food that she has opened a cookery school in the old milking parlour. Inside: patterned carpeting, a quaint melée of dark furniture, a parlour set with tables for games. Bedrooms, some with brass beds and Edwardian wardrobes, have good little bathrooms (some with stencilled Victorian baths) which look onto the front garden – or over the whitewashed old farm buildings to the hills. Outside this hive of activity lie 300 acres of pasture, the lovely forested hills of Wicklow for superb walking, the Carrig Mountain on the doorstep – peace by the basinful. (Two great Irish gardens too, Powerscourt and Mount Usher, and gorgeous Brittas Bay beach.) Leave your boots in the drying room and head to supper: Catherine's modern-Irish country dinners, made with imagination and the finest produce, are served in a modest Georgian-red dining room with checked tables and gleaming parquet floors.

Price	€118-€134. Singles €69-€100.
Rooms	10: 4 doubles, 2 twins, 3 twins/doubles, 1 triple
Meals	Dinner, 4 courses with sherry & canapés, €45 (Fri/Sat). Book ahead. Midweek supper, 3 courses, €38. Wine €21.95.
Closed	Mid-December to January.
Directions	From Dublin N11 to Ashford 48km; there, right after Chester Bealty pub for Glenealy 5km. House on right signposted, 4km.

Catherine Byrne-Fulvio
Glenealy, Ashford, Co. Wicklow
Tel +353 (0)404 44627
Fax +353 (0)404 44696
Email cfulvio@ballyknocken.com
Web www.ballyknocken.com

Travel Club Offer. See page 266.

Ethical Collection: Food.
See page 270.

Entry 218   Map 5

Co. Wicklow   Self-catering

The Old Milking Parlour

Bowl down a gravel track and land in a courtyard surrounded by low buildings. To the left is The Old Milking Parlour, built (circa 1670) when the main house was used as a meeting place for the Quakers. Now Delphine and Philip live here and it is they, green architects both, who have designed the lovely space you get to stay in. Enter a huge open-plan living area with black floor tiles, bright white walls, a ceiling that soars, criss-crossed by ancient knobbly beams, and all brightened with colourful rugs and a wicker sofa and chairs with red cushions. You are toasty warm with geothermal underfloor heating and a wood-burner, huge velux windows pull the light in, and round the corner of one of the original animal stalls is a kitchen with all you need to rustle up meals. Bedrooms are at the top end; the first a double with pretty yellow walls, and the master bedroom up another level. There's a modern light wood bed, rough whitewashed walls, simple furniture and pictures, a walk-in shower cabinet. The house opens from all living areas onto its own mature south-facing garden. Eco chic at its best.

Price	€700–€1,200 per week.
Rooms	Cottage for 4–5.
Meals	Pubs 1.6km.
Closed	Rarely.
Directions	N11 motorway south from Dublin, left 0.25 miles after Beehive pub. Right onto gravel lane after 1.6km. Proceed to end of lane, 200m.

Travel Club Offer. See page 266.

Delphine & Philip Geoghegan
Ballymurrin House, Kilbride, Wicklow,
Co. Wicklow

Tel	+353 (0)404 48206
Fax	+353 (0)404 48206
Email	oldmilkingparlour@o2.ie
Web	www.ballymurrin.ie

Entry 219   Map 5

Getting around Ireland

Cycling

Currently there are five long-distance cycle routes which span Northern Ireland and dip into the borders of the Republic.

Belfast to Ballyshannon
(231 miles/372km)
Ireland's first coast-to-coast route starts in Whiteabbey and ends at the Atlantic Ocean, taking you through the cathedral city of Armagh, busy market towns and the rugged Sperrin mountains.

Ballyshannon to Ballycastle
(236 miles/380km)
This route takes you inland from the coast and over the border towards Lough Erne, then up to Derry and some fine north-coast beaches. You can stop to see Enniskillen Castle, the Giant's Causeway and Bushmills Irish Whiskey Distillery.

Kingfisher Trail
(230 miles/370km)
The first long-distance cycle trail in Ireland, this takes you through fairly minor country roads into the border counties and their rivers and lakes. Highlights include Castle Coole, the Marble Arch Caves and the Lough Scur Dolmen.

Loughshore Trail
(110 miles/184km)
A watery delight taking you all the way round Lough Neagh – you choose the direction. Mostly minor roads and lanes with some stretches of off-road track.

See small beaches, a 1,000 year-old Celtic cross and the railway viaduct at Randalstown.

The North West Trail
(202 miles/326km)
Meander through Yeats country in County Sligo, glimpse the Atlantic Ocean in Donegal, link up with parts of other long distance routes, and enjoy some traffic-free sections beside rivers and mountains.

Of course you don't have to do any of these routes from start to finish! Pick and choose your sections carefully: cycling through cities can be tricky for the uninitiated or less than brave, and some roads outside of the cities and towns can be busy. There are plenty of shorter rides and the best way to decide which traffic-free part you would like to join is by buying a map from the Sustrans website (www.sustrans.org.uk).

Photo: www.istockphoto.com

Walking

The beauty and variety of the Irish landscape make it perfect for walking. Whether you are a serious rambler or only wanting to take a short stroll there is something here to delight.

Highlights in the North include Binevenagh with its dramatic cliffs, and the Causeway coast with its sprinkling of picturesque fishing villages. March through the Sperrins – the second highest mountain range in Northern Ireland – then discover the Glens of Antrim and the coastal area between Larne and Ballycastle. Don't miss Rathlin Island, a rare and beautiful place of extraordinary ecological value. For more information about walking in Northern Ireland visit www.walkni.com and download a free brochure.

In the Republic there are several long-distance walking routes, including the three mentioned below, and more information is available at www.walkireland.ie.

The Wicklow Way
(79 miles/127km)
Now part of a network of long-distance self-guided walking trails, this is the most westerly section of the E8 footpath which extends across much of Europe. It begins in a Dublin suburb and travels across the Dublin and Wicklow uplands, taking in mountains, lakes, forests and farmland, to finish in the small village of Clonegal.

The Dingle Way
(111 miles/179km)
Taking you on a circuit of the Dingle Peninsula, starting and ending in Tralee, the capital of Kerry, this is a popular trail; the diversity of landscape from the foothills of the Slieve Mish Mountains to golden beaches and crashing Atlantic waves will leave you exhilarated.

The Kerry Way
(134 miles/215km)
Ireland's longest signposted walking trail, and also one of the busiest, so best tackled in the quieter spring or autumn months. It starts and finishes in Killarney, looping in between around the Iveragh Peninsula through some of the most isolated and dramatic scenery in the country. The trail avoids most of the higher peaks and takes you along lower mountain ridges, but is nevertheless demanding.

Photos: www.istockphoto.com

Driving

Expect to take twice as long as 'normal' to drive from one place to another – and enjoy it. There are few motorways, main roads tend to go through old town centres, country roads are narrow lanes with high hedges, surprise bends and dogs sleeping in patches of sun.

As part of the United Kingdom the North uses miles, the Republic uses kilometres.

You drive on the left and speed limits are:
- 75mph/120kph on motorways
- 50mph/80kph on regional & local roads
- 30mph/50kph in built-up areas.

With the boom has come an increase in traffic and house building on the main roads, so plan your routes carefully with a good map. The Michelin motoring map of Ireland is generally considered to be the best. It covers the whole island at a scale of 1cm = 4km.

Irish literature

Where to start? So many great writers, so many great works. From the ancient *Book of Kells* to 2007 Booker Prize winner Anne Enright, Ireland has a long and proud literary history. For a country that still only has a population of just over four million, Ireland has made a disproportionate contribution to world literature. Four Irish writers – William Butler Yeats, George Bernard Shaw, Samuel Beckett and Seamus Heaney – have won the Nobel Prize for Literature (although James Joyce, possibly the most influential Irish writer of the 20th century, never did).

The space here can't even begin to cover the panoply of writers in a tradition spanning over 1000 years. The role call of dramatists alone would be the pride of most nations – from late 17th and early 18th century playwrights Oliver Goldsmith, William Congreve and Richard Brinsley Sheridan, to 20th century masters and re-inventors of the form George Bernard Shaw, John Millington Synge, Seán O'Casey, Samuel Beckett and Brian Friel. Eminent novelists include the father of satire, Jonathan Swift; the father of gothic, Bram Stoker; and the father of modernism, James Joyce. Add to that list Flann O'Brien, Edna O'Brien, Elizabeth Bowen, William Trevor and four Booker prize winners – Iris Murdoch, John Banville, Roddy Doyle and Anne Enright. And then there are the poets. No nation can be more proud of its poets. WB Yeats is without peer, in any century, in any language. Seamus Heaney, Patrick Kavanagh, John Montague, Eavan Boland, Paul Muldoon, Derek Mahon and Paul Durcan are amongst the myriad of other talents.

But epithets such as 'poet' or 'playwright' seem inadequate for so many of the great Irish writers. Oscar Wilde produced some of the most memorable comic plays of the late Victorian era, but he also penned possibly his greatest work – *The Ballard of Reading Gaol* – in verse, as well as publishing a novel (*The Picture of Dorian Gray*), a beautiful fairy tale (*The Selfish Giant*), and a thousand quotable lines. James Joyce wrote poetry and one play, *Exiles*; Yeats, the autodidact, wrote 26. Beckett, the dramatist, wrote a trilogy of novels. Is Brendan Behan a novelist who wrote a memorable play, or a playwright who wrote a great novel?

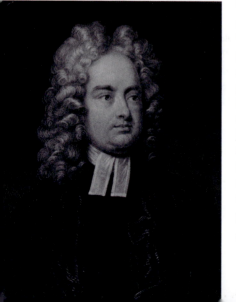

Photo of Jonathan Swift: www.istockphoto.com

So many great writers, so many great works. Where to start?

Well here's a very personal reading list.

James Joyce
Best to start with *Dubliners* and if you only read one story in the collection make sure it's "The Dead". Move on to *A Portrait of the Artist as a Young Man*, then you'll be ready for *Ulysses*. If you've stayed with the man this far, then *Finnegans Wake* awaits you. If you are an "ideal insomniac" and manage to finish it, well done – you will be one of a select few.

John Millington Synge
There's Shakespeare then there's Synge, and in the years between there is nothing. A bold statement, but Synge's Aran Island play, *Riders to the Sea*, produced in 1904, was the first dramatic tragedy written in the English language since *Macbeth*, four hundred years earlier. As versatile as the Bard, Synge then produced a work of surreal comic genius, *The Well of the Saints*, which greatly influenced Samuel Beckett. He followed this with his masterwork, *The Playboy of the Western World*, which caused a riot on its first performance at Dublin's Abbey Theatre. (WB Yeats had to step in to pacify the angry crowd.)

Seán O'Casey
Like Synge before him O'Casey caused riots at the Abbey Theatre with his play *The Plough and the Stars*, and again Yeats had to calm the audience, as he had done nearly twenty years before, allegedly telling them "You have disgraced yourselves again. Is this to be an ever-recurring celebration of the arrival of Irish genius? Synge first and then O'Casey?". One of Alfred Hitchcock's early films is an adaptation of O'Casey's *Juno and the Paycock*.

Samuel Beckett
Beg, steal or borrow a recording of Patrick Magee reading *Krapp's Last Tape*. Watch Conor McPherson's film of *Endgame*. Scour YouTube for Max Wall and Leo McKern in *Waiting for Godot*.

WB Yeats
Unlike most poets, William Butler Yeats produced some of his greatest works late in his life, many after his marriage in 1917 to George (Georgie) Hyde-Lees. His four collections of poems after the marriage – *The Wilde Swans at Coole*; *Michael Robartes and the Dancer*; *The Tower*; and *The Winding Stair and Other Poems* – show a poet without peer. If you need convincing, simply read "The Second Coming" and shiver.

JP Donleavy
Not Irish at all and yet perhaps the most Irish of them all. *The Ginger Man* is the great Dublin novel.

Rob Richardson

Sawday's Travel Club

Becoming a member of Sawday's Travel Club opens up hundreds of discounts, treats and other offers at many of our Special Places to Stay in Britain and Ireland, as well as promotions on Sawday's books and other goodies.

Where you see the symbol in this book it means the place has a special offer for Club members. It may be money off your room price, a bottle of wine or a local tour. The offers for each place are listed on the following pages. These were correct at the time of going to print, but owners reserve the right to change the listed offer. Latest offers for all places can be found on our website, www.sawdays.co.uk.

Membership is only £25 per year. To see membership extras and to register visit www.sawdays.co.uk/members. You can also call 01275 395433 to set up a direct debit.

The small print
You must mention that you are a Travel Club member when booking, and confirm that the offer is available. Your Travel Club card must be shown on arrival to claim the offer. Sawday's Travel Club cards are not transferable. If two cardholders share a room they can only claim the offer once. Offers for Sawday's Travel Club members are subject to availability. Alastair Sawday Publishing cannot accept any responsibility if places fail to honour offers; neither can we accept responsibility if a place changes hands and drops out of the Travel Club.

Ulster
Co. Antrim
5   Pre-dinner drink each evening.

Co. Armagh
7   10% off Monday-Thursday. Pre-dinner drink.

Co. Donegal
9   Late checkout (12pm).
14   Half-hour holistic treatment.

Co. Down
22   10% off Monday-Thursday (October-March).
26   A nightcap of Anna's sloe gin each evening.

Co. Fermanagh
28 House cocktail each evening.

Co. Monaghan
32 20% off stays of 2+ nights. Round of golf.
33 Bottle of house wine with dinner on one night of stay.

Co. Tyrone
34 10% off room price after first night.

Connacht
Co. Galway
35 Bottle of house wine.
40 Glass of wine on arrival.
42 Bottle of house wine.
44 Afternoon tea on arrival.
45 Bottle of wine with dinner.
46 Welcome pack of local brown sodabread & organic smoked salmon.
49 Picnic lunch packed for boating.
50 Holistic seaweed body wrap.
51 Home baking or elderflower aperitif on arrival.

Co. Mayo
55 Drink on arrival or specialist coffee/herbal tea & homemade scones.

Co. Roscommon
63 10% off Monday-Thursday.

Co. Sligo
66 Guided visit around the Coopershill Fallow Deer Farm (the bambi kind!).
67 Bottle of house wine with dinner for 2.
68 10% off January-May & September-December (not Christmas & New Year).

Munster
Co. Clare
70 10% off stays of 3+ nights.
71 3 nights for the price of 2, 15 October-10 March (not Christmas Eve & 2 January).
76 10% off Monday-Thursday (for 2+ nights).
79 5% off room rate.

Co. Cork

85   12% off stays of 2+ nights.
91   Pre-dinner aperitif. Bottle of wine with dinner. After-dinner liqueur.
92   Glass of wine with dinner. Free collection at pier.
100 Bottle of wine. Box of luxury chocolates.
101 Bottle of house wine with dinner.
104 Dinner (excluding wine) for 2, for 2-night stays (Tuesday-Thursday).

Co. Kerry

113 Pre-dinner drink each evening.
114 10% off Sunday-Thursday.
121 10% off Sunday-Thursday.
126 Selection of home baking. Bottle of wine.
128 Drink on arrival.
129 Bottle of champagne.
131 Evening meal & wine for 7+ nights. Aperitif with wine. Traditional Irish song & dance provided by family.
132 5% off room rate.

Co. Limerick

138 Room upgrade subject to availability.
141 30% off Sunday nights. Extra night free on 3+ nights.

Co. Tipperary

147 Natural horsemanship lesson. Extra night free if you can identify either 10 species of birds or 3 Bronze Age remains at Rusheen.
149 10% off stays of 2+ nights.

Munster
Co. Waterford

152 10% off 3+ nights, 5% off 2+ nights, Monday-Thursday. Local products in room.
153 10% off Monday-Thursday. Afternoon tea.
161 Bottle of house wine with dinner.
164 10% off Sunday-Thursday. Tours of private local gardens. Late checkout (12pm).
165 10% off 3-night stays.

Leinster
Co. Dublin
170 10% off January-May & September-December (not Christmas & New Year).
172 Dublin City Tour per person for 3-night stays.

Co. Kilkenny
182 10% off Monday-Thursday.
183 Seasonal produce, when available, delivered to cottage.

Co. Laois
186 Bottle of house wine with dinner.
187 Late checkout. Pick-up from local bus/train station. House cocktail.

Co. Meath
190 10% off October-March.
193 Sandwiches and tea/coffee on arrival.
195 15% off all beauty treatments. Wine and chocolates on arrival.

Co. Offaly
199 Guided hill walk or 2 hours art tuition (still life) or packed lunch.
200 Tea/coffee on arrival. Walking maps.

Co. Westmeath
203 Welcome pack of local produce.
205 10% off room rate.
206 Bottle of house wine with dinner.

Co. Wexford
207 10% off Monday-Thursday. Drink on arrival. Late checkout (12pm). Courtesy car to local restaurants.
208 10% off Monday-Thursday. Late checkout (12pm).
209 Homemade chocolate cake on arrival.
210 Pick up from local station. Late checkout (12pm).

Co. Wicklow
218 One picnic (min. 3-night stay). 10% off (Sunday-Tuesday).
219 5% off. Bottle of wine.

Ethical Collection

Many of you may want to stay in environmentally friendly places. You may be passionate about local, organic or home-grown food. Or perhaps you want to know that the place you are staying in contributes to the community? To help you we have launched our Ethical Collection, so you can find the right place to stay and also discover how each owner is addressing these issues.

The Collection is made up of places going the extra mile, and taking the steps that most people have not yet taken, in one or more of the following areas:

• **Environment** Those making great efforts to reduce the environmental impact of their Special Place. We expect more than energy-saving light bulbs and recycling – in this part of the Collection you will find owners who make their own natural cleaning products, properties with solar hot water and biomass boilers, the odd green roof and a good measure of green elbow grease.

• **Community** Given to owners who use their property to play a positive role in their local and wider community. For example, by making a contribution from every guest's bill to a local fund, or running pond-dipping courses for local school children on their farm.

• **Food** Awarded to owners who make a real effort to source local or organic food, or to grow their own. We look for those who have gone out of their way to strike up relationships with local producers or to seek out organic suppliers. It is easier for an owner on a farm to produce their own eggs than for someone in the middle of a city, so we take this into account.

How it works

To become part of our Ethical Collection owners choose whether to apply in one, two or all three categories, and fill in a detailed questionnaire asking demanding questions about their activities in the chosen areas. You can download a full list of the questions at www.sawdays.co.uk/about_us/ethical_collection

We then review each questionnaire carefully before deciding whether or not

Photo: Ballyroon Mountain, entry 85

to give the award(s). The final decision is subjective; it is based not only on whether an owner ticks 'yes' to a question but also on the detailed explanation that accompanies each 'yes' or 'no' answer. For example, an owner who has tried as hard as possible to install solar water-heating panels, but has failed because of strict conservation planning laws, will be given some credit for their effort (as long as they are doing other things in this area).

We have tried to be as rigorous as possible and have made sure the questions are demanding. We have not checked out the claims of owners before making our decisions, but we do trust them to be honest. We are only human, as are they, so please let us know if you think we have made any mistakes.

The Ethical Collection is a new initiative for us, and we'd love to know what you think about it – email us at ethicalcollection@sawdays.co.uk or write to us. And remember that because this is a new scheme some owners have not yet completed their questionnaires – we're sure other places in the guide are working just as hard in these areas, but we don't yet know the full details.

Ethical Collection in this book
On the entry page of all places in the Collection we show which awards have been given.

Photo: Anna's House, entry 26

A list of the places in our Ethical Collection is shown below, by entry number.

Environment
26 • 41 • 46 • 66 • 69 • 83 • 85 • 92 • 101 • 117 • 215

Community
46 • 50 • 92 • 117

Food
22 • 26 • 41 • 43 • 46 • 66 • 76 • 83 • 85 • 90 • 92 • 101 • 113 • 117 • 215 • 218

Ethical Collection online
There is stacks more information on our website, www.sawdays.co.uk. You can read the answers each owner has given to our Ethical Collection questionnaire and get a more detailed idea of what they are doing in each area. You can also search for properties that have awards.

Fragile Earth

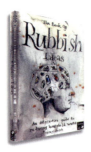

The Book of Rubbish Ideas
An interactive, room by room, guide to reducing household waste
£6.99

This guide to reducing household waste and stopping wasteful behaviour is essential reading for all those trying to lessen their environmental impact.

Ban the Plastic Bag
A Community Action Plan
£4.99

In May 2007 Modbury in South Devon became Britain's first plastic bag free town.
This book tells the Modbury story, but uses it as a call to action, entreating every village, town and city in the country to follow Modbury's example and… BAN THE PLASTIC BAG.

One Planet Living
£4.99

"Small but meaningful principles that will improve the quality of your life."
Country Living

Also available in the Fragile Earth series:

The Little Food Book   £6.99
"This is a really big little book. It will make your hair stand on end" *Jonathan Dimbleby*

The Little Money Book   £6.99
"Anecdotal, humorous and enlightening, this book will have you sharing its gems with all your friends" *Permaculture Magazine*

To order any of the books in the Fragile Earth series call 01275 395431 or visit www.fragile-earth.com

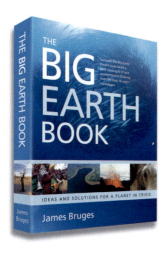

The Big Earth Book
Updated paperback edition
£12.99

We all know the Earth is in crisis. We should know that it is big enough to sustain us if we can only mobilise politicians and economists to change course now. Expanding on the ideas developed in *The Little Earth Book*, this book explores environmental, economic and social ideas to save our planet. It helps us understand what is happening to the planet today, exposes the actions of corporations and the lack of action of governments, weighs up new technologies, and champions innovative and viable solutions. Tackling a huge range of subjects – it has the potential to become the seminal reference book on the state of the planet – it's the one and only environmental book you really need.

What About China? £6.99
Answers to this and other awkward questions about climate change

"What is the point of doing anything when China opens a new power station every week?"

All of us are guilty of making excuses not to change our lifestyles especially when it comes to global warming and climate change. *What About China?* explains that all the excuses we give to avoid making changes that will reduce our carbon footprint and our personal impact on the environment, are exactly that, excuses! Through clear answers, examples, facts and figures the book illustrates how any changes we make now will have an effect, both directly and indirectly, on climate change.

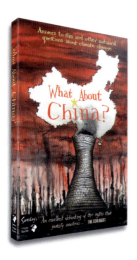

"An excellent debunking of the myths that justify inaction" *The Ecologist*

Alastair Sawday's

British self-catering

A whole week self-catering in Britain with your friends or family is precious, and you dare not get it wrong. To whom do you turn for advice and who on earth do you trust when the web is awash with advice from strangers? We launched Special Escapes to satisfy an obvious need for impartial and trustworthy help — and that is what it provides. The criteria for inclusion are the same as for our books: we have to like the place and the owners. It has, quite simply, to be 'special'. The site, our first online-only publication, is featured on www.thegoodwebguide.com and is growing fast.

Cosy cottages • Manor houses

Tipis • Hilltop bothies

City apartments and more

www.special-escapes.co.uk

Slow down with Sawdays

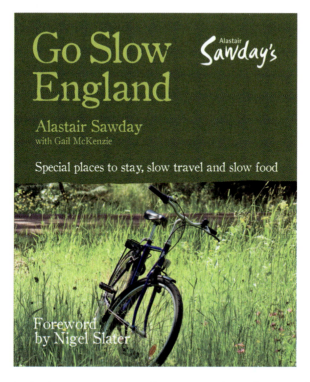

Special places to stay, slow travel and slow food

The Slow Food revolution is upon us and this guide celebrates the Slow philosophy of life with a terrific selection of the places, recipes and people who take their time to enjoy life at its most enriching. In this beautiful book that goes beyond the mere 'glossy', you will discover an unusual emphasis on the people who live in Special Slow Places and what they do. You will meet farmers, literary people, wine-makers and craftsmen – all with rich stories to tell. *Go Slow England* celebrates fascinating people, fine architecture, history, landscape and real food. A counter-balance to our culture of haste.

Written by Alastair Sawday, with a foreword by Nigel Slater.

RRP £19.99. To order at the Reader's Discount price of £13.00 (plus p&tp) call 01275 395431 and quote 'Reader Discount IR'.

"*Go Slow England* is a magnificent guidebook" *BBC Good Food Magazine*

Special Places to Stay series

Have you enjoyed this book? Why not try one of the others in the Special Places to Stay series and get 35% discount on the RRP *

British Bed & Breakfast (Ed 13)	RRP £14.99	Offer price £9.75
British Bed & Breakfast for Garden Lovers (Ed 5)	RRP £14.99	Offer price £9.75
British Hotels & Inns (Ed 10)	RRP £14.99	Offer price £9.75
Devon & Cornwall (Ed 1)	RRP £ 9.99	Offer price £6.50
Scotland (Ed 1)	RRP £ 9.99	Offer price £6.50
Pubs & Inns of England & Wales (Ed 5)	RRP £14.99	Offer price £9.75
Ireland (Ed 7)	RRP £12.99	Offer price £8.45
French Bed & Breakfast (Ed 11)	RRP £15.99	Offer price £10.40
French Holiday Homes (Ed 4)	RRP £14.99	Offer price £9.75
French Hotels & Châteaux (Ed 5)	RRP £14.99	Offer price £9.75
Paris Hotels (Ed 6)	RRP £10.99	Offer price £7.15
Italy (Ed 5)	RRP £14.99	Offer price £9.75
Spain (Ed 7)	RRP £14.99	Offer price £9.75
Portugal (Ed 4)	RRP £11.99	Offer price £7.80
Croatia (Ed 1)	RRP £11.99	Offer price £7.80
Greece (Ed 1)	RRP £11.99	Offer price £7.80
India (Ed 2)	RRP £11.99	Offer price £7.80
Green Places to Stay (Ed 1)	RRP £13.99	Offer price £9.10
Go Slow England	RRP £19.99	Offer price £13.00

*postage and packing is added to each order

To order at the Reader's Discount price simply phone 01275 395431 and quote 'Reader Discount IR'.

Feedback form

If you have any comments on entries in this guide, please tell us. If you have a favourite place or a new discovery, please let us know about it. You can return this form or visit www.sawdays.co.uk.

Existing entry

Property name: _____

Entry number: _____ Date of visit: _____

New recommendation

Property name: _____

Address: _____

_____

Tel/Email/Web: _____

Your comments

What did you like (or dislike) about this place? Were the people friendly? What was the location like? What sort of food did they serve?

_____

_____

_____

_____

_____

Your details

Name: _____

Address: _____

_____

_____ Postcode: _____

Tel: _____ Email: _____

Please send completed form to:
IR, Sawday's, The Old Farmyard, Yanley Lane, Long Ashton, Bristol BS41 9LR, UK

Quick reference indices

Wheelchair-accessible

At least one bedroom and bathroom accessible for wheelchair users. Phone for details.

Co. Antrim 1
Co. Donegal 8 • 14
Co. Down 24 • 26
Co. Londonderry 29
Co. Monaghan 33
Co. Galway 47
Co. Leitrim 53
Co. Mayo 55
Co. Sligo 64 • 65
Co. Clare 75 • 79
Co. Cork 101 • 106 • 108
Co. Kerry 116 • 119
Co. Limerick 138 • 141
Co. Tipperary 144
Co. Waterford 153 • 154 • 161
Co. Dublin 175
Co. Kildare 178
Co. Longford 188
Co. Meath 192 • 193 • 195
Co. Offaly 200
Co. Westmeath 202
Co. Wexford 208 • 213

On a budget?

These places have a double room for £70/€100 or under.

Co. Donegal 9 • 11 • 16
Co. Down 18 • 19 • 20 • 21 • 22
Co. Fermanagh 28
Co. Londonderry 31
Co. Galway 39 • 41 • 44 • 45 • 52
Co. Mayo 55
Co. Sligo 69
Co. Clare 71 • 73 • 77
Co. Cork 81 • 83 • 85 • 88 • 90 • 91 • 92 • 93 • 96 • 97 • 101 • 102 • 103 • 107
Co. Kerry 110 • 111 • 115 • 125 • 126 • 131 • 132 • 135
Co. Limerick 137 • 139
Co. Tipperary 145 • 146 • 147 • 149 • 151
Co. Waterford 154 • 155 • 159 • 160 • 161 • 164
Co. Carlow 168
Co. Dublin 171
Co. Kildare 177
Co. Kilkenny 182 • 185
Co. Meath 193 • 195
Co. Offaly 199 • 200
Co. Westmeath 201 • 204
Co. Wexford 210 • 211
Co. Wicklow 217

Singles

Single room OR rooms let to single guests at half the double room rate or under.

Co. Antrim 5
Co. Donegal 8 • 10 • 14 • 16
Co. Down 19 • 21 • 23
Co. Galway 37 • 42
Co. Sligo 65
Co. Cork 92 • 106 • 109
Co. Kerry 119 • 131
Co. Limerick 138

Co. Tipperary 146
Co. Waterford 157
Co. Kilkenny 184
Co. Laois 187
Co. Louth 189
Co. Meath 191 • 197
Co. Westmeath 206
Co. Wexford 208 • 211

Gardens
These gardens are of particular interest to garden lovers/horticulturalists.

Co. Antrim 2 • 4
Co. Armagh 7
Co. Donegal 9 • 10 • 11 • 12 • 14 • 15 • 17
Co. Down 18 • 23 • 26
Co. Londonderry 29
Co. Monaghan 32
Co. Galway 36 • 39 • 41 • 43 • 46 • 48 • 52
Co. Leitrim 53
Co. Mayo 55 • 58
Co. Roscommon 62
Co. Sligo 67 • 69
Co. Clare 70 • 72 • 76
Co. Cork 81 • 82 • 83 • 84 • 92 • 93 • 94 • 97 • 98 • 99 • 101 • 102 • 106 • 107 • 108
Co. Kerry 112 • 113 • 114 • 118 • 119 • 120 • 124 • 129
Co. Limerick 138 • 140 • 141
Co. Tipperary 144 • 151
Co. Waterford 152 • 153 • 156 • 158 • 160 • 162 • 164 • 166
Co. Carlow 168
Co. Dublin 172
Co. Kildare 176 • 177
Co. Kilkenny 179 • 180 • 181 • 183 • 185
Co. Laois 186 • 187
Co. Longford 188
Co. Louth 189
Co. Meath 190 • 192 • 193 • 194 • 196 • 197 • 198
Co. Westmeath 205
Co. Wexford 208 • 210 • 213 • 214 • 216
Co. Wicklow 217 • 218

Riding
Riding can be arranged nearby.

Co. Donegal 9 • 10 • 14
Co. Down 19 • 21 • 22 • 23 • 27
Co. Monaghan 33
Co. Tyrone 34
Co. Galway 35 • 36 • 40 • 41 • 42 • 43 • 44 • 45 • 46 • 47 • 48 • 49
Co. Leitrim 53 • 54
Co. Mayo 55 • 56 • 61
Co. Roscommon 63
Co. Sligo 64 • 65 • 66 • 67 • 68 • 69
Co. Clare 72 • 76 • 77 • 78 • 79
Co. Cork 94 • 95 • 99 • 101 • 105 • 107 • 108
Co. Kerry 111 • 112 • 113 • 114 • 116 • 119 • 120 • 121 • 122 • 124 • 125 • 126 • 127 • 128 • 129 • 131
Co. Limerick 136 • 137 • 138 • 139 • 141

Quick reference indices

Co. Tipperary 142 • 143 • 144 • 146 • 147 • 148 • 149 • 151
Co. Waterford 152 • 153 • 156 • 164 • 165 • 166
Co. Carlow 167
Co. Dublin 174
Co. Kildare 176 • 177
Co. Kilkenny 179 • 181 • 183 • 184 • 185
Co. Laois 186 • 187
Co. Meath 191 • 192 • 193 • 195 • 196 • 197 • 198
Co. Offaly 199 • 200
Co. Westmeath 201 • 203 • 204 • 205
Co. Wexford 207 • 208 • 210 • 211 • 212 • 214
Co. Wicklow 217 • 218

Travel without a car
Within 10 miles of a bus/coach/train station and owner can arrange collection.

Co. Antrim 5
Co. Armagh 7
Co. Donegal 9 • 12 • 14 • 16
Co. Down 18 • 19 • 21 • 22 • 23 • 27
Co. Fermanagh 28
Co. Londonderry 29 • 30 • 31
Co. Monaghan 32
Co. Tyrone 34
Co. Galway 36 • 37 • 38 • 40 • 41 • 42 • 43 • 44 • 46 • 48 • 50 • 51
Co. Leitrim 54
Co. Mayo 55 • 57
Co. Roscommon 62 • 63
Co. Sligo 64 • 65 • 66
Co. Sligo 67
Co. Clare 71 • 72 • 74 • 78 • 79
Co. Cork 81 • 82 • 83 • 84 • 88 • 92 • 93 • 96 • 97 • 99 • 100 • 102 • 104 • 105 • 107 • 109
Co. Kerry 110 • 111 • 114 • 116 • 119 • 121 • 122 • 123 • 126 • 131 • 132 • 134
Co. Limerick 137 • 140 • 141
Co. Tipperary 144 • 145 • 146 • 147 • 151
Co. Waterford 152 • 156 • 158 • 159 • 160 • 161 • 162 • 164
Co. Dublin 171 • 172 • 173
Co. Kildare 176 • 177 • 178
Co. Kilkenny 180 • 181 • 184 • 185
Co. Laois 186 • 187
Co. Louth 189
Co. Meath 190 • 191 • 192 • 193 • 194 • 196 • 197 • 198
Co. Offaly 199
Co. Westmeath 201 • 202 • 206
Co. Wexford 208 • 210 • 211 • 212 • 213 • 214 • 216
Co. Wicklow 217 • 218

Photo: www.istockphoto.com

Index by town

Abbeyfeale	139
Achill Island	56
An Ghlaise Bheag	113
Aran Islands	51-52
Ardara	11
Arthurstown	207
Ashford	218
Athlone	201-202
Athy	178
Bagenalstown	167
Ballinasloe	48
Ballinfull	69
Ballingarry	138
Ballintoy	2
Ballitore	177
Ballycastle	3
Ballyconneely	42
Ballyduff Upper	154
Ballymacarbry	162
Ballymena	5
Ballymote	67
Ballyvaughan	70-72
Balrath	192
Bandon	97-98
Bantry	82-85
Beara	81
Belfast	6
Belmullet	55
Bettystown	190
Birr	199-200
Blarney	102-103
Borris-in-Ossory	187
Borrisokane	142
Bushmills	1
Butlerstown	163
Caherdaniel	124-125
Caherlistrane	47
Callan	182
Campile	208
Cappoquin	156-157
Carlingford	189
Carrick-on-Shannon	54
Carrigans	16
Cashel	149
Castlebaldwin	64
Castlecoote	62
Castlecove	126-127
Castlelyons	108
Castlemaine	117
Castlerea	63
Clifden	38-40
Clones	32
Clonmel	151, 161
Cobh	105
Collinstown	206
Colloney	68
Comber	26
Cong	61
Coom	80
Cork	104
Corofin	73-74
Craigavon	7
Crossmolina	58
Culdaff	17
Cushendun	4
Derry	31
Dingle	114-116
Donegal	9
Downpatrick	23
Dromore	18-19
Dublin	169-172
Duleek	191
Dunamaggan	183
Dundrum	22
Dunfanaghy	12
Dungannon	34
Dungarvan	158-160
Dunkineely	10
Durrus	86
Enfield	193
Enniscorthy	214-215
Enniskillen	28

Fanad	13
Feeny	29
Fingal	175
Fordstown	194
Glencairn	155
Glin	140
Goleen	89-90
Gorey	216
Graiguenamanagh	185
Hillsborough	20
Holywood	27
Kanturk	109
Kenmare	130-135
Kilbrittain	94-96
Kildare	176
Kilkenny	179
Killarney	121-123
Killiney	173
Killorglin	118-120
Killucan	203
Killurin	210
Killyleagh	21
Kilmallock	136-137
Kilrush	78
Kiltegan	217
Kilternan	174
Kinsale	99-101
Kinvara	50
Laghey	8
Lahinch	75-76
Leenane	35
Letterfrack	36
Limerick	141
Listowel	110-111
Londonderry	30
Longford	188
Maddoxtown	180
Midleton	106-107
Milltown Malbay	77
Monaghan	33
Mountrath	186

Moyard	37
Mullinahone	150
Mullingar	204-205
Navan	195
Nenagh	143-145
New Ross	209
Newtownards	25
Oldcastle	197-198
Oughterard	43-45
Pontoon	59-60
Portaferry	24
Ramelton	15
Rathmullan	14
Riverstown	65-66
Rossinver	53
Rosslare	212-213
Roundstone	41
Schull	87-88
Sherkin Island	92
Sixmilebridge	79
Skibbereen	91
Slane	196
Sneem	128-129
Spiddal	46
St Mullins	168
Stonyford	181
Templemore	146
Thomastown	184
Thurles	147-148
Tralee	112
Union Hall	93
Waterford	164-165
Westport	57
Wexford	211
Wicklow	219
Woodford	49
Woodstown	166
Youghal	152-153

Index by property name

Aberdeen Lodge	172
Abocurragh	28
Allcorn's Country Home	103
Allo's Townhouse	110
An Tigh Beag	112
Anna's House	26
Annesbrook	191
Arbutus Hotel	121
Ard Na Breatha Guest House	9
Ard Na Sidhe Country House	120
Ardmore House	200
Ardroe Cottage	13
Ardsallagh Lodge	152
Ardtarmon House	69
Ash Hill Stud	137
Ashley Park House	144
Ballaghmore Manor House & Castle	187
Ballaghtobin	182
Ballinakill House	193
Ballinkeele House	214
Ballyduff House	184
Ballyknocken House	218
Ballylickey House	82
Ballymagarvey Village	192
Ballymaloe House	106
Ballymote House	23
Ballyogan House	185
Ballyportry Castle	74
Ballyroon Mountain	85
Ballyvolane House	108
Ballywarren House	61
Bantry House	84
Barr Hall Barns	24
Barraderry House	217
Bath Lodge	3
Bayly Farm	145
Beech Hill Country House	27
Berry Lodge & Cookery School	77
Blairs Cove House	86
Blanchville House	180
Boland Townhouse	100
Brendan House	199
Bruckless House	10
Bushmills Inn Hotel	1
Butler House	179
Cafe Paradiso & Paradiso Rooms	104
Camillaun	45
Carrig Country House	119
Casino Cottage	96
Castle Leslie	33
Castlecoote House	62
Castlegar Stables	48
Churchtown House	212
Clanmurry	18
Clonalis House	63
Clonleason Gate Lodge	194
Cnoc Suain	46
Coopershill House	66
Coursetown House	178
Coxtown Manor	8
Croan Cottages	183
Crocnaraw Country House	37
Cromleach Lodge	64
Cuasnóg	211
Currarevagh House	43
Decoy Country Cottages	195
Delphi Lodge	35
Derry Farm Cottages	30

Dolphin Beach House	38	Grove House	88
Drom Caoin	55	Grove House & Courtyard Cottages	91
Dromana House	156	Hagal Healing Farm	83
Druid Lodge	173	Hanora's Cottage	162
Drumcovitt House Cottages	29	Healthfield Manor	210
Drumcreehy House	71	Hilton Park	32
Dualla House	149	Hollywell	54
Dufferin Coaching Inn	21	Horseshoe Cottage	92
Edenvale House	25	Inch House	148
Emlagh Country House	116	Inis Meáin Restaurant & Suites	51
Emlaghmore Lodge	42	Iskeroon	124
Enniscoe House	58	Johnny's Cottage	17
Fergus View	73	Kelly's Resort Hotel & Spa	213
Fitzgerald's Farmhouse	139	Kilbrogan Coachhouse	98
Flemingstown House	136	Kilbrogan House	97
Fleur & Kizzie Cottages	118	Killarney Royal	122
Fortview & Elacampane Cottages	89	Kilmaneen Farmhouse	151
Fortwilliam Country House	20	Kilmokea Country Manor	208
Foxmount Country House	165	Kinvara Suites	50
Frewin	15	Knockbrack Grange	198
Gaultier Lodge	166	Knockeven House	105
Ghan House	189	Kylenoe House	143
Glasha	161	Laragan Lodge	59
Glencairn Inn & Pastis Bistro	155	Lawcus Farm Guesthouse	181
Glendine Country House	207	Lis-ardagh Lodge	93
Glenlohane	109	Lisdonagh House	47
Glin Castle	140	Little House on the Hill	154
Gorman's Clifftop House	113	Lorum Old Rectory	167
Gort-Na-Nain Vegetarian Guest House	101	Lough Bishop House	206
Grange Lodge Country House	34	Lough Owel Lodge	204
Greenhills	203	Loughcrew House	197
Greenmount House	114	Man of Aran Cottage	52
Gregans Castle Hotel	72	Maranatha Country House	102
Griesemount	177	Marlagh Lodge	5

Index by property name

Martinstown House	176		Shelburne Lodge	130
Mornington House	205		Sion Hill House & Gardens	164
Mount Cashel Lodge	79		Sliabh gCua Farmhouse	160
Mount Rivers	111		Somerton	134
Mount Royd Country House	16		Sunville House	107
Mount Vernon	70		Sylvan Hill House	19
Moy House	76		Tahilla Cove Country House	128
Mulvarra House	168		Tankardstown House	196
Newforge House	7		Temple House	67
Newtown House	153		The Anglers Return	41
No. 1 Pery Square	141		The Barnhouse at Drumkeerin	4
Number 31	169		The Bastion	201
Number Fifty Five	115		The Bervie	56
Old Parochial House Cottages	78		The Cahernane House Hotel	123
Picín	125		The Carriage House	22
Pier House	99		The Castle Country House	159
Powersfield House	158		The Coach House, Butlerstown	163
Railway Lodge	44		The Coach House, New Ross	209
Rathmullan House	14		The Cottage, Kilbrittain	95
Ravenhill House	6		The Cottage, Kilternan	174
Redbank House & Restaurant	175		The Cottage, Mullinahone	150
Richmond House	157		The Cottages	190
Rock Cottage	87		The Crooked Cottage	60
Roosky Cottage	53		The Glen Country House	94
Rosleague Manor Hotel	36		The Green Gate	11
Ross House	65		The Heron's Cove	90
Rosturk Woods	57		The Humble Daisy	49
Roundwood House	186		The Lake House	135
Rusheen House	147		The Merchant's House	31
Sallyport House	133		The Merrion Mews & Stables	170
Saratoga Lodge	146		The Mill Restaurant	12
Sea Mist House	39		The Mustard Seed at Echo Lodge	138
Seal Rock Cottage	129		The Old Milking Parlour	219
Seanua	131		The Phoenix	117

The Quay House	40	Waterloo House	171
The Schoolhouse	68	Westcove Farmhouse	126
Tir na Fiúise Cottages	142	Westcove House	127
Ulusker House	81	Whitepark House	2
Vaughan Lodge Hotel	75	Wineport Lodge	202
Viewmount House	188	Woodbrook House	215
Virginia's Guesthouse	132	Woodlands Country House	216

Photo: www.istockphoto.com

What's in each entry?

① B&B ② Co. Cork

③ **Horseshoe Cottage**

④ Joe and Fiona, the happy owners of little old Horseshoe, are wonderfully warm fun characters who have achieved much, including raising unnumbered goats and nine children. Joe, a retired commercial fishing skipper, has sailed the Atlantic, can take you whale or dolphin watching, show you his film on humpback whales near the Cap Verde Islands or his book of sea-faring yarns. Fiona, a registered homeopath and massage therapist, expends her exuberant energy re-vamping the garden, collecting eggs from her hens for your delicious breakfast, baking bread and flapjacks and cooking delicious, mostly organic, dinners – maybe mackerel caught that day and sizzled on the garden barbecue. This is three, 400 year old cottages, now rolled into one. The bedrooms are small and cosy, newly painted with colourful soft rugs on wooden floors, views are dizzying, the corridor is lined with books – but linger not, you are here to walk, swim, sail, discover. After breakfast sally forth to experience the peace and solitude of this beautiful little island (pop. 120): the Franciscans thoughtfully left a ruined friary to explore.

⑤	Price	€80–€95. Singles €40–€50.
⑥	Rooms	3: 1 double, 1 twin/double, 1 single.
⑦	Meals	Dinner from €25. By arrangement only. Pubs within short walking distance. Packed lunch.
⑧	Closed	Rarely.
⑨	Directions	Ferry from Baltimore (all year) or Schull (summer only). Up hill past friary ruins; left at telephone box; cottage on right.

Fiona & Joe Aston
Horseshoe Harbour, Sherkin Island,
Co. Cork
Tel   +353 (0)28 20598
Email joe@gannetsway.com
Web   www.gannetsway.com

Travel Club Offer. See page 266. ⑩

Ethical Collection: Environment; Community; Food. ⑪
See page 270.

⑫ Entry 92 Map 6 ⑬